Data Base
Administration

APPLICATIONS OF MODERN TECHNOLOGY IN BUSINESS

Series Editor: **Howard L. Morgan**
University of Pennsylvania

Data Base Administration

JAY-LOUISE WELDON

Graduate School of Business Administration
New York University
New York, New York

PLENUM PRESS • NEW YORK AND LONDON

Library of Congress Cataloging in Publication Data

Weldon, Jay-Louise.
  Data base administration.

  (Applications of modern technology in business)
  Includes index.
  1. Data base management. 2. Business—Data processing. I. Title. II. Series.
QA76.9.D3W45   658'.05   80-20467
ISBN 0-306-40595-4

First Printing—March 1981
Second Printing—April 1983

© 1981 Plenum Press, New York
A Division of Plenum Publishing Corporation
233 Spring Street, New York, N.Y. 10013

Printed in the United States of America

To my parents

Preface

In modern organizations, data has been added to the classical economic assets of land, labor, and capital. Data on company products, finances, and operations are gathered into data bases that are used to support management reporting and decision making. Effective use of these data bases requires control over their design and development and coordination among the various users. The exercise of these management functions is called data base administration (DBA).

DBA is an evolutionary area. In many organizations, it was formed as a response to the problems created by the installation of sophisticated systems for data base management. As a result, the practice of DBA has been strongly influenced by its technological and organizational environment. The size, organizational position, staffing, and defined role of DBA vary from firm to firm. However, certain fundamental tasks and responsibilities are, or should be, recognized as the province of DBA.

To date, literature on the DBA function is sparse. Most texts on data base management systems (Date, 1975; Kroenke, 1977; Martin, 1978; Sprowls, 1976; Tsichritzis and Lochovsky, 1977)*discuss DBA as one aspect of that technology.

---

*Date, C. J. *An introduction to Database Systems.* Second edition, Addison-Wesley, Reading, Mass., 1977; Kroenke, D. *Database Processing,* Science Research Associates, Palo Alto, Ca., 1977; Martin, J. *Computer Database Organization,* Prentice-Hall, Englewood Cliffs, N.J., 1978; Tsichritzis, D. and F. Lochovsky.*Data Base Management Systems,* Academic Press, New York, 1977; Lyon, J. *The Database Administrator,* Wiley-Interscience, New York, 1976; Sprowls, R. C. *Management Data Bases,* Wiley/Hamilton, Santa Barbara, Ca., 1976.

Lyon (1976) has provided a broader description of DBA within a CODASYL data base environment. His coverage is introductory and emphasizes the basic principles of DBA.

This book provides a comprehensive description of DBA: its objectives, its tasks, and the organizational issues raised by its existence. Part I provides an overview of the DBA function and a discussion of the organization and staffing of the DBA group. Parts II–V are devoted to major classes of DBA tasks: planning, design, operation and control, and user support. Part VI contains case histories of DBA in practice.

For individuals in the DBA area, this book can serve as a guide to the scope and content of their responsibilities. For individuals in general management or data processing management, it is a detailed view of this new management area. Finally, this book may be used as a text for graduate business or executive courses on the management of data base systems.

Many people contributed in various ways to the research necessary for this book and to the preparation of the manuscript. In particular, many Data Base Administrators in the New York area took time from their busy schedules to meet with me and share their experiences and views. Without their participation this book would not have been possible. Frank Lowell extended some of the DBA interviews and I am indebted to him for the material on which the case studies (Chapter 16) are based. Thanks are also due to Howard Morgan and to the reviewer for their helpful comments and criticisms. I am grateful to my colleagues in the Computer Applications and Information Systems (CAIS) Area at the New York University Graduate School of Business Administration (NYU–GBA) for their support and encouragement. Finally, I wish to thank the various members of the CAIS secretarial staff, the NYU–GBA Manuscript Center, and the NYU–GBA Computer Center for assisting with the preparation of this manuscript.

Jay-Louise Weldon

Contents

PART II • DATA BASE PLANNING

PART III • DATA BASE DESIGN

PART IV • DATA BASE OPERATION AND CONTROL

11 • Maintaining Data Base Integrity   133

12 • Controlling Data Base Access   145

13 • Monitoring Data Base Performance   159

PART V • MANAGING THE USER INTERFACE

14 • Data Administration   173

15 • Data Base Standards   187

PART VI • CASE HISTORIES

Part I

The Organization of Data Base Administration

Chapter 1

Managing the Data Resource

Effective management of organizations, both private and public, depends on information concerning the firm's operations, finances, and the allocation of its resources. With such information management can control costs and maximize profits (private industry) or operational efficiency (public institutions). Such information also provides a basis for planning for future developments, i.e., new products, new services, improved operations.

Since the first nonscientific use of the computer in 1953, organizations have relied increasingly on the use of computers to store and manipulate this information (see Figure 1.1). Today certain industries, e.g., banking and insurance, are virtually dependent on computers. The information explosion of the 1960s and 1970s has made computer data processing a cost-effective operational tool for organizations of almost every type.[1] Recent technological advances, resulting in the availability of low-cost data processing systems, are extending this trend to organizations of almost every size.

To make proper use of these technological tools, the firm must capture data on operations, finances, and resources and convert the data to computer-readable form. The data must be stored, processed, and made available as needed to management. The accuracy and timeliness of the data must be carefully controlled and the processing continually refined to meet new needs. In essence, the data need to be managed.

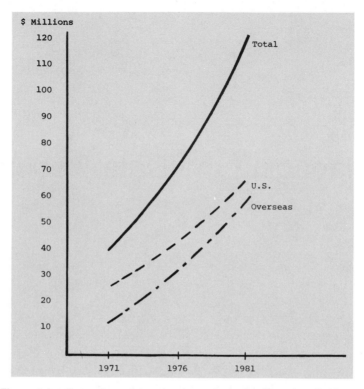

Figure 1.1.   General purpose computer systems, $ millions installed base.

1.1. THE TRADITIONAL APPROACH TO DATA MANAGEMENT

1.1.1. Specialization by Application

Anthony[2] has classified management decision making into three categories: operational, tactical, and strategic (see Figure 1.2). Operational decisions govern the day-to-day activities of the firm. The alternatives and decision rules for each are well defined. They also focus on specific functions or events. Tactical decisions are concerned with the allocation of resources and planning. These decisions are more complex and often involve estimates or probabilities in addition to factual information. The highest level of decision making, strategic decisions, is concerned with long-range planning and policymaking. Information for strategic decisions must be gathered from areas both inside and outside the firm.

Data processing (or information) systems can be similarly classified according to the level of decision making that they support. Initially most data processing systems were concentrated at the operational level.[3,4] Information systems that support operational-level decisions emphasize transaction processing and recordkeeping. Check processing, order entry, and inventory systems are of this type. The data to support this level are the most detailed and voluminous. As a result, the cost savings of operational-level systems could easily be demonstrated by comparison with the labor-intensive systems required for manual processing of the same data.

Over time, systems were developed to support tactical decisions as well. Usually these systems received their input from one of the operational systems. For example, models were applied to improve reordering strategies in inventory control; sales analyses were developed using data from orders received. The benefits of tactical systems are often difficult to quantify, however, so their acceptance and use has been slower than that of operational-level systems.

Even fewer strategic-level systems exist, reflecting the complex, unstructured nature of such decisions and the habits of high-level decision makers. Systems which have been successful at this level are designed to gather, integrate, and display data from a variety of sources in support of the human decision maker.

The operational or tactical nature of most information systems has resulted in system specialization. Information systems have traditionally been developed

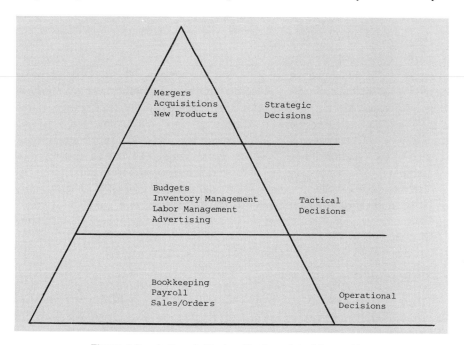

Figure 1.2. Anthony's[2] classification of decision making.

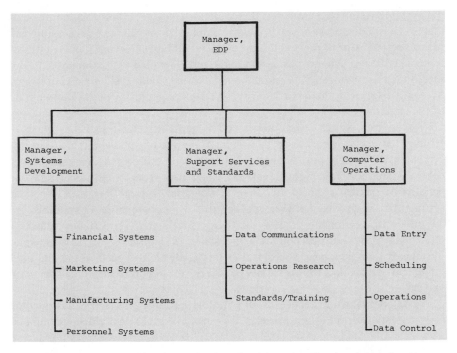

Figure 1.3. A traditional organization of a data processing (EDP) department.

in support of the functional areas of the firm's operations. Thus systems could be identified as financial systems, personnel systems, manufacturing systems, or marketing systems. This classification was reflected in the organization of the data processing staff (see Figure 1.3). The systems analysis and programming staff was organized into groups. Each group developed and supported systems for one of the functional areas. Further, each system was viewed as a separate application of data processing technology to the relevant functional area.

In this model, data were identified, organized, and processed independently for each application. Data files created by one application could be used by others and several reports could be run against one data file. However, the extent of such sharing was limited.

1.1.2. Process Orientation

In the traditional system development process, the data items to be collected and stored were determined by the processes that the system would perform. For example, a data file for a payroll system would contain for each employee those data items needed by the payroll computation and check writing process. Other employee data, e.g., information concerning job history or skills, would not be included.

The process also influenced the method of data storage. If a file of customer accounts was designed for a billing process (in which every record in the file was accessed), its records were stored sequentially. A credit inquiry process, on the other hand, required a random-access file. If the same data were used for two different processes requiring different types or sequences of access, elaborate procedures were used to convert the data from one form to another. For example, a random file of credit information might be created daily from the sequential customer account file to support credit inquiries.

1.1.3. Decentralized Controls

Traditionally the data supporting any given application system were the responsibility of the data processing subgroup that designed the system and ultimately of the users in the functional area for whom the system was developed. Controls on the accuracy of the data and the validity of the processing were developed and applied in this context. Little attempt was made to preserve accuracy or consistency across applications. For example, a customer's address in an accounts receivable file was not checked against the address for that customer in a sales promotion file.

Access to any data file was controlled by operating procedures that limited the use of the physical files (i.e., tape reels or card decks) to specified programs and systems. Also access to the data was controlled by the fact that file names and descriptions were the property of the applications group that created them.

1.1.4. Specialized Software Support

Methods of data storage and retrieval were also highly specialized and varied from one system, and even one program, to another. A certain amount of generality existed at the lowest levels through the use of standardized access methods provided as part of operating system software. However, different high-level languages, e.g., FORTRAN and COBOL, provided different and incompatible choices for data storage and retrieval. A system written in FORTRAN, for example, could not directly access a data file developed as part of a COBOL language system.

The file manipulation necessary to handle specific access requirements, e.g., "locate record X," was coded separately for each system in which it was needed. Further, the coding necessary differed according to the format and the structure of the data file being searched.

1.1.5. Shortcomings of the Traditional Approach

The traditional approach to data management presented several difficulties. The emphasis on specialization created a great deal of redundancy. Data items were stored and sometimes collected by several different systems. Redundant application programs were required to perform the same file manipulation operation on different data files. Control depended on diverse individuals and groups and was not sensitive to inconsistency.

Most significant, the files of data created to support specialized application systems could not readily be used to support requests for information that spanned two or more areas. Further, traditional data files could not support management's ad hoc requests for reports, even if all the data items necessary existed somewhere in the organization's data files. The items could vary from file to file in terms of data codes, timeliness, and degree of detail. These incompatibilities made seemingly straightforward requests difficult, if not impossible, to fulfill.

1.2. THE DATA BASE APPROACH

The data base approach to data management evolved in response to the problems of traditional methods. In its broadest sense the data base approach embodies two radical changes in philosophy. The first change is a redefinition of what constitutes a data base. The second is a change in the management of the data base.

1.2.1. A Definition of Data Base

Conceptually the data base consists of all information about things of interest to the organization. Some of these "things" might be employees, sales, customers, or raw materials. Information about these things might be recorded on paper forms, index cards, in notebooks, or as part of magnetic coded records in data files.

For most organizations only a portion of its data base exists in computer data files. It is generally this computerized portion that is referred to as the data base. This latter usage is followed in this book, except where specifically noted.

A collection of data files does not automatically qualify as a data base. To qualify, the files must be
  • Integrated: Incorporating little or no redundant data items.
  • Interrelated: Linked to provide complete and consistent information about the organization.

- Information oriented: Focused on the things of interest to the organization.
- Independent: Existing separately from the processes that they support.

1.2.2. Data Base Management

The data base approach to data management, called data base management, is designed to promote data sharing, preserve data independence, increase data availability, and reduce redundancy in application coding.

If data can be shared by two or more processes, redundant data storage can be eliminated and the consistency of the data can be assured. Data base management systems provide for a common description of data and the integrated storage of that data. All processes rely on the data base description to locate the data that they require.

Data independence refers to the situation in which changes in data file formats and access methods do not force modifications in the application programs which use the files. Data base management accomplishes this by removing both data descriptions and detailed data management coding from application programs. The former are replaced by references to a common data base description. The latter are replaced by data manipulation commands which are carried out by generalized data management software. In this way the application programs are isolated from most changes in data base content and storage structure.

A common, integrated description of an organization's data base makes that data more readily available. In addition, generalized data manipulation commands simplify the development of application programs that require data base access. Finally, data base inquiry systems and high-level reporting languages are available to provide access for users who are not programmers.

Initially the objectives of data base management were tackled individually.* Report generator packages were developed to produce reports from standard, e.g., COBOL, file formats. Next, more complex file management systems were developed. These provided flexible inquiry, reporting, and data sharing at the expense of nonstandard data file formats. Fully generalized data management software emerged almost simultaneously from plans to enrich the data management capabilities of COBOL[6] and from techniques developed to meet the needs of specialized applications.[7,8] Today several commercially available data base management systems (DBMS) exist,† and the data base approach is virtually synonymous with their use. It is possible, however, to have a data base and to apply the principles of data base mangement without a commercial system.

---

*See Fry and Sibley[5] for a detailed discussion of the evolution of data base management systems.
†Synopses of the features of several DBMS packages are included as Appendix A.

1.3. CRITERIA FOR USING THE DATA BASE APPROACH

While the data base approach promises many benefits over traditional data management, it may not be feasible or cost-effective in all situations. To assess whether or not a given organization would profit from the data base approach, four factors must be considered.

1.3.1. Commonality of Data

How much redundancy exists in the organization's data files? How costly is this redundancy? Extensive overlap among files, duplication of data collection and verification, and problems with inconsistent data items all suggest the need for the data base approach.

1.3.2. Integrated Processes

The number of systems or reports that require data from two or more data files should be computed. If this number is large or is expected to grow in the near future, the data base approach would be beneficial.

1.3.3. Need for Inquiry or Ad Hoc Access

The data base approach achieves the flexibility to handle inquiries and ad hoc requests easily. There is a price paid for this flexibility, however, since for any given inquiry or request a customized data structure and access method might be more efficient. If this flexibility is required, there is virtually no other way to achieve it.

1.3.4. Dynamic Application Requirements

Like flexibility, the ability to produce application programs quickly in response to new requirements is purchased at the price of maximum efficiency for each program. An organization in which processing requirements are relatively static, e.g., one that runs mostly production systems, would gain little from the data base approach.

1.3.5. Cost Trade-offs

Although use of a commercial DBMS is not necessary to the data base approach, an organization that satisfies all four criteria may have no alternative. A commercial system represents a substantial initial cost but promises long-range benefits and supporting software commensurate with state-of-the-art development. In-house development of comparable software would surely exceed the cost of a commercial system and would limit the organization's flexibility in the future.

If only one or two of the four criteria are met, however, the superiority of a commercial DBMS is no longer clear. Unless a change in the criteria is anticipated, it may be more cost-effective to follow the data base approach using in-house software.[9]

1.4. IMPLICATIONS FOR MANAGEMENT

The data base approach to data management will have an impact on company management, management of the functional user areas, and data processing (EDP) management.[10]

1.4.1. Company Management

The benefits of the data base approach will be apparent to company management in the form of increased responsiveness on the part of the data processing group to requests for information or new systems. It should also have an impact on data processing costs by reducing system development time and costs. The transition to the data base approach should also create an awareness among corporate management of the value of the data resource and its importance as a basis for management decision making.

1.4.2. Functional User Management

Managers in the functional user areas should observe a trend toward decentralization in both the development of application systems and the use of the data base. Initial data base design should find user management heavily involved in data definition and structuring. Once operational, the data base should facilitate the development of systems to meet the user's changing requirements. Inquiry and reporting systems will also allow the user to manipulate the data base directly.

1.4.3. Data Processing Management

The positive effects of the data base approach on managers outside EDP will be balanced by certain problems and issues which the data base approach will raise within the EDP group. Changes will be required in staff skills, individual responsibilities, and organizational structure.

New technical skills will be required to support the DBMS and to design and monitor the data base. System development methods must be modified to include

Table 1.1. DBA Job Specification

Function	Data base administration
Purpose	To support and manage the corporate data base(s). (See Chapters 1, 2, 16.)
Position in organization	Manager of DBA reports to highest-level EDP manager. (See Chapters 3, 5, 16.)
Group structure	Functional; subgroups for data base design, data dictionary support, and data base operation and control (possibly including DBMS support). (See Chapters 4 and 16.)

Areas of responsibility	Tasks (interfaces)	Chapter number
Planning	Define data base goals in support of EDP and organizational goals (company management)	6
	Develop and revise plans to achieve data base goals; in particular plan and direct the transition to a data base environment (system developers, operations, users)	6
	Assess impact of changes in technology and/or business information requirements on data base (vendors, consultants, users)	6
	Evaluate and select hardware and software, including DBMS, data dictionary, etc., to support data base (operations, systems programmers)	7
Design	Control the data base design process, through the integration of data needs and the scheduling of application development	8
	Provide expertise on methods for requirements analysis, data base design, and on the DBMS (system developers, users, operations, and systems programming)	8
	Articulate design trade-offs (system developers, users)	8
	Guide and consolidate logical data base design; provide expertise in data modeling; define data; integrate user views	9
	Perform physical design, evaluate design trade-offs, and select storage and access methods	10
	Maintain physical data description	10
Operation and control	Set and enforce standards for data definition, application coding, testing, and system design	11
	Develop and install procedures for error detection and resolution	12
	Set policies and procedures for data base backup and recovery	12

(continued)

Table 1.1 (*continued*)

Areas of responsibility	Tasks (interfaces)	Chapter number
	Formulate and apply a data base security policy, including user authorization, internal controls, and controls on personnel	12
	Develop and monitor data base performance measures	13
	Resolve data base operational problems through tuning, reorganization, or redesign	13
	Maintain DBMS and related software	13
Usage	Build, maintain, and distribute data about the data base (users, system developers, operations)	14
	Select data dictionary package	14
	Define and enforce standards for data naming, coding, documentation, and system development procedures (users, system developers)	15

data definition and the design of data base structures. Integration of the data will require a new kind of cooperation and planning among application support groups. Plans must be made for overall data base growth, access priorities must be set, and other conflicts among applications must be resolved. Finally, many issues concerning data base protection and control (such as data integrity, security, and reliability) must be addressed across all application areas instead of within each one.

The characteristic common to these changes is the centralization of responsibility for and control over the data base. This fact suggests that technical and managerial responsibility for the newly integrated data base should be vested in one organizational unit, a central authority with expertise in and control over the data base and its environment. Data base administration (DBA) is the name assigned to this new functional group. Table 1.1 contains a comprehensive job specification for a DBA function. The table also lists the chapters that elaborate on the tasks, responsibilities, and interfaces described.

Chapter 2

The DBA Function

The data base concept offers many advantages to organizations that adopt it. The pooling of formerly diverse data files into an integrated data base can reduce redundancy of data and promote consistency in the reports and processes that use the data base. The use of generalized software to store and access the data base can reduce the duplication in application programming and system development that existed when these tasks were the province of each individual system. Finally, the existence and use of DBMS-related software, such as query languages and data dictionaries, makes the data base more available and more accessible to both programmers and end users of the data.

However, these benefits are achieved at the expense of new problems. The integration of data requires data sharing among groups which previously had responsibility for their own data. The success of this new environment requires coordination among users and centralization of control over the integrity and security of the data base. New levels of technical expertise are also required, both for data base design and for the support of operational data bases and the DBMS itself.

2.1. AN OVERVIEW OF THE DBA FUNCTION

In recognition of these problems a new functional area called data base administration (DBA) has come into existence. The DBA is assigned the administrative responsibilities that must be centralized as a result of data integration and the technical responsibilities that are specifically related to the data base and the use of a data base management system. The tasks normally ascribed to the DBA function [1,2] can be classified into four categories related to the stages of data base development: planning, design, operation and control, and usage.

2.1.1. Planning

As the resident expert on data base systems, the DBA has an important role in both data processing and organizational planning. The DBA is involved in the evaluation and selection of data-base-related software and hardware. The DBA works with end users in the organization to establish realistic operational goals and requirements for application systems and data bases. The DBA must insure that priorities for application development and operation are consistent with organization's goals. Finally, the DBA is involved in long-range planning through forecasts of data base growth and technological trends.

2.1.2. Design

The DBA provides technical support to application system developers for both logical and physical data base design. The DBA controls the logical design process to produce a consistent, integrated picture of the organization's data resources. As new data needs arise, the DBA determines the manner in which they should be integrated into the existing data base and controls any modifications required. Physical data base design requires the DBA's skill and expertise with the DBMS. As a consultant or sole agent, the DBA generates a description of the data base suitable for the DBMS (called a schema). The DBA also determines the access methods and physical storage allocations necessary to meet the requirements of applications systems.

2.1.3. Operation and Control

The DBA is responsible for developing and administering policies that ensure the integrity of the data base, including procedures for data base backup and recovery. Preserving the security of the data base, through access controls and DBMS features, is also the province of the DBA. Finally, the DBA continually monitors the performance of the data base to insure that cost–performance goals are met.

2.1.4. Usage

The DBA is the primary liaison with the users of the data base. Thus the DBA has responsibility for setting standards for data base content and use. The DBA collects and maintains data about the data base and makes this information available to potential data base users. The DBA also maintains specialized software tools needed for data base use, such as data dictionaries,* query languages, or design aids. The DBA may also provide educational support for data base users, on any or all data base–related software.

2.2. THE HISTORY OF THE DBA FUNCTION

The creation of the DBA function is in some sense a managerial response to a technological change. With the introduction of generalized systems for data base management, DBA was put forth as the instrument of management control over the newly integrated data. Early definitions of DBA show this emphasis on control.

> The data base administrator is . . . responsible for the data base. [3]

> The DBA determines the rules which control the access to the data, and determines the manner in which the data will be stored. [4]

> The ownership of the data in the data base was to be transferred from the application programming and user groups to the DBA. [5]

As data base systems came into broader use and organizations gained experience in the use of these systems, the role of the DBA expanded. First, the task of data base definition and design become a recognized part of the DBA function. [1] User conflicts over data element definitions and names had to be resolved. Data base structures had to be designed to support multiple, and sometimes conflicting, application requirements. Thus a central figure with data base expertise was needed in the design activity.

Next, as managers and users in the organization's functional areas came to appreciate the data base approach, planning and user support were added to the DBA's tasks. [6,7] Writing in the *Harvard Business Review* in 1973, Richard Nolan said:

> Companies seem to agree that the administrator should concentrate his energies in the areas of planning and designing the data base; . . . they . . . view the administrator as a useful focal point from which the whole issue of computer data can be viewed as an integrated whole. [7]

As a result, the DBA function came to be synonymous with a whole range of activities throughout the development cycle of data base systems (i.e., design, creation, operation, performance, reorganization, documentation).

In recent years an attempt has been made to differentiate the roles of data

---

*Synopses of the features of several data dictionary packages are included as Appendix B.

base administrator (DBA) and data administrator (DA). [8,9] The latter is defined as the person

> responsible for developing and administering the policies, procedures, practices and plans for the definition, organization, protection, and efficient utilization of data within a corporate enterprise. [8]

This view broadens the scope of the DA to include all corporate data, not simply that portion which is computer based and specifically DBMS supported. According to this model the DBA would cede most of its managerial responsibilities to the DA and assume a solely technical role in the design and maintenance of DBMS-supported data bases.

While the development of a separate data administrator holds some appeal, notably the emphasis on a conceptual model of the organization's data, it has not been widely accepted in practice. As a result, in this book DA tasks are treated as part of the administrative responsibilities of the DBA.

2.3. THE NATURE OF DBA TASKS

The tasks included in the DBA function are numerous and diverse. They vary in their orientation along two different dimensions: administrative or technical tasks, and application-oriented or system-oriented tasks. These distinctions are of interest because the nature of the work influences the organization and staffing of the DBA group.

2.3.1. Administrative versus Technical Tasks

Administrative tasks are those that involve policy formulation, interpretation of organizational policies, or management direction. These activities affect the way in which work is done, both by individuals within the DBA group and by those outside the group who interact with the data base. Administrative tasks generally require organizational authority and the prerogative of control, or enforcement.

Technical tasks are those which rely on specialized knowledge and skill in a specific area. DBA technical tasks require expertise in data base areas, e.g., knowledge of a particular DBMS or skill in designing data base logical structures. The activities classified as technical are operational in nature. They are the tasks through which the data base is developed and maintained. Technical tasks may be performed in conjunction with, or in support of, data base users.

2.3.2. Application-Oriented versus System-Oriented Tasks

Application-oriented tasks are concerned primarily with the content and use of the data base. These tasks could also be called user oriented. Such tasks

Table 2.1.   A Classification of Representative DBA Tasks

Classification	Applications	Systems
Administrative	Set operational goals Set policies on access Set data element standards Set application priorities	Select hardware, software Set policies on data base recovery Set coding standards
Technical	Create data definitions Develop data structures (views) Educate users Maintain data dictionary Document data base	Support DBMS Develop physical structures Monitor data base performance Tune data base operation

require a thorough knowledge of the end uses of the data base, the requirements of those uses, and the relative importance of the various applications to the organization as a whole.

System-oriented tasks are concerned primarily with the hardware/software environment in which the data base operates. A detailed knowledge of the DBMS, of techniques for physical data storage, and of operational issues such as recovery and performance are required for these tasks. In addition, these tasks are closely tied to general systems support tasks, such as operating system support and data communications.

As Table 2.1 shows, DBA tasks can be classified along both of these dimensions simultaneously. For example, the task of setting data element standards is an administrative task concerned with the content of the data base (hence an administrative–application task). Similarly, physical data base design requires special technical skills and is concerned with the physical implementation of the data base; hence it is a technical–system task.

It will be convenient to classify different organizational approaches to DBA using these same two dimensions. To do so we shall define a DBA group with X–Y orientation as a group in which the tasks in subclass X–Y predominate. For example, a DBA group which emphasizes DBMS support more than all other tasks would be classified as a DBA group with a technical–system orientation.

2.4. DBA ORGANIZATION AND STAFFING

Initially the DBA function was described as the role of one individual, the data base administrator. However, as the number of activities assigned to the DBA grew, it became obvious that a staff group for DBA was needed. Nevertheless, it is common usage to refer to this group as a whole as the DBA.

While the literature has placed a great deal of emphasis on the tasks assigned to the DBA, very little has been said about the organizational aspects of the DBA function. Other than a general exhortation that the DBA should have management support and be placed in a high-level position (to establish authority for the DBA's administrative responsibilities), most writers have left organizational questions unspoken. Three organizational issues and their impact are raised briefly here and treated in more detail in Chapters 3–5.

2.4.1. Organizational Position

Organizational position refers to the placement of the DBA group with respect to related groups within the organization. It also includes the concept of the level, or rank, of the DBA. The position of the DBA influences its ability to successfully perform its responsibilities. For example, a DBA placed below and reporting to a specific application area will have difficulty supporting other application areas. Organizational position also influences the manner in which the DBA performs its tasks. A DBA located within an applications development group will play a different role in system design than a DBA located elsewhere in the organization.

2.4.2. Internal Structure of the DBA Group

The internal structure of the DBA group is heavily influenced by the size and orientation of the group. The group may be organized into functional subgroups along the administrative-technical dimension or along the application-system dimension. Small groups may have no internal structure but may instead assign roles to individuals within the group. The degree of internal structure in the DBA group influences the amount of functional specialization which can be developed or tolerated within the group.

2.4.3. The DBA Staff

The DBA function requires a diverse mix of staff skills. Application-oriented groups may seek individuals with extensive background in the application areas being supported and little background in data processing. Groups emphasizing technical–system tasks may opt for system specialists. A look at the staff rosters of DBA groups will show programmers, analysts, systems programmers, librarians, clerks, and data communications specialists among the positions listed. The major challenge for the DBA manager is to properly balance in-company knowledge with data processing expertise, and interpersonal skills with technical skills. In an effective DBA group, staff skills should match the orientation of the group and the tasks performed.

2.5. DBA IN PRACTICE

Recent surveys[10–13] have shown that there is no single approach to DBA. DBA groups vary in tasks performed, orientation, organizational position, internal structure, and staffing. Theoretically, all the tasks enumerated for the DBA should be performed somewhere in the organization. However, they may be performed outside DBA, e.g., DBMS support in the computer operations group or logical data base design in the user area. Not performing certain tasks has consequences which may or may not be tolerable to the organization. For example, the lack of standards for naming data elements may be tolerable for a small installation or where the integration among applications is minimal. However, the redundancy and inconsistency caused by duplicate data elements could have significant costs in a larger, more integrated environment.

The correct approach to forming and placing a DBA group within an organization is the following.

1. Understand the data base approach.
2. Be familiar with the full range of DBA tasks.
3. Understand the ramifications of the performance (or omission) of these tasks.
4. Be familiar with alternative DBA organization possibilities and their implications.

With this background, management can form the DBA function in a way that is best for their environment.

The remainder of this book provides a comprehensive background for this task. Chapters 3–5 address various approaches to DBA organization and staffing. Parts II–V contain detailed descriptions of the four major classes of DBA tasks: planning, design, operation and control, and usage. Finally, Part VI provides three case studies of different approaches to DBA in practice.

Chapter 3

DBA within the Organization

The activities of data base administration require that the DBA interact with several different groups, both within and outside the organization. These interactions and the DBA's role in each affect the proper location for the DBA function within the organization. Thus, to understand the impact of alternative positions for DBA within an organization, one must first understand the nature of these interfaces.

3.1. DBA INTERFACES

To properly perform the tasks assigned to it, the DBA must work with company management, with groups within data processing, with data base users, and with groups external to the organization, such as software vendors and consultants.[1]

3.1.1. Company Management

As manager of the data resource of the organization, the DBA is responsible to company management for the correct and efficient use of that resource. Plans for new technologies and for the implementation of new application systems must be reported to company management. Reports on the performance of operational systems must also be provided. Further, the DBA must be aware of management policies or plans which affect the data base and must see that data base plans and policies are consistent with these.

3.1.2. The Data Processing Organization

The DBA works with the system development staff, i.e., application analysts and programmers, during the design and implementation of application systems supported by the data base. The DBA must supply the technical expertise necessary for defining the data needed and for structuring the data to support the processes being implemented. Once the system is operational, the DBA continues to interact with the system development staff to resolve operational problems and to tune the data base to meet performance requirements.

The operational and control duties of the DBA require close cooperation with the computer operations staff. Policies and procedures for backup, recovery, and retention that are promulgated by the DBA are usually carried out by the operations staff. Enforcement of data and coding standards, application testing, and performance monitoring must all be performed in conjunction with operations.

The DBMS becomes a major part of system software in an installation. As a result, the DBA must work closely with the systems programming staff. Even if DBMS support is not the responsibility of the DBA, close coordination must be maintained. Changes in operating system software or in other elements of the installation's hardware/software environment can have an impact on the operation and performance of DBMS-supported systems.

3.1.3. Data Base Users

By users we mean individuals or groups in the organization, external to the data processing group, who ultimately use the information contained in the data base and the reports generated from that data. The DBA interacts with these individuals during system specification and initial data base design. Rules developed during this stage for data access and integrity must be formulated and applied by the DBA during the rest of system development and operation. The DBA must also provide the users with proper documentation on the data base and see that training in data base concepts and procedures is available as needed.

3.1.4. External Groups

As the organization's focal point for data base activities, the DBA acts as primary liaison with the vendors of the DBMS and other related software products. This is especially true of technical (nonlegal) interactions, such as vendor-provided training and ongoing operational support. For research and planning activities the DBA must keep abreast of developments in data-base-related software and must interact with vendors to obtain information on new products as required.

The DBA is also the organization's contact with external consulting firms who may be called in for specialized data-base-related tasks, such as data base design or data base performance measurement.

3.2. THE DBA AND DATA PROCESSING

The DBA must work closely with all aspects of the data processing organization. Data processing management may play the role of company management for the DBA, i.e., articulating the policies of the organization and monitoring data base plans and performance. In fact, in most organizations the DBA is part of the data processing organization and reports to data processing management.

To understand the reason for this placement, one need only review the tasks of the DBA. With few exceptions these tasks are identical to those which would be performed by groups within a traditional data processing department. [2] Except for DBMS-related tasks, DBA represents a centralization of existing design and control tasks. That such a redistribution of tasks is a source of conflict goes without saying. (These conflicts are treated in full in Chapter 5.) Thus it is logical that DBA be placed, initially at least, within the data processing department.

Within the data processing (or EDP) organization there are still several locations where the DBA may be placed. Before discussing these, a brief review of the organization of EDP departments is in order.

3.3. THE DATA PROCESSING ORGANIZATION

Two organizational issues related to the EDP group are of interest: the internal organization of the group and the placement of the EDP group within the context of the whole organization. The former reflects the work style of the EDP group itself, and the latter reflects the organization's philosophy with respect to the role of EDP.

3.3.1. The Internal Organization of EDP Department

Internal EDP organizational structures can be classified as functional, project, or mixed. [3] In a functional organization each specialty within the group, e.g., programming, is represented by an organizational subunit. This approach allows maximum interaction among specialists in each area and provides pools of resources to be tapped as needed.

In a project approach the system development staff, including systems analysts and programmers (and at times other specialists), are organized into subunits in support of specific application system projects (or project areas). So, for example, one group addresses the development of financial systems, another marketing systems, and so on. This approach provides more continuity and support for the several project areas, but it may result in a misallocation of resources when one project group is overstaffed and another is understaffed.

A mixed structure for EDP results when project teams are formed as needed from an underlying functional organization. These teams become temporary subunits of the organization, and the team members are responsible both to their superior in the functional group and to the project manager. This results in a matrix structure which achieves the benefits of each of the functional and project approaches at the expense of complexity.

3.3.2. Centralization versus Decentralization of EDP

The second issue of interest is the degree of centralization or decentralization of data processing with respect to the rest of the organization. A strongly centralized EDP group has all data processing activities and facilities concentrated in one organizational location and under the control of a manager of EDP. A decentralized approach to EDP has data processing activities and facilities dispersed throughout the organization, and the managers of each data processing group report to the operational management at their location.

In practice, of course, there are many variations combining aspects of both extremes. For example, a company might have centralized computer hardware and operations and decentralized system development staffs. The argument has been made that this results in more effective information system design [4] since the system developers are close to the end users. Another alternative, in a largely decentralized environment, might be a corporate EDP group charged with designing and operating those systems which cross organizational boundaries.

3.4. PLACEMENT OF THE DBA

The DBA should be placed at the organizational location from which it can best perform the tasks assigned to it. The assigned tasks vary from company to company and are related to the organization of the EDP department. They even vary over the lifetime of a single DBA group. Thus no one organizational position can be put forth as best regardless of these factors.

Five common locations for the DBA within an EDP organization have been identified. [5] These can be described by their orientation (project or functional) and by the nature of the role that the DBA assumes (advisory, support, consultant, or management).

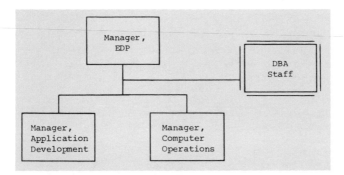

Figure 3.1. The advisory DBA.

3.4.1. The Advisory DBA

The advisory DBA is a staff group that reports to a high level of EDP management (see Figure 3.1). It is usually a small group of individuals with considerable background in data processing and longtime experience with the organization. The tasks of the advisory DBA are limited to planning, research (into new software, tools, and techniques), and administrative tasks, such as policy formulation and standards.

The advisory DBA may be a precursor of the data base approach in an organization. In this role the DBA may concentrate on standardizing procedures and data elements. The selection of the DBMS and other related software may be handled by the DBA. Once a DBMS has been introduced into the organization and application development has begun, the advisory DBA will no longer suffice.

Another circumstance that favors an advisory DBA is an organization with decentralized EDP groups, managed by a corporate group. In this model the technical and operational roles of the DBA are assigned within the decentralized groups, while the advisory DBA exists within the corporate management group.

3.4.2. The Project/Support DBA

The project/support DBA reports to the manager of a project system development group (within a project EDP organization) or the manager of a project team (within a matrix EDP organization) (see Figure 3.2). The project/support DBA performs a broader spectrum of tasks than the advisory DBA, but the scope of these tasks is limited to the project area of the DBA's manager. Design tasks and those supporting data base operation and control are emphasized by the project/support DBA.

The DBA's role in this structure is clearly supportive. Project management is in control of the direction and scope of data base development. DBA is an instrument of that control. Further, all operational and performance information on the data base is relayed to data processing management through the project manager.

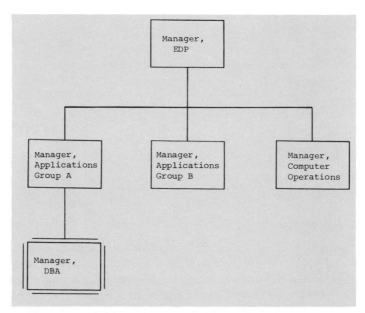

Figure 3.2. The project/support DBA.

While the project/support DBA must interact with computer operations and systems support groups, there is no interaction with other project groups. In fact, in large organizations that follow this approach, it is not unusual to find more that one DBA group, each servicing a different project area. However, when the DBA's services are needed by other project groups, this organizational position becomes dysfunctional. To achieve the benefits of the data base approach across several application areas requires a different organizational structure.

3.4.3. The Functional/Support DBA

The functional/support DBA reports to data processing management along a line different from that of the project manager or system development manager. The manager to whom the DBA reports, e.g., the manager of support services, is on the same level as the project managers or the manager of system development (see Figure 3.3). Thus, while not reporting directly to the system development manager, the DBA is at a lower organizational level.

As a result, the functional/support DBA plays a supporting role in system development, as does the project/support DBA. However, the functional/support DBA is not limited to supporting one application area. The DBA's services are available to all project groups as needed. This is analogous to the provision of data communications support or statistical support in traditional, functional data processing organizations.

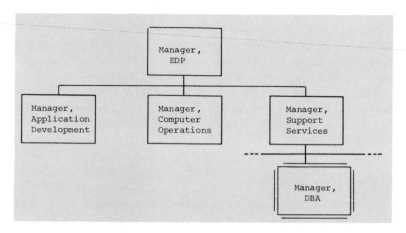

Figure 3.3. The functional/support DBA.

The support DBA's (both project and functional) have no coordinating role or real management control over the data base. Decisions on application priorities, data base content, and compliance with standards are made at a level above the DBA. Thus, the DBA can do no more than provide input to the project managers (or system development manager). If data processing management is explicitly reserving control over the data base for itself, this organizational approach suffices. However, if the DBA is expected to set and enforce standards and control the content and use of the data base, the support role is inadequate.

3.4.4. The Consultant DBA

The consultant DBA is a subunit of the data processing organization on a par with the system development group or the project groups (see Figure 3.4). The

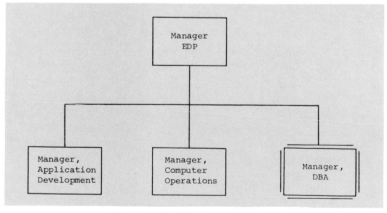

Figure 3.4. The consultant DBA.

consultant DBA performs the full range of DBA tasks. At this level the DBA manager participates in decision making across applications and can make recommendations directly to data processing management. The consultant DBA is the most common organizational position for DBA in practice.

During system development the DBA acts as a consultant to application development teams (in functional EDP groups) or may assign DBA staff to those teams (in matrix EDP groups). The DBA is a full participant in these efforts and serves as expert on matters relating to the data base.

3.4.5. The Management DBA

The management DBA reports to the top EDP manager and is located higher than the managers of projects or system development (see Figure 3.5). This DBA has high visibility and can exert personal control over the direction and nature of data base development within the organization. The existence of a management DBA indicates a strong commitment on the part of data processing (and company) management to the data base approach or the use of the DBMS.

The management DBA staff performs the full range of DBA tasks, functioning as consultant to the system development staff. However, in this model the DBA is able to promulgate and enforce procedures for system development and standards for data control.

3.4.6. The Impact of Decentralization

The DBA function is predicated on the centralization of various tasks related to data base planning, design, operation, and control. This makes the DBA func-

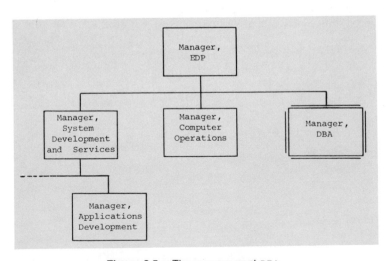

Figure 3.5. The management DBA.

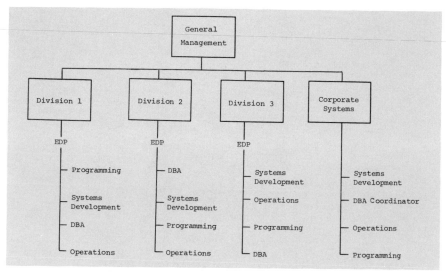

Figure 3.6. Coordination of decentralized DBA's.

tion somewhat incompatible with decentralized data processing activities. However, the organization's requirements for coordination or for centralization of certain data processing tasks can result in the formation of DBA groups in decentralized environments.

In the most extreme case, where all hardware and system development activities are decentralized, DBA group(s) will usually be formed as needed within the decentralized groups. If a coordinating body exists for data processing, e.g., a corporate systems group, a DBA liaison may be created to foster cooperation and coordination among the several DBA's (see Figure 3.6). This may result in a move

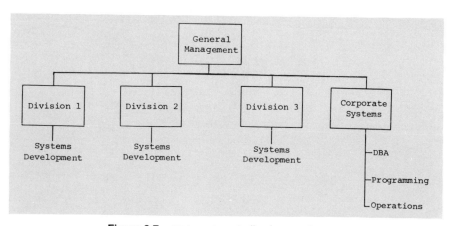

Figure 3.7. DBA as a centralized support group.

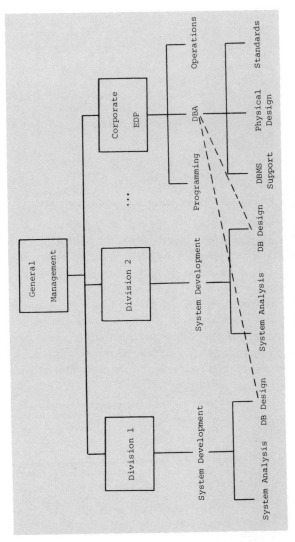

Figure 3.8. Partially decentralized DBA.

toward organization-wide standards, savings in software evaluation, and information sharing among the several DBA's.

In organizations in which only the system development function has been decentralized, two other DBA structures are possible. First, the DBA could exist as part of the centralized facility, acting in a support, consultant, or management role with respect to the decentralized system development groups (see Figure 3.7). Since the system development groups now report to operational management at their decentralized locations, the DBA's level is of crucial importance to the success of the function. The management DBA is most effective in this situation.

Second, the DBA staff can be partitioned and assigned in response to the decentralized environment. In particular, most of the DBA staff, expecially the technical portion of the staff, e.g., DBMS support and physical designers, could remain centralized while the data base design staff is decentralized with the systems development staff (see Figure 3.8). For best results, the data base design staff would report directly to operational management at their location, with a dotted line responsibility to the manager of DBA.

3.5. OTHER FACTORS AFFECTING ORGANIZATIONAL POSITION

In practice other factors, some unrelated to the nature of data base administration, influence the position occupied by the DBA. One is the history of the data base concept in the organization. Where did the idea for taking a data base approach originate in the firm? A data processing manager who originates the idea is most likely to set up an advisory DBA. A project manager is likely to have his or her job description rewritten to include DBA. The position of the DBA that originates in an internal management study or reorganization may reflect management's desire for improved controls or reassignment of personnel.

The immediate background of the individual chosen to manage the DBA group also affects position. A high-level EDP manager is likely to retain that position after becoming manager of DBA. The selection of a technical staff member is most likely to lead to a lower-level DBA.

The nature of the organization's business may indirectly influence the position of the DBA. In organizations which rely heavily on information resources, e.g., insurance and public utilities, and which require a high degree of internal consistency, the pressures for and rewards from an integrated data base approach are greatest. In these industries, then, one expects to see DBA at the highest levels. The lowest levels are expected in highly decentralized and diversified organizations, such as manufacturing conglomerates.

The complexity of the hardware/software environment may also indirectly affect the DBA's position. Organizations that use complex DBMS systems, requiring the support of a large and specialized support staff, may assign that staff to the DBA. The size and responsibility of such a staff may increase the DBA's level without regard for other factors.

Finally, and perhaps most important, the DBA's position is influenced by the maturity and performance of the DBA staff. As data base applications are developed successfully and become operational, the responsible DBA group may expect to move up in the organization, e.g., from support to consultant status. On the other hand, a management DBA that is unsuccessful in developing or controlling data base systems may be demoted to support status or disbanded entirely.

Chapter 4

DBA Organization and Staff

The DBA group is the organizational subunit charged with carrying out the tasks and responsibilities of data base administration. Typically the DBA group reports within the data processing department and draws its staff primarily from that department. Reflecting both its organizational position and internal policies on naming, the DBA may be called Manager of Data Base Administration, Director of Data Base Services, Manager of Information Resources, or any of a number of similar titles. Where no DBA group exists, the administrative and technical tasks of data base administration are assigned to existing groups within EDP. Technical tasks are performed by groups within the computer operations or system services department, sometimes called DBMS Support, Data Base Design, On-line Systems. Administrative tasks are assumed largely by data processing management.[1]

The actual size of the DBA group varies from organization to organization. Typically the DBA manager and staff make up 3.5% of the EDP staff. Thus DBA is generally much smaller than the computer operations or system development groups and on a par with other specialized support groups such as systems programming or data communications support. However, the experience level required of the DBA staff is generally greater than that required of any other group within the data processing department, for two reasons. First, to design an integrated data base to support diverse applications requires a broad knowledge of and experience with those applications. Second, the operational success of the data base depends on technical expertise with the DBMS, i.e., both knowledge of the DBMS and experience with its use.

The internal organization of the DBA group and the skills required of its staff are influenced by the scope of the group's tasks and the role that it plays, or is perceived to play, in the organization. For example, DBA's that assume the tasks of data base planning require skills, and perhaps an internal subgroup, dedicated to those tasks. Similarly, a DBA that plays an intermediary role between end users and technical data base designers requires a staff with highly developed interpersonal skills.

4.1. DBA SKILLS INVENTORY

The skills required within a data base administration group are independent of the individuals or staff positions through which they are practiced.[2] A large DBA group may have a very finely structured internal organization, with functional groups for each skill area. In a smaller group, however, one individual or position may be assigned tasks that require several different skills. This section presents a full inventory of the skills that may be needed within the DBA group (see Table 4.1). These skills are grouped into three broad categories: data processing skills, data base–specific skills, and interpersonal skills.

4.1.1. Data Processing Skills

The basic skills necessary to the DBA staff include several that would be found in any data processing group. While the DBA may not practice these skills in their purest sense, it may be assumed that each DBA staff member has some background and experience in at least one of the data processing skills.

Table 4.1.   Skills Needed on DBA Staff

Data processing skills	Data base skills	Interpersonal skills
EDP management	Logical data base design	Oral and written
Systems analysis	Physical data base design	communication
Applications	DBMS software operation	Diplomacy
programming	and maintenance	Negotiation
Systems	Data dictionary operation	
programming	and maintenance	
Data communications		
Technical writing		
Clerical skills		

4.1.1.1. Systems (or Applications) Analyst

Systems (or applications) analysis is the process by which application requirements are specified and application systems are designed to meet those requirements. The DBA staff requires this skill for both the design of the data base and for the design of application systems supported by an existing data base.

In addition to analytical skills and experience with system design procedures, a systems analyst has experience in working closely with the end user of the application system. Experience in such a liaison role is valuable to any member of the DBA staff who assists or consults with users.

4.1.1.2. Applications Programmer

An applications programmer is knowledgeable in one or more high-level programming languages, e.g., COBOL or PL/I, and the data file structures supported by that language. Experience in developing program modules for application systems gives the applications programmer skills in program construction, testing, debugging, and documentation. An applications programmer also has detailed knowledge of the data and processing requirements of one or more application areas, depending on his or her experience and project assignments.

The DBA staff needs applications programming skills for the design and testing of data base systems and the development of data base utility programs. Such skills also serve as a basis for setting standards for data base system development and application coding.

4.1.1.3. Systems Programmer

Systems programmers understand the architecture of hardware/software systems and the facilities and limitations of operating system software. They are familiar with assembly language and have experience in locating and solving operational problems by means of computer memory dumps and program traces. Systems programmers may also have experience in monitoring the performance of both hardware and software.

The DBA staff requires systems programming expertise for its dealings with the operation and support of the DBMS itself and the application data bases supported by the DBMS. To identify the source of operational problems, the DBA staff must be able to track each problem, separating the effects of the DBMS from those of other system software. The DBA's responsibility to monitor and tune the performance of data base applications also requires systems programming skills.

4.1.1.4. Data Communications Specialist

DBAS supporting on-line systems must have staff with expertise in the design and operation of data communications networks. Data communications specialists are proficient in assembly language programming, are knowledgeable about communications protocols and network design, and have experience with one or more of the software systems supporting data communications, e.g., TCAM, CICS, TSO. Experience with the specific teleprocessing monitor associated with the DBMS is desirable but not always necessary.

4.1.1.5. Manager

The DBA manager—the data base administrator—should be an experienced data processing manager. The data processing manager's skills include an ability to direct projects to successful and timely conclusion, supervisory abilities, the ability to coordinate diverse and highly technical staff groups, and the ability to interact diplomatically and productively with management colleagues and superiors.

The DBA manager need not have any direct experience with the DBMS being used. In this position company background, including experience with a wide range of application areas and a proven management record, is more important than technical skills. In fact, the narrow orientation of a DBA with a strong technical background may be detrimental to the success of the DBA function.

4.1.1.6. Other Skills

Two other skills in a data processing group may be valuable to the DBA group as well: technical writer and clerk. A technical writer is skilled in written communication and the presentation of ideas. With some training in the terminology of data base systems and the DBMS, a technical writer is valuable for the production of data base documentation and standards manuals.

Clerical skills in filing, tabulation, data entry, and verification are all needed within the DBA staff. Such tasks as the generation and maintenance of data base descriptions have a heavy clerical component. Creating and maintaining a data dictionary also involve clerical tasks.

4.1.2. Data-Base-Specific Skills

In addition to the data processing skills previously enumerated, some new skills related specifically to the design and operation of data base systems are needed by the DBA staff. Individuals can acquire these data-base-specific skills through education or previous experience with data base systems in another organization.

4.1.2.1. Logical Data Base Designer

An individual qualified to do logical data base design (or serve as a design consultant) must be thoroughly versed in the data base approach. He or she must be familiar with several different data models and must be expert in the data model and data description language used by the DBMS. It is desirable that the logical data base designer also be familiar with the application areas to be supported by the data base.

The logical data base designer works with the systems (or application) analysts and users during requirements specification and data base design. The logical data base designer may also consult with the applications team when operational problems occur or when the data base needs modification.

The logical data base designer is the primary interface between the users (or project team) and the data dictionary activity. It is the responsibility of the logical data base designer to see that the elements and relationships in the data model are accurately described by the data dictionary. This activity controls the accuracy of the data base descriptions and of any documentation produced from the dictionary.

The skills of the logical data base designer can best be developed within the organization. Individuals with broad systems analysis or applications programming background can be trained in data base techniques. Many universities and professional organizations offer courses in data base design and data models. The DBMS vendors themselves offer training and courses in data description languages and data base design.

4.1.2.2. Physical Data Base Designer

The role of the physical data base designer is to select the appropriate physical forms, e.g., access methods or record layouts, to realize the logical data base on physical storage devices. The physical designer requires a detailed knowledge of the access methods and data formats provided by the DBMS. He or she must also be familiar with the capacity and timing characteristics for secondary storage devices. A knowledge of programming, especially file design and file-searching techniques, is also required.

After the logical data base has been designed but before that logical design has been converted into the data description language of the DBMS, the physical designer interacts with the full project team to determine the processing requirements of the data base. The designer selects storage and access methods based on these requirements and assists in the production of the data base description. The physical designer also directs the initial data base load.

When the data base becomes operational, the physical designer is responsible for evaluation of performance results and for any reconfiguration that must be performed to tune the data base. The physical designer also assists the project team in the development of backup and recovery procedures for the data base and advises them on statistics to be monitored as an indication of the need for reorganization.

A physical data base designer should have a systems or applications programming background. Operational experience with the specific DBMS is also important. Exposure to application areas and company background are of lesser importance in this role.

4.1.2.3. DBMS Software Specialist

The DBMS software specialist is the most technical member of the DBA staff. This position requires detailed knowledge of the architecture and facilities of the DBMS in use in the organization. A DBMS specialist should have intensive training by the DBMS vendor and experience in installing and maintaining the DBMS in a hardware/software environment similar in complexity to that of the DBA's organization.

The DBMS specialist is responsible for installing the DBMS and all related software such as the utility load program and the teleprocessing monitor. The DBMS specialist also applies and tests all modifications to the DBMS. The DBMS specialist must be familiar with all features of the DBMS, whether in use or not, and their potential impact on system operation.

The DBMS specialist works most closely with systems programmers and the operating system support staff. All operational problems tracked to the DBMS must be verified by the DBMS specialist and corrected. The DBMS specialist works with the physical designer to solve performance problems as required. The DBMS specialist is also the technical liaison with the DBMS vendor.

An individual with systems programming background and experience in system software support is the most likely candidate for DBMS specialist. However, DBMS training and experience are necessary before one can function effectively in this role.

4.1.2.4. Data Dictionary Specialist

The data dictionary specialist is responsible for creating and maintaining a dictionary of the data elements included in the organization's data base(s). A name, description, edit specifications, access rules, and other information on usage must be kept for each element. The data dictionary specialist may also be responsible for developing conventions for data naming and other standards and procedures regarding the content of the data base.

The data dictionary specialist works primarily with the data base users (i.e., the project team) and the data base designers in the specification and naming of data elements. The data dictionary specialist also reports on data base content, both periodically and on request, to application development teams, data base designers, and management.

The data dictionary specialist should have a working knowledge of the operation and features of the data dictionary/directory system (DDDS) in use by the organization. He or she need not, however, have an extensive data processing background. It is much more important for the data dictionary specialist to have a detailed understanding of the organization's applications areas and the data elements of importance to each application. An ability to organize and classify information and a desire for accuracy and precision are also required. Some organizations have trained individuals with library science backgrounds for positions as data dictionary specialists.

4.1.3. Interpersonal Skills

The basic skills inventory of the data base administration staff shows DBA as a largely technical and highly specialized group. The close relationship of the DBA to the DBMS and DBA's responsibility for the operation and performance of data base systems enhance this view. However, the DBA's role in the introduction of the data base approach, in general, and in the development of new systems, in particular, makes a purely technical staff untenable.

With perhaps the exception of the DBMS specialist, all members of the DBA staff work with system development teams and end users at some time during the life of a data base system. In this interaction the DBA staff assumes a support, or at most, a consulting role with respect to the other members of the team. In such cooperative efforts interpersonal skills are of the utmost importance. The DBA staff must be able to communicate effectively with the rest of the group, to effect design compromises where necessary, and to focus the design on true organizational requirements, as opposed to the whims of a particular application area (or analyst). The DBA staff must be able to convey the strengths and limitations of the DBMS to potential users in terms that they can understand.

Diplomacy and interpersonal skills are especially required in a DBA group, for DBA owes its existence to the centralization of tasks from the groups that it serves. The DBA staff must build a reputation for competency and professionalism, so that DBA may be viewed as a worthy recipient of these responsibilities. Continued misunderstandings or personal antagonism will result in the development of specialized skills within the project teams, in competition with DBA.

4.2. INTERNAL ORGANIZATION OF DBA

The internal organization of the DBA group is influenced both by its size and by the range of tasks in its charge.[3] DBA staffs of six or more individuals, including the DBA manager, can be organized along functional or project lines into subgroups focusing on particular specialty areas or on project support. Smaller groups usually have a flat structure, with each staff member reporting directly to the DBA manager.

The range of the DBA's tasks affect the orientation of assignments given to

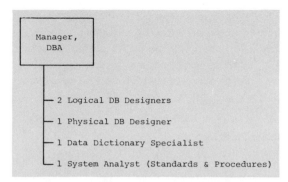

Figure 4.1.   Unstructured DBA, design emphasis.

the internal subgroups or to individuals in a flat organization. These assignments usually correspond to one or more of the major classifications of DBA tasks: planning, design, operation and control, and user support. DBMS support is often considered a separate group because its responsibilities are highly specialized.

4.2.1. The Flat or Unstructured DBA Group

In flat or unstructured DBA groups, either specialty tasks are shared among several experienced individuals or the group emphasizes one class of tasks to the exclusion of all the others. Figure 4.1 shows the staffing of an unstructured DBA group that focuses on system development. Personnel are included for logical and physical data base design and for the maintenance of a data dictionary. A systems analyst with an extensive and broad background in the organization's application areas is assigned the responsibility of developing data element standards and procedures for data base development. DBMS and other operational support are provided within computer operations with no relationship to DBA.

The DBA group shown in Figure 4.2 is smaller and focuses only on the use of the data dictionary. Data element definitions and data base descriptions are

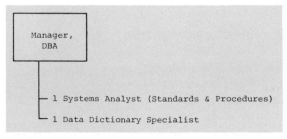

Figure 4.2.   Unstructured DBA, data dictionary emphasis.

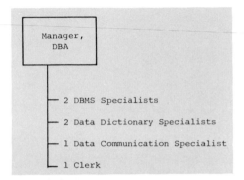

Figure 4.3. Unstructured DBA, data base operation emphasis.

managed by means of the data dictionary under the DBA's supervision. In this organization data base design tasks are performed by the system development staff, and DBMS support is provided by the system software group.

Figure 4.3 shows a flat DBA group that emphasizes data base operation. The staff is quite technical and is responsible for physical data base design and DBMS support. This DBA is responsible for maintaining the data dictionary and for developing standards for data elements and data base documentation. However, the logical data base design, including the definition of data elements, is done by the system development staff.

Unstructured DBA groups cannot adequately perform the full range of DBA tasks. As a result, these organization types are usually adopted in the early stage of DBA development or by organizations not fully committed to the data base approach.

4.2.2. Functionally Organized DBA Groups

The most typical internal structure for a mature DBA group is a functional organization. Frequently the DBA manager supervises three functional groups, each headed by a lower-level manager. Figures 4.4 and 4.5 show two examples of this approach.

Figure 4.4 shows a functionally organized DBA group that includes the DBMS support group as part of its staff. The other two functional groups are the data base design group and the data dictionary group. The former interacts with the system development staff and data base users during both the design and the operation of data base systems. The data dictionary staff develops data base standards and procedures, maintains the data dictionary, and provides data base documentation. Data base planning tasks are assumed by the DBA manager in consultation with the data base design staff and the DBMS specialists. The DBMS staff not only handles all DBMS maintenance but is also instrumental in determin-

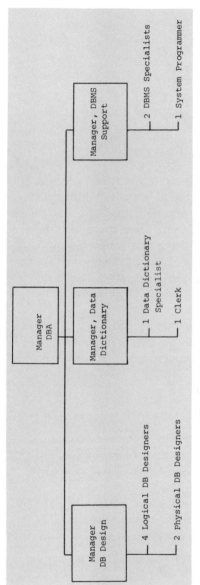

Figure 4.4. Functional DBA with DBMS support.

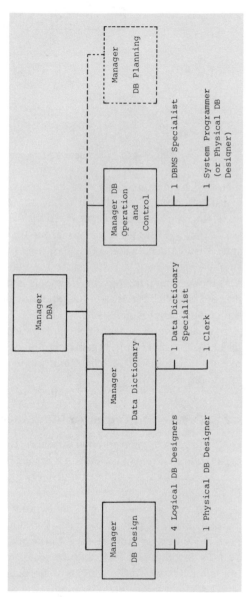

Figure 4.5. Functional DBA without DBMS support.

ing and controlling operational tasks, such as data base backup and recovery and performance monitoring.

In many organizations DBMS support is considered virtually indistinguishable from other systems software support, e.g., operating system support or data communications support. Such organizations prefer that the DBMS group report with these others within a computer operations or system support group. When this occurs, the DBA group may adopt a structure similar to that shown in Figure 4.5. In this structure the DBMS support group has been replaced by data base operation and control staff who assume the application-oriented tasks formerly performed by the DBMS support group. The other two functional groups remain the same. However, the number of physical data base designers needed in the data base design group may be reduced, since the data base operation and control group can assist with this task.

In DBA groups that are in the midst of large-scale development efforts or changes in their hardware/software environment, the data base planning effort may be formalized into a functional group (shown by dotted lines in Figure 4.5). This group would draw staff from the existing functional groups on a temporary basis to accomplish the planning tasks assigned, e.g., software evaluations.

4.2.3. A DBA Group Organized by Project

As noted in Chapter 3, during the initial application of DBMS within an organization the DBA group may provide exclusive support to a given application or project area (i.e., a project/support DBA). This special support may also be provided by a consultant DBA group in which the data base design subgroup is organized by project (see Figure 4.6). In this case the logical and physical data base designers on the DBA's staff are assigned to two or more subgroups that support data base and system development for specific application areas. The other specialty groups, that is, the DBMS support and data dictionary groups, remain unchanged.

This structure may be beneficial and, in fact may exist informally in a DBA group organized by function, when system development is active in several application areas simultaneously. It allows the data base designers to become thoroughly familiar with the requirements of a given application area. However, over the long run this structure is inappropriate. It fosters the traditional lack of integration among areas.

4.2.4. A Matrix Organization for DBA

Some organizations have attempted a matrix organization for DBA. In this approach certain DBA tasks are assigned to subgroups in other organizational units but retain an indirect reporting relationship (i.e., a dotted line) to the DBA

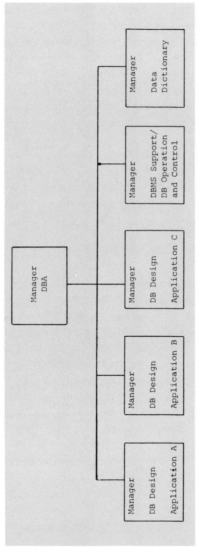

Figure 4.6. Project-oriented DBA.

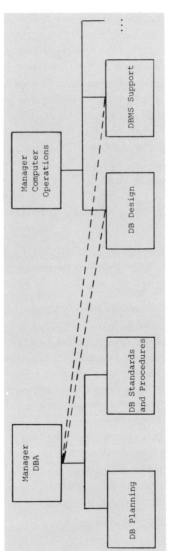

Figure 4.7. DBA with matrix organization.

manager. This approach allows DBA groups to place data base designers within decentralized system development groups, while retaining the ability to coordinate their actions and promote professional contact among the designers.

Another use of the matrix organization[4] permits the separation of technical and administrative DBA task groups (see Figure 4.7). In this case the data base designers and DBMS support specialists report within the computer operations area along with system software support and others with whom they work closely. They also retain a dotted line responsibility to the DBA manager, who directly supervises administrative groups for data base planning, standards and procedures, and data protection policies.

While the matrix approach allows the DBA group organization to adapt itself to specific organizational conditions, it has several disadvantages. The complexity of the structure increases the difficulty of coordination. The dual reporting channels become sources of conflict both within the DBA group and between the DBA manager and the manager of the other responsible group. And, finally, the loss of direct control over portions of the DBA staff reduces the power of the DBA manager and limits his or her effectiveness.

Chapter 5

Organizational Dynamics

The introduction of the data base approach, often accompanied by a data base management system, represents a major change from traditional methods of data processing. The new technology, along with the new philosophy of data owner-ship and control, has a profound effect on the development and administration of systems. This change in work content is also accompanied by changes in the organization of the data processing staff, namely the introduction of the DBA function. Thus the DBA has a central role in this drama of organizational change.

Initial use of a DBMS and the conversion of application systems to this new technology has been likened to the major upheaval caused by the conversion of such systems from manual to computerized form.[1] The DBMS software, now vital to the success of any application system, is unfamiliar and sometimes unreliable. Analysts and programmers are forced to follow new procedures for system design and to submit to rigorous constraints on data definition and data base content. Project management and costs may be adversely affected by the inability of project leaders to accurately forecast the time and resources needed for system development.

The change in system development tasks is accompanied by changes in the way in which the work is done. The centralization of control over data represents a loss of authority by the system development groups. Data integration forces data sharing and thus closer cooperation among groups that have formerly worked independently. Each of these changes holds the potential for organiza-tional conflict.

To successfully cope with these problems the organization must have a strategy for effecting and maintaining the desired change.[1,2] Such a strategy should include a series of short-range objectives, i.e., intermediate change goals, against which the progress of the transformation can be measured. This will allow early detection and resolution of barriers to change. In addition, the strategy should include a long-range plan for the institutionalization and thus continuance of the change.

The DBA group can be instrumental in the introduction and institutionalization of the data base approach within an organization. Whether or not DBA is a conscious part of management's strategy for effecting this change, its work responsibilities and organizational position put DBA at the center of this dynamic situation. For DBA to play an effective role as an instrument of change, management must understand the relationship between the evolution of the DBA function and the maturation of the organization's commitment to the data base approach. Further, both management and the DBA staff must understand the inherent conflicts in the DBA role and develop effective means for resolving them.

5.1. THE EVOLUTION OF THE DBA FUNCTION

Observation of DBA in practice has provided evidence for identifying four stages in the evolution of this organizational unit.[3–5] These stages are defined in terms of the scope and degree of integration of data base–supported applications. They begin with management's first interest in the data base approach and lead to the point where a data base integrating several major application areas is operational. At each step the DBA's task emphasis, organizational position, and internal structure may vary (see Table 5.1).

Table 5.1.   Stages in the Evolution of the DBA Function

Stage	Task emphasis	Data base scope	Organizational position	Organizational structure
Introduction	Planning	—	Advisory or support	Unstructured
Initiation	Development	Individual applications	Support	Project or functional
Integration	Development and operation	Integrated applications	Support or consultant	Functional
Maturity	Operations	Integrated applications	Consultant or management	Functional or matrix

5.1.1. Stage 1: Introduction

The introduction stage occurs when a DBA group is organized before the introduction of a data base management system.* The group's primary tasks are data base planning, especially the evaluation and selection of data base–related software. The creation of a data dictionary and the development of standards may also be part of the introduction stage.

During the introduction stage the DBA group is usually small. It may consist of a manager and one or two staff members with experience in data processing technology and the applications of the organization. The group reports to data processing management (i.e., an advisory DBA) or within the system development group having the most likely initial aplication for the DBMS (i.e., a project/ support DBA).

5.1.2. Stage 2: Initiation

Once an initial, or pilot, application is identified for the DBMS, the DBA group becomes a technical support group for that application. Thus DBA assumes a project/support or functional/support position within the data processing organization.

During this phase the DBA concentrates on developmental tasks, such as designing the data base and developing procedures for backup and recovery. Maintenance of the data dictionary, of data base descriptions, and of the DBMS also begins during this stage. As a result, the DBA staff may grow in size and may assume a functional structure internally.

In many organizations the DBA group does not exist until the initiation stage. The developmental process described by Ross[4] begins with a transition stage which is identical to initiation. In these cases a task force or study team considers the data base approach and selects software. Then the DBA group is set up to follow through on the team's recommendations by implementing the initial data base application.

5.1.3. Stage 3: Integration

During the initiation stage, data base development was limited to one application area in order to simplify the process and to gain experience with the methodology and the software. While the DBA manager and the data dictionary staff maintained a broader outlook, data base development focused on the needs of the specific application area supported.

Once these initial data bases are operational, however, the DBA enters the integration stage. The planned links among data bases are realized, and the

*The names for the stages used here are those coined by DeBlasis and Johnson.[3]

development of application systems that use this integration is begun. At this point the organization should begin to reap the major benefits of the data base approach.

The DBA group should be functionally, rather than project, oriented by this stage. It should also be moving from a supporting position to one of consultation or management. Internally it should be organized by function, with subgroups supporting the full range of DBA tasks, i.e., planning through operation and control.

In the integration stage the emphasis of DBA tasks shifts from development to operation and control. Since most of the organization's data bases have been implemented or planned, the DBA's attention is drawn to performance improvements and control over the quality and reliability of the data base. However, the data base designers continue to assist with new applications and with modifications to the existing data base. The DBA must continually plan for data base growth and the advent of new technology.

5.1.4. Stage 4: Maturity

According to DeBlasis and Johnson, DBA reaches maturity when "the DBA is involved from the beginning in all data base work and also has the final power to make operational decisions."[3] This implies that the DBA has risen from a consulting to a management role in charge of a highly integrated data base environment. Other than the change in organizational position, this stage is identical to the preceding integration stage.

To date, few if any mature DBAs have been observed or described in the literature. Some DBAs have achieved high organizational position but minimal integration of their application area data bases. Others are attempting to develop highly integrated systems early in their evolution, e.g., during the initiation stage, but are acting without the power of a mature DBA. Still others have been absorbed back into data processing management.

This lack of maturation is due in part to the relative newness of the data base approach. However, in greater measure it is due to the inability of the DBA staff to deal effectively with conflicts and to a failure to tap the organizational power inherent in the DBA position.

5.2. CONFLICTS IN THE DBA'S ROLE

Interactions between organizational units may lead to conflict between the units. When such conflicts go unresolved, the effectiveness of both groups may be reduced and the impact on the organization may be undesirable. As was shown in Chapter 3, the DBA group serves as a focal point for all activities affecting the data base. In this capacity the DBA interacts with many different groups in the organization. Thus the potential for conflict is inherent in the DBA's role.

5.2.1. Sources of Organizational Conflict

In their studies of individuals and group behavior, sociologists and social psychologists have identified several conditions that lead to conflict among organizational units.[6,7] Among these, five are particularly relevant to the DBA's position.

5.2.1.1. Task Interdependence

Task interdependence refers to the degree to which two groups depend on each other for services or direction. A high degree of interdependence can cause conflicts over the assignment of praise or blame related to the groups' joint efforts. Further, if the dependence is not mutual, i.e., if one group is more dependent or less powerful or less knowledgeable, the conflict is exacerbated.

5.2.1.2. Poor Communication between Groups

When staff members from two organizational groups cannot communicate with each other, cooperation is difficult and the potential for conflict is great. Differences in background and lack of understanding of the other group's operations can lead to unreasonable expectations.

5.2.1.3. Differences in Goals

The possibility of conflict between two groups is increased if the goals of the two groups differ. There may be an actual difference in goals, as articulated by the groups' managers, or a perceived difference, based on observation of the group's behavior.

5.2.1.4. Interpersonal Skills of Group Members

A certain level of interpersonal skills is required of individuals who must work closely with individuals from other groups within an organization. A person lacking such skills may not have the flexibility to adapt to such cooperation. The result could be either direct conflict or a refusal to participate in the joint activity.

5.2.1.5. Ambiguity

The potential for conflict in a given situation is increased by ambiguity. If the assignment of responsibility for tasks in a joint effort is unclear, misunderstanding and conflict may occur. The lack of unambiguous performance criteria for a joint effort may lead the two groups to pursue contradictory goals. Finally, a group whose role in the organization is unclear, whether due to its newness, its origin, or its organizational position, may suffer resentment or lack of cooperation from other groups.

5.2.2. Conflict Situations for the DBA

Conflict situations may arise from either the technical or the administrative responsibilities of the DBA. The cooperative nature of system development and operation strains the relationships between the DBA and the other groups that participate in these technical tasks. The DBA's administrative role in policymaking, enforcement of standards, and arbitration among data base users presents similar difficulties.

5.2.2.1. Interaction with System Development Staff

In the design of data bases and the development of data base application systems the DBA staff serve as data base experts. However, they must work closely with the system development staff during the specification of user needs, data definition, and data base design. The system development staff depends on the DBA for knowledge of data structures and the features and limitations of the DBMS. The DBA staff depends on system development for its experience with and understanding of user needs. The objective of their cooperative effort should be an operational data base that supports user requirements.

The degree of interdependence between these groups is high and not always symmetrical. If the data base designer is a former systems analyst with a background in the user applications area, the system development staff may be more dependent on DBA than vice versa. On the other hand, the newness and low organizational position of the DBA group could put DBA at a disadvantage with respect to the more established and prestigious position of the system development group.

Communication can also be a problem. A technically oriented DBA staff, imbued with DBMS jargon, may be unintelligible to the system development staff and the end users. A staff selected for technical ability and experience alone may lack the interpersonal skills needed for the interaction with system development.

Finally, a difference in goals may be perceived by members of the two groups. The system development staff may feel that DBA is superfluous and merely striving to build an organizational empire. DBA may perceive that the system development staff is preventing access to necessary design information in order to preserve the traditional approach to system design.

5.2.2.2. Interaction with the System Software Staff

DBMS support, while not a joint effort, certainly requires close cooperation between the DBA staff and the system software support staff. In this case the DBA depends on the system support staff for expertise on system architecture and operation. The system support staff, however, is not equally dependent on the DBA group. System support requires DBMS expertise only when an operational problem is found, or suspected, to be the result of the DBMS.

Isolating the cause of operational problems in a complex hardware/software environment is difficult at best. When two groups, such as DBA and system support, are involved, this ambiguity can cause conflict between them.

Since the DBMS support staff and the system software support staff have similar education and experience, the two groups are not likely to have communication problems. However, this similarity and the similarity of their tasks, e.g., software maintenance, performance monitoring, operational support, may foster competition rather than cooperation.

5.2.2.3. Setting Policies and Standards

The DBA's role as manager of the data resource includes setting policies and standards on matters related to the development and use of the data base. Policies may be an articulation of the organization's objectives, e.g., "data base backup will be provided to allow reconstruction of data over no more than a four-hour period." They may also be more specific guidelines, such as policies governing the necessary steps in a data base development project. Standards go further than policies and specify rules for detailed interactions with the data base. Rules for data element names and coding conventions are examples of standards.

Normally policies or standards are formulated by management and used to guide the individuals or groups within their span of control. These individuals or groups perceive the guidelines to be management instruments for assuring that their work is consistent with organizational goals. Compliance is assured by the formal authority of management. In the case of the DBA, however, policies and standards relating to the data base can affect the actions of any group or individual that interacts with the data base. Often the formal authority of the DBA is not apparent to these individuals or groups. Indeed, it may be lacking, perhaps due to the DBA's low organizational position. This ambiguity in the DBA's authority can lead to conflict.

Standards can cause additional problems since their precision leaves little or no room for flexibility for those who must follow them. Further, standards often deal with matters that are of interest to several groups, each of which has a different goal. For example, the DBA may wish to assign unique data element identifiers using codes that facilitate cross-referencing among systems. Application programmers, however, may wish to assign their own codes to maximize consistency within one application system.

The relationship between the DBA group and system developers and users may be compared with that between a staff group and the line groups that it serves. Conflicts between staff and line usually center around questions of staff authority.[8] Similar conflicts between the DBA and the groups it serves will result if users perceive that the DBA has exceeded its authority in setting policies or standards.

5.2.2.4. Arbitration

The integration of data into a shared data base will result in disagreements among users of the data base over data base plans, data base design, and data base use. The DBA has administrative responsibility for each of these tasks and thus becomes the most likely arbiter for these disputes. Decisions concerning the priorities for application systems, the content and format of shared data elements, the assignment of responsibility for data update, and rules for data access all involve compromise among the users involved. Since DBA is the instrument of these compromises, ambiguity over the DBA's role and authority can intensify rather than resolve these conflicts.

5.2.3. Conflict Resolution

Some measure of conflict is inevitable for the DBA. The large number of interfaces between the DBA and other groups involved with the data base is fundamental to the job function. The sweeping changes brought about in a traditional data processing group by the transition to a data base approach cannot be avoided. Disputes over data use and priorities are bound to occur in this environment. Finally, the DBA's staff role in support of the line users presents a classical situation for conflict.

In some cases confict between groups can have a positive impact on the organization.[6] For example, competition between two sales groups can improve morale and result in improved performance for both groups. Likewise, the conflicting interests of the DBA and system developers can result in a beneficial balance between long-range optimization (DBA) and short-range efficiency (system developers). However, excessive or inappropriate conflict can limit the DBA's effectiveness and hinder the development of data base systems.

While conflict cannot be avoided, it can be confronted and its negative impact reduced. Both general management and the DBA group itself must be alert to conflict, and both have a role in the prevention and resolution of those conflicts.

5.2.3.1. Management's Role

Management's first responsibility is to provide clear and unambiguous direction for the transition to the data base approach and for continued development in this new environment. Goals for each organizational group, e.g., users, DBA, and application programmers, must be clear and consistent. Performance criteria must be stated and must clearly reward activities that promote the overall objective of the several groups. These actions will foster the internalization[9] of the common goal by each of the separate groups.

Management can promote cooperation through the use of development teams or steering committees that include members from each of the groups. Formal procedures for intergroup activities, such as data base development, will reduce conflicts over roles and responsibilities. Procedures for handling disputes among data base users, perhaps including provision for appeals to management or to a representative steering committee, will ease the arbitration process.

Finally, a full and unambiguous articulation of DBA's responsibilities and authority will be an effective deterrent to conflicts over the DBA's role. While the organizational position of the DBA implicitly conveys authority, simply placing the DBA is not enough. Management must clearly state the degree of authority being vested in the DBA, e.g., advisory or functional responsibility, and then support that authority.

5.2.3.2. The DBA's Role

The DBA group must approach each of its tasks with an awareness of the potential for conflict inherent in that task. This recognition will foster the development of procedures and protocols least likely to engender conflicts. For example, if standard data definitions become a point of disagreement among data base users, the DBA may choose to have an advisory board of user representatives participate in defining the data.

The DBA manager must also be actively seeking staff members with the interpersonal skills necessary to function effectively in this environment. Very large DBA groups may be able to employ technical specialists lacking in interpersonal skills. But this is the exception rather than the rule.

Finally, the DBA must become aware of the potential for organizational power that exists within the DBA function. Once familiar with the types of power that exist and their manifestations in the DBA's own organizational environment, the DBA is prepared to use this power to reduce conflicts and to achieve both the DBA's and the organization's goals.

5.3. POWER AND THE DBA

Power can be defined as the ability to direct or control the actions of others. In an organization a group is considered powerful if other groups within the organization act in conformance with its wishes or objectives. This conformity is desirable since it reduces conflicts between the powerful group and the other groups within the organization.

Power is both relative and dynamic. It is relative in that a group's power is measured, or weighed, in relation to the power of the groups with which it interacts. For example, group B may be less powerful than group A but more powerful than group C. The dynamic nature of power means that the power of a group can change over time and be influenced by organizational and behavioral factors.

It is important for the DBA to be familiar with the concepts of organizational power and the factors that affect it. By seeking to increase its own power relative to the groups with which it interacts, e.g., users, system development and computer operations, the DBA can reduce the conflicts that can prevent DBA from being effective.

5.3.1. Types of Power

The extremes of power within an organization are represented by authority and influence.[10] Authority is power conveyed both by formal organizational position and by the accompanying control mechanisms. Authority is institutionalized power. Thus the manager of a group has authority over the members of the group. The manager's power comes from the formal description of his or her position. Such a position usually includes the authority to hire and fire personnel, set goals for the group, and set priorities for group actions.[11]

A group with no formal position of authority nor any means of exercising control over other groups must rely on influence. The group must suggest its ideas to others and try to persuade the others to conform. Low-level groups attempt to influence the actions of higher-level groups. Similarly, staff groups rely on influence to affect line operations.

It is possible, however, for a group with no formal authority to transform its influence into power through other means.[10,12] Two types of power achieved in this manner are particularly relevant to the DBA: expert power and reward power. A group with expert power has gained the ability to control other groups by virtue of its own special knowledge or expertise. The group's expertise has engendered respect from the other groups who then defer to the more powerful group in matters in which that expertise is relevant. To sustain this power the expert group must maintain its credibility over time by demonstrating its abilities. If this credibility is lost, the group will lose its power.

A group can also become powerful if it has the ability to influence the success or failure of other groups. It can then use this ability to reward or coerce other groups into conformity. For example, a marketing group could have a strong influence on the success or failure of a product developed by a research and development group. As with expert power, reward power lasts only as long as the group is capable of influencing success or failure. If success is promised and does not occur, or if threatened failure is avoided, the group will lose its power.

Other factors concerning the group's performance and the nature of the group's tasks affect the power of a group.[13] In particular, the power of a group is affected by the group's ability to cope with uncertainty, the substitutability of the group's tasks, and the centrality of the group's function. If a group shows itself capable of coping well with an uncertain environment, its power will increase. However, if the group's tasks can be performed as well by another group, its power will diminish. The more important the function of the group, i.e., the more central it is to the organization, the more powerful the group. Even with outstanding performance, a group whose tasks are peripheral to the objectives of the other groups will have little power.

5.3.2. The Power of the DBA

DBA is potentially a very powerful group. The integration of data under the administrative control of the DBA puts DBA in a very central and influential position vis-à-vis the data base users. Further, the background of the DBA staff gives DBA the expertise necessary for successful development of data base systems and makes the DBA function difficult to replace.

Few DBA groups enjoy formal authority by virtue of their high level in the organization. Most act in advisory, support, or at best consulting roles with their users. However, the DBA's credibility and demonstrated expertise can substantially increase the DBA's power. If the DBA has shown strong leadership throughout the transition to the data base environment and an ability to cope with the uncertainties involved in that process, its power will increase. Users and the other groups within the data processing department will respond favorably to a DBA staff whose skills are valuable to them and who is perceived as dedicated to the organization's goals. If DBA fails to establish its credibility, is inept, or perceived as pursuing its own narrow goals, the other groups may react by assuming some of the DBA tasks themselves (e.g., a system development group doing data base design) or by seeking to avoid or limit data base use. Either of these responses erodes the DBA's power.

Part II

Data Base Planning

Chapter 6

Components of Data Base Planning

One of the major administrative tasks assigned to the DBA is the responsibility for data base planning. This responsibility entails setting goals and objectives for data base content and operation as well as selecting technical and organizational alternatives that most effectively utilize company resources to achieve these goals. Goals must be set in the context of organizational goals and management objectives. The selection of alternatives must reflect a knowledge of current and projected technological developments as well as an appreciation of the organizational implications of managing data as a resource.

Most literature on data base planning emphasizes two tasks. The first task is introducing the data base approach within an organization. The second is selecting the hardware and software required to support data base activities. While these are certainly crucial to the successful implementation of data base systems, data base planning cannot cease once the DBMS has been selected and the first application system installed. The direction of data base development should be continually reassessed in the light of organizational objectives and alternatives should be revised to reflect new constraints.

To be an effective planner, the DBA must understand the nature of the planning process, must be able to define data base goals in a manner consistent with the organization's goals, and must be able to execute a variety of planning tasks for both the initiation and the continuation of effective data base systems.

6.1. THE PLANNING PROCESS

The starting point for any planning process is the statement of objectives.[1] Objectives are assertions of fact or accomplishments that are deemed desirable to attain. Objectives can describe the desired state of being for the organization at some point in the future. For example, a school may aspire to being ranked among the top five schools of its type. Or an objective can describe desirable changes in organization's activities or characteristics. For example, a consumer products firm may want to alter the composition of its market share to favor product X over product Y (the former may be considered to have more growth potential).

Once objectives have been established, they should be ranked according to their importance to the firm. Changing the composition of the market share may be deemed more important than reducing the annual turnover rate for manufacturing personnel. The ranks assigned to objectives can be used to determine priorities for the allocation of resources and the order of activities in support of the objectives.

By their nature, objectives are broad statements oriented to results rather than means. Before any efforts can be started to attain the objectives, they must be broken into a series of more specific, short-term goals. For example, one goal that is consistent with the objective of changing the composition of the consumer products firm's market share is to increase the market share for product X by 5%. This goal may in turn be broken down into subgoals, e.g., broaden advertising coverage for product X. A full hierarchy of subgoals may be developed in support of the overall objectives (see Figure 6.1).

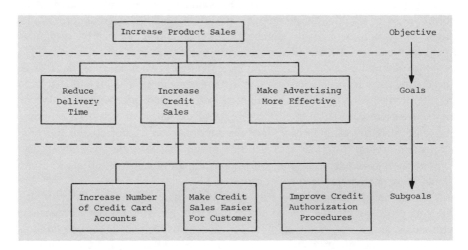

Figure 6.1. Hierarchy of organizational objectives and goals.

Both objectives and goals serve to guide the operational activities of the organization. Managers develop plans governing how the resources under their control can be best used to achieve the stated goals and objectives. Plans are action statements, e.g., institute a coupon sales campaign for product X. They describe a full set of activities which, if accomplished, assure the goals and objectives sought. The activity statements in the plan can be used to organize staff projects or to direct line operations. Each activity also carries a budget describing the resources available for its completion.

The planning process does not end with the initial articulation of the plan. To be effective the plan must be managed. The activities initiated by the plan must be monitored and their results compared with those that were projected. If results diverge from projections, if goals are modified, or if external conditions change the assumptions on which the plan was based, the plan should be modified. Even if no specific event triggers a reevaluation, plans should be reviewed periodically to determine whether resources are being used in an optimal way.

The goals of an organizational line or staff group may be different in scope and quite far removed from those of the organization as a whole. For example, the goals of the distribution group within a consumer products firm are not stated in terms of market share for specific products. However, the efficient distribution of products, including product X, is consistent with and supportive of the broader organizational goal. Thus more efficient product distribution can be established as a goal of the distribution group, and the group manager will develop plans to accomplish this goal.

The data base planning process follows the same procedure as other types of organizational planning. The DBA, as data base manager, establishes data base goals which are consistent with the goals and objectives of the organization as a whole.[2] These goals address questions of data base content and scope, data base performance, and the priorities that are assigned to data base applications. In support of these goals the DBA defines and manages data base plans which include tasks such as evaluation and selection of data base hardware and software, the staffing and organization of the DBA group, effecting the transition to a data base environment, and forecasting internal and external changes that affect the data base plan.[3]

6.2. DATA BASE GOALS

Data base goals are short-term objectives that guide the development of the organization's data resource and the activities of the data base administration group, as manager of that resource. These objectives must be consistent with organizational goals; in fact, they are the means of translating organizational goals into terms that are meaningful with respect to the data base (see Figures 6.2

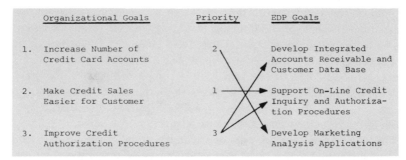

Figure 6.2.   Organizational goals and EDP goals.

and 6.3). Data base goals apply the mandate of organizational goals to questions of data base scope, data base operation, or data base use.

6.2.1. Data Base Scope

Goals related to data base scope govern the content of the data base. For example, one such goal might state that the data base should support each of the major line activities of the firm; another might be that the data base should support all corporate financial operations, integrating financial data from each division within the company. Each of these goal statements, though broad in nature, establishes a reference point against which questions of data base content

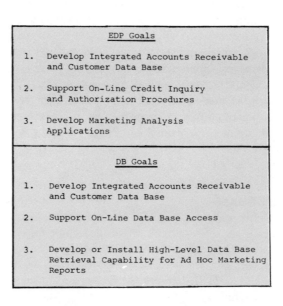

Figure 6.3.   EDP goals and data base goals.

can be measured. For example, is the activity supported by a proposed data base system a major line activity? Does the data support a corporate financial operation?

Goals can also address the level of decision making to be supported by the data base—for example, ''the data base will support manufacturing operations'' or ''data base support will be provided for marketing analysis.'' The level of decision-making support provided will guide in the selection of data base content, the size of the data base, and the level of aggregation of data base content.

6.2.2. Data Base Operation

Data base operational goals govern the mode and performance level of data base systems. Goals such as ''provide immediate updating of warehouse inventory'' or ''produce daily sales analysis reports'' have ramifications for the processing alternatives that can be considered for systems consistent with those goals. The former require on line processing support, while the latter may be met through a batch system.

The selection of hardware and software needed to meet data base goals is also influenced by operational goals. The requirement for on-line processing with specific response time goals serves as a standard when evaluating software for data communications support as well as terminals and other data communications hardware. The need for a high-level query language for the data base and the specific features required will also be determined with respect to goals defining how the system should operate.

The DBA's role in formulating operational goals includes bringing data base expertise and knowledge of the current state of the art in technology to bear on the issue. Data base operational goals should be not only desirable in terms of meeting users' needs but also realistic in terms of the technology which will support them. Unrealistic goals will eventually reflect badly on the DBA group, since they will be interpreted as unfulfilled due to the DBA's inability to accomplish them.

6.2.3. Data Base Use

Goals concerning data base use will identify the applications that are most supportive of organizational goals. Acknowledging the dependencies among applications, the DBA can assign priorities for both development and operation. The priorities can then be used to formulate an implementation schedule that assures the development and implementation of the system(s) with the highest impact first.[4] Priorities can also be used during data base design, to select the most effective physical structure, and also during operation, to schedule batch processing or transactions.

Since these priorities reflect organizational goals, they change over time.

The DBA must be ready and able to respond to such changes so that data base development is not geared to outmoded objectives. The DBA must use the feature of data independence and reconfigure the data base as necessary to remain responsive to organizational needs. To maintain this flexibility, requests from within the DBA group or from users to compromise data independence in return for efficiency should be carefully evaluated and granted only on an exceptional basis.

6.3. DATA BASE PLANS

Data base plans are a collection of related activities which if undertaken and accomplished will result in the attainment of data base goals (see Figure 6.4). Plans address three issues: the activities themselves, the resources required for each, and problems which are likely to be encountered.[5] Each activity is specified as a series of subtasks, some independent, some dependent on the outcome of others. The whole set of activities may also be sequenced. For each activity, resources in terms of personnel, time, computer usage, and hardware/software acquisitions must also be specified. Since the activities are competing for both DBA and data processing resources, the assignment of resources should reflect the priorities of data base and organizational goals.

The identification of possible problems in fulfilling the data base plan is one

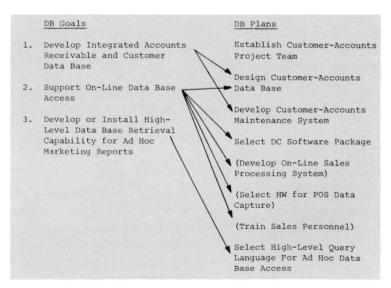

Figure 6.4. Data base goals and data base plans. DC = data communications; POS = point of sale.

way of coping with the uncertainty of the future. Activities specified in the present, based on certain assumptions (about needs, technology, data base size, priorities, personnel availability) may run into difficulty in the future should any of these conditions change. Thus plans must contain contingency actions that could be taken to resolve or at least mitigate anticipated problems.

6.3.1. Initial Data Base Planning

The change from a traditional data processing environment to a data base environment has both technical and organizational ramifications. Organizationally, tasks and responsibility for data are being shifted from individuals and groups who formerly exercised them and are being centralized under the DBA. The whole process of designing and implementing application systems is revised, with data being emphasized over processes. Data sharing makes the need for data standards paramount and requires cooperation among formerly independent groups. Technically, system success is tied to a new and complex piece of software, the DBMS. New technical skills, and possibly new personnel, are required. In addition, the risks and the full costs of a successful implementation are not known.

The transition process (see Figure 6.5) begins with a statement of data base objectives and goals, based on an analysis of user needs. With these requirements as guidelines, the necessary software tools (for example, a DBMS and a data dictionary) can be selected. The benefits of the data base approach and these new tools can be demonstrated by means of the design and implementation of a pilot application system. The entire transition process sets precedents for continued development of data base applications by yielding not only an operational data base but sets of procedures and standards for each of the tasks involved.[6]

It is the DBA's responsibility to take charge of the transition effort and thus improve the chances for a successful and permanent change. The transition plan has three main components: organization of the DBA group, the evaluation and selection of a DBMS, and the initial data base design and conversion effort.

6.3.1.1. Organization of the DBA Group

The DBA group should begin as a planning team to investigate the need for the data base approach in the organization. This team may include representatives from each of the application development areas in data processing plus representatives of the user group(s) served. Their first task is to analyze user requirements in a way that allows the quantification of the benefits of data sharing, data independence, and data security and integrity for comparison with the costs of data base introduction, e.g., the DBMS, training, hardware, disruption of the work flow.[7-9] If the data base approach is cost justified, then the DBA group should be formally established to select the DBMS and manage the transition process.

The DBA manager is responsible for establishing the structure and staff composition of the DBA group. Both of these characteristics change with respect to the maturity of the group and the organizational environment in which it is to

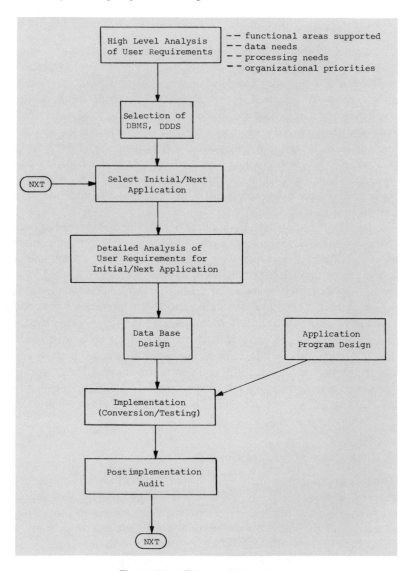

Figure 6.5. The transition process.

work. At the outset the most important skills are those related to knowledge of user applications and processing needs. Next, skill in the selected DBMS in vital. Finally, skills in creating and maintaining operating programs in the data base environment are required. The DBA manager should plan to obtain these skills as they become necessary. The group's growth should follow the natural evolution, emphasizing the tasks most crucial to the organization's stage of development.

6.3.1.2. Hardware/Software Evaluation and Selection

The evaluation and selection of data base–related hardware and software is a major planning task of the DBA. The DBA is concerned primarily with software selection and serves as a consultant to the manager of computer operations, or to the data processing manager, who is responsible for hardware selection. However, even when final authority to acquire a product does not rest with the DBA, the DBA is responsible for providing recommendations based on data base plans and goals to the decision maker. Data base–related hardware/software is of three types: the data base management system (DBMS) itself, the host hardware/software system, and related software packages such as data dictionaries and query languages.

The selection of the DBMS is a fundamental and complex task.[10] It is covered in detail in Chapter 7.

The host hardware/software system includes the host central processing unit (CPU), secondary storages devices, data communications hardware, and the host operating system, including data communications support. For many installations this configuration is fixed without regard for data base needs. However, where data processing represents a major part of installation processing the needs of the data base should be reflected. For example, the number and capacity of disk storage devices should reflect data base size and projected growth. Also the choice of data communications software should be made with the full knowledge of facilities and limitations of the DBMS and any data communications software provided by the DBMS vendor. The size of internal memory of the host CPU must be adequate to support DBMS applications without unnecessary overhead. Finally, the interaction between the DBMS and the host operating system should be considered when selecting operating system features at system generation or when evaluating the impact of changing to a new operating system release.

In addition to the DBMS itself, proper support of the data base may require a number of other software tools. In particular, a data dictionary/directory system (DDDS) is needed to document data base content and structure and to assist in the maintenance of DBMS data descriptions. The selection of the DDDS should be based on an analysis of DDDS features in the light of the emphasis of the DBA's data dictionary responsibility. Compatibility with the data description language of the DBMS is a prime consideration for DBA's using the dictionary to maintain

DBMS data descriptions. DBA's using the DDDS primarily for documentation and design purposes will look for more extensive and flexible reporting and cross-referencing capabilities.

The selection of an end-user query language requires both knowledge of user requirements and familiarity with available query languages and their compatibility with DBMS systems. The DBA is in the best position to evaluate the trade-offs between fulfillment of user needs and the cost of the query language, including the direct costs of acquiring the package plus the indirect cost associated with its impact on data base processing.

Other software selection decisions that are the province of the DBA are those concerning data base design aids, data base performance monitors, and data compression utilities.

6.3.1.3. Application Selection and Conversion

The selection of the first application to be brought up under a data base environment is critical to the success of the data base approach.[11] A careful balance must be struck between the breadth of the application, in terms of the number and complexity of data interrelationships required, and the centrality of the application, i.e., how crucial it is to the organization's functioning. The DBA may select a project of tangential importance to the company if the project allows a thorough experimentation with the capabilities and features of the DBMS. On the other hand, the DBA may wish to demonstrate the contribution of the data base approach by selecting a small, well-defined portion of a more crucial application which can be used as a basis for gradual expansion to include and support other applications. In either case all those involved—users, data processing analysts, and DBA staff—must be fully aware of the scope and objectives of the application. In addition, all must have realistic expectations for the results to be achieved and the costs (in terms of time and people) to achieve those results. Anything less will leave the DBA vulnerable to charges that the data base approach does not achieve the promised benefits.

6.3.2. Revising the Data Base Plan

Organizational planning generally follows a two-stage cyclic process.[12] Stage 1 involves long-range, or strategic, planning for the organization as a whole. During this process objectives and goals for the company for the next five years are stated and communicated to managers throughout the company. In stage 2 short-range, or operational, planning is done to determine how resources will be used to attain the long-range goals. These two planning cycles trigger action periodically, e.g., annually or biannually, and are synchronized so that long-range corporate objectives can be reflected in the operational goals.

The data base planning cycle follows the same pattern (see Figure 6.6). For

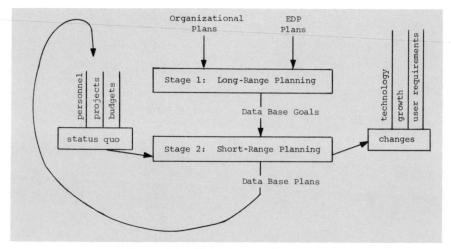

Figure 6.6.   The data base planning cycle.

each short-term planning cycle all data base activities must be reviewed. Then forecasts must be made of changes anticipated in the near future. These two—status quo and changes—are then combined to develop a plan for the next short-term cycle.

Both internal and external changes must be considered in revising the data base plan. Internal changes include data base growth, changes in user requirements, and changes in organizational priorities, e.g., as a result of organizational objectives. External changes that can affect data base plans are software trends (such as new packages or new features in existing packages), hardware trends, and the nature and quality of vendor support.

The DBA must be able to respond to changes in the organizational and technological environment through revision of the data base plan. Thus projects mounted in support of the plan should be of shorter duration than the short-term planning cycle. Also such projects should be modular, i.e., self-contained, so that changes in direction or technological tools will cause the least disruption and cost.

6.4. SUMMARY

Planning, especially in information systems, is something that everyone agrees must be done, but few agree on its methodology or procedures. However, if the data base is to be supportive of organizational and EDP goals, the DBA must properly plan the transition to the data base environment and must direct its development over time. The DBA must become and remain cognizant of organizational and technological directions and must guide activities in synchronization with these goals.

Chapter 7

Evaluation and Selection of Data Base Management Systems

A major decision in adopting the data base approach to data management is the choice of a data base management system (DBMS). The DBMS is a complex software system used for the storage and subsequent manipulation of the organization's data. All application systems rely on the DBMS to provide the interface they require to the data base. The DBMS may also provide facilities for data base users to manipulate their data directly. In this central role the DBMS is certainly crucial to the success of the data base environment.

Figure 7.1 shows the general architecture of a DBMS. Descriptions of the data elements, data groups or records, and relationships among the data are captured using a data description language (DDL) and stored in tables. A data manipulation language (or data sublanguage[1]) is provided by which the application programs request operations (e.g., retrieval or update) against the data base. The actual physical storage structure of the data is known only to the DBMS routines.

While all DBMS systems follow this same general architecture, they vary with respect to options and features provided to accomplish the necessary functions. The process of evaluating and comparing DBMS's for one environment thus becomes a process of matching DBMS features and capabilities against the requirements and constraints of the environment.

Any analysis for evaluation and selection must begin with a thorough study of user needs. This analysis is usually completed as part of the study to determine whether the data base approach is warranted.

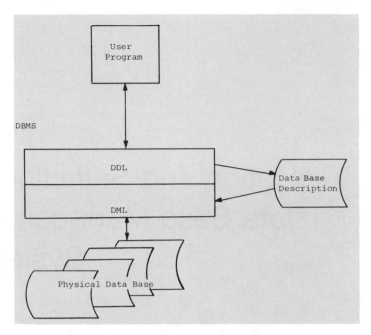

Figure 7.1.   The architecture of DBMS systems.

Ideally, for the purposes of DBMS evaluation, the study of user needs should yield a complete list of the data to be stored, including estimates of data volumes; a prioritized list of processes to be run against the data base, especially including the parameters by which the data are to be accessed; a description of the relation between data items and data files in the data base; and requirements, in terms of transaction times and costs, for data base performance. While it is unlikely that all these requirements will be known prior to the evaluation, the evaluator should be capable of making reasonable estimates for each category.

The processing environment in which the DBMS is to function must also be considered. The relevant characteristics of this environment include the type and size of the main frame processor; the operating system environment, including possibly data communications support; the availability and extent of secondary storage resources; and the number and skill levels of the systems programming and applications programming staffs.

With this information the evaluator can take one of two approaches: feature analysis or performance analysis.[2] The objective of feature analysis is to match the features of the DBMS to user requirements under the assumption that the system which provides the best match will also yield the best performance. The performance analysis approach assumes that since all DBMS features are roughly comparable, only the bottom line, namely performance, need be considered to make the choice. Ideally, the selection process should combine these two approaches. Feature analysis is used to narrow the field of alternative DBMS's, and performance analysis is used to make the final selection.

7.1. DBMS FEATURES

In reviewing and evaluating the features of alternative DBMS's the evaluator should consider four types of capabilities: data definition, data manipulation, physical data base support, and other factors related to the DBMS vendor and the resources required for DBMS acquisition and operation.[3,4]

7.1.1. Data Definition Capabilities

Table 7.1 lists some of the characteristics of interest when the data definition features of a DBMS are being evaluated. These characteristics can be summarized as describing the data model supported and the nature of the data description language. The data model is the fundamental approach taken by the DBMS to representing entities and relationships in the data base. (This concept is treated in more detail in Chapters 8 and 9.) The data model describes the view of data and data relationships which is most "natural" to the DBMS. User requirements which conform to this natural view are more easily supported than those which vary from it.

The data description language is a language used by the DBA, and sometimes by other data base programmers, to describe the content and structure of the data base to the DBMS. The evaluator should look to the DDL both to ascertain its own

Table 7.1. DBMS Data Definition Features

Data model	Data description language
Basic unit of data (character, field, group, record)	Language type (keyword, positional, free format)
Relationships supported (1:1, 1:n, n:m)	Readability
Sequencing allowed	Ease of learning
Unique identification required, duplicates allowed	Degree of data independence
Structural validation performed	Maintenance requirements
Support for user views	Accessibility (reports, data lists)
	Security (authorization) procedures
	Elements of description (data types, size, name, alias, occurrences)

characteristics (e.g., ease of use and readability) and to discover constraints placed on data by the DBMS (e.g., data types supported or provisions for access constraints). It is also important to assess the frequency with which data descriptions must be prepared and revised. Utilities for maintaining these descriptions and for effecting necessary revisions must also be investigated. With this information the evaluator can estimate the operational burden of anticipated data base activities such as changing the data model, adding new data items, or changing data storage structures.

7.1.2. Data Manipulation

Data manipulation features of interest concern the ways in which the data base can be accessed and the language(s) with which to do so (see Table 7.2). The evaluator should be concerned with how data groups can be accessed, e.g., in physical sequence, in a logical sequence (based on the value of a data item), or directly through the record key. For each manipulation operator provided by the DBMS it is important to note the type of record identification required. For example, in a hierarchical system access to a record at the lowest level can only proceed given the keys of all records above it in the hierarchical path.

Most DBMS's have a data manipulation language (DML) which the user or application programmer uses to invoke data base processing operations. The following characteristics of that DML are of interest. With what host (high-level) languages is it compatible? How easy or difficult is the DML to learn? How procedural is it? If the DML is quite procedural, does a nonprocedural query language exist for this DBMS?

The relation of the DML to existing languages is important in matching the DBMS to the existing data processing environment. Similarly, its ease of use and ease of learning have ramifications for systems development under the DBMS. The degree of procedurality is a measure of data independence for programs. The less procedural a language is—i.e., the less it says about how data are to be accessed,

Table 7.2. DBMS Data Manipulation Features

Access features	Data manipulation language
Sequences supported	Interface to standard languages
Keys required for access	Ease of use
Record or field retrieval	Degree of procedurality, data independence
	Query language available
	Control over concurrent processing
	Report generator available

restricting itself to what data are required—the less likely it is that programs written in that language will have to change when new accessing modes or even new data structures are introduced into the DBMS.

A final consideration under data manipulation is related to the question of concurrent processing. What provision does the DBMS provide to preserve the integrity of a data base that is being used simultaneously by more than one application? Normally, some restrictions are placed on access for all but one of the concurrent processes. An important consideration is the extent of these restrictions. For example, if a program is updating a data base record, are concurrent processes denied access to the field being changed, the record, or the whole physical file of which the record is a part?

7.1.3. Physical Data Base Support

A major objective of the data base approach is to provide independence of the logical data base and application programs from the physical data base storage methods. However, the physical storage has a strong impact on the performance of DBMS-supported systems. Thus the DBMS evaluator should investigate the access methods provided by the DBMS. It is especially important to note the types of retrieval supported (direct, indexed, inverted, sequential) and the proportion of overhead information required.

The facilities provided for data base backup and recovery are also of interest. In particular, the ability to request automatic logging of data base activity is valuable. DBMS routines to assist the recovery process, e.g., data base reload and log tape processing, are also desirable.

Other utility routines or DBMS-related software of interest include data base load routines, a trace feature for debugging, and routines for collecting and analyzing operational performance statistics.

If the data base is to support on-line processing applications, the evaluator must gather data on the type of data communications support available as part of

Table 7.3.   DBMS Physical Data Base Support Features

Access methods	Backup and recovery	DP support	Utilities
Indexing	Logging	Monitor available	Load
Inversion	Restart	Reentrant	Trace
Sequential	Checkpoint	Message, transaction handler	Tuning
Data		Interface with standard	Performance
compression		communication handlers	measurement
Overhead			

the DBMS. If no such support is provided as part of the DBMS, one must investigate other software that is compatible with the DBMS either by the same vendor or other vendors. The most important features of interest are the facility for message and transaction handling, the way in which multiple applications are supported, and the way in which DBMS code common to all the concurrent processes is handled.

Table 7.3 summarizes the physical support features to be evaluated.

7.1.4. Other Factors

A number of other factors that are not directly related to the capabilities of the DBMS are important for the success of implementing the DBMS in an organization, and these must also be considered in the evaluation (see Table 7.4). The stability and reliability of the vendor must be considered. The depth of the vendor's product line, the number of users for its DBMS, and the satisfaction of those users should be determined. Services provided by the vendor, including software maintenance, consultation, and training, should be enumerated and costed. The quality of the documentation provided should be rated, and its availability, i.e., how much is provided with the DBMS and the costs of additional documentation, should be determined.

To fully estimate system costs, the evaluator must look at both the charges levied by the DBMS vendor and the indirect costs of modifying or expanding the operating installation to accommodate the DBMS. The former include both one-time acquisition costs and recurring software license or maintenance costs. Initial training costs must also be estimated. Indirect costs might include additional core memory for the host processor, changes in the operating system, or additional secondary storage devices.

7.2. METHODS OF EVALUATION

The objective of evaluating several DBMS systems is to find the system that meets the organization's needs in the most cost-effective way. Since DBMS sys-

Table 7.4.   Other DBMS Features for Evaluation

Vendor	Documentation and training	HW/SW requirements	Cost
Stability	Availability	Core	One-time charge
Other products	Cost	Operating system	License fees
Other users	Quality	Incremental change in	Maintenance
Service		existing configuration	
		Compatibility	

tems vary widely in the way in which they provide the features described in the preceding section, evaluating and then comparing them is a complex process. Without a clear articulation of user needs, both in terms of the types of data to be supported and in the processing required, an objective evaluation is impossible. In spite of this fact, some organizations have selected a DBMS on the basis of cost or vendor characteristics alone. For a DBMS selected in such a way to succeed, applications must be designed to fit its features, rather than vice versa, and tuning must be employed to produce acceptable performance in applications for which the DBMS is unsuited.

In most DBMS selection projects, however, a thorough analysis of user needs is the first step. Then one or more of the following methods are used to evaluate and compare alternative DBMS systems in the light of those needs.

7.2.1. Feature Analysis and Scoring

Feature analysis is the most common method of DBMS evaluation. The features of DBMS systems in general are enumerated, as in Tables 7.1–7.4, and weighted to reflect the importance of each feature to the organization's needs. For example, the capability for multikey access to the data base might be crucial to an organization that expects frequent ad hoc inquiries into its data base. The same feature may be irrelevant or even detrimental for an organization whose inquires are infrequent or well known in advance. For each feature, the evaluator rates each DBMS with respect to whether and how well it meets the requirements. The DBMS that is rated highest is selected.

Data used in preparing the ratings include detailed documentation of user requirements, DBMS documentation, consultation with the DBMS vendors, discussions with other DBMS users, and perhaps the advice of an experienced data base consultant.

To formalize the rating process and to make the results comparable across various DBMS systems, a scoring methodology [5] can be used. With this approach, scoring sheets are prepared for each class of features and requirements evaluated (see Figure 7.2). The evaluator rates each feature in two ways: whether it exists in the DBMS being considered, and the quality of the capability provided. The latter is rated on a standard scale, say from 1 (very poor) to 10 (excellent). Each quality rating can be multiplied by the weight assigned to the feature rated to produce a score for that feature. A score for the entire class of requirements is computed by summing the weighted scores of the features.

The full capabilities of a DBMS can be viewed as a hierarchy of classes of features, each class being further decomposable into more detailed component features (see Figure 7.3). At each level of the hierarchy weights can be assigned to reflect the relative importance of the features on that level. An overall score for the DBMS can then be constructed by computing the weighted sum of the feature

DBMS _____ Vendor _____			Evaluator _____ Date _____	
Requirement/Feature	Existence (Y/N)	Quality (1-10)	Weight (% of total)	Score
Multikey Access	Y	7	.4	2.8
Hashed Access	Y	3	.3	.9
Indexed Access	Y	2	.2	.4
Sequential Access	Y	10	.1	1.0
TOTAL		5.5 (unweighted)	1.00	5.1 (weighted)

Figure 7.2. A feature analysis scoring sheet.

scores at each level of the hierarchy. Figure 7.3 shows a hypothetical example of this computation process. For each DBMS rated the weights remain unchanged; only the ratings vary.

This weighting and scoring process provides two immediate benefits, in addition to that of quantifying the analysis variables. First, it reflects user needs in the scores computed. It prevents an unnecessary feature, which happens to be of excellent quality, from biasing the results. For example, in Figure 7.2 the rating of 10 for sequential access inflates the unweighted score even though sequential access has low priority with respect to the user's needs.

The second benefit of this type of scoring is that the final scores for each DBMS can be decomposed into more detailed components, also scored, for discussion or negotiation with the vendors. For example, an evaluation of two DBMS systems X and Y not only yields the fact that X scores higher than Y but also that Y's weakness was related to data description facilities, in particular that Y's DDL was difficult to learn and to maintain.

Feature analysis and scoring is basically a staff analysis activity. As such the resources required are staff persons to perform the analysis and data gathering. The depth of the analysis can be cursory or quite detailed, or even refined iteratively. One disadvantage to this approach, however, is that it is static. Observations on performance and other operational issues must be based only on interpretations of the features provided. The nature of the trade-offs, e.g., between retrieval speed and updating overhead, cannot be made explicit. Also the quality and reliability of the analysis depends on the skills and knowledge of the

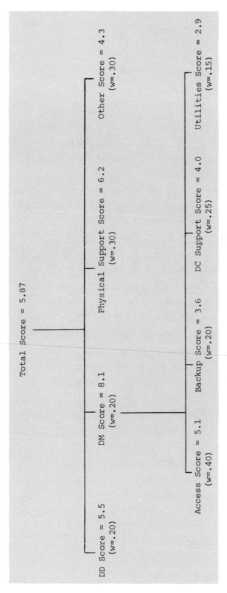

Figure 7.3. Computation of overall score for a DBMS.

evaluator. For an analyst new to data base systems, the decision on how well a particular feature or requirement is met can be a difficult one.

As a result, the feature analysis approach is best suited as a method to narrow the field of alternatives, and then cost and performance measures can be used to make the final selection.

7.2.2. Benchmarking

Benchmarking is a procedure for assessing the performance characteristics of a hardware/software system given a specific application environment. Application programs typical of the organization's work load are selected and run on an existing installation having the hardware/software system characteristics of interest. For example, when deciding whether to upgrade to the next model of a particular CPU, one could measure the performance of selected benchmark programs on the new model CPU at the vendor's or another user's site.

The use of benchmarking to compare DBMS systems requires more preparation than benchmarking two different models of a CPU. A test data base must be designed and stored which is a representative though scaled-down version of the organization's data base. Then the processing requirements of existing and anticipated applications must be modeled using the data manipulation facilities of the DBMS. Finally, the benchmark tests are run using the candidate DBMS in a system environment comparable to that of the evaluating organization.

Since the preparation for DBMS benchmarking—data base creation and application coding—requires a thorough knowledge of the DBMS, the evaluator may have no alternative other than entrusting this preparatory work to the DBMS vendor. Few vendors will allow the evaluating organization the necessary training in and use of their package without a commitment to acquire the package. Thus the benchmark will be reduced to one well-defined application and a test data base designed and implemented by the vendor. The performance statistics from this benchmark can be compared across DBMS's, but the evaluator gains no insight into the reasons for differences in the performance figures or how those statistics might change for another application or data base.

One approach to this problem is to develop a general test data base and a set of representative transactions that reflect the range of processing capabilities that might be required.[6] The test data base might be a subset of an existing data base or a synthetic data base created to embody the types of data and relationships desired. The test processes, or transactions, represent the basic processing functions to be supported by the DBMS. In the example described by Fong[6] the test involved eight test transactions including on-line update, delete, data entry, and data retrieval requests with various types of qualifications. By prespecifying the test data base and transactions, the evaluator is assured a measure of uniformity among the benchmark results. Further, the performance statistics can be related to types of processing, e.g., one DBMS may excel on update, another on multikey retrieval.

The advantage of benchmarking is that real performance of the DBMS's can be observed and compared. Even if the vendors take responsibility for setting up the test data base and processes, the evaluator can get some feel for the difficulty or ease with which the DBMS handles the required processing, such as by the number and complexity of the DML commands needed or the size of the data base or the length of the data base description. However, in order for such realism to be achieved within reasonable cost limits, the scope of the tests is limited and many simplifying assumptions must be made. No conclusions can be drawn about the performance of the systems tested when, say, the data base increases in size or the volume or distribution of processing requests changes. Finally, such tests are performed on the assumption that the installation on which the tests are run is comparable to that of the evaluator. This condition may not be met in many situations.

7.2.3. Simulation and Modeling

With simulation and modeling the evaluator uses mathematical expressions and quantitative representations to describe the actions of the DBMS. These models of DBMS activity relate the objective of the evaluation, perhaps to test processing time, to the other factors that affect that objective. For example, processing time for a transaction might be expressed as a function of the number of disk accesses required, the amount of data transferred, and the CPU time necessary to form the required response. Since each of these factors is affected by the way in which the DBMS stores the data and the access strategies used, different models will result for different DBMS systems. Once developed these models can be used to estimate the processing time or costs required by each DBMS for a variety of processing conditions, such as different data base sizes, different blocking factors, or different access techniques.

Simulation and modeling are used most frequently in research environments by researchers trying to understand the relative importance of various factors affecting system costs or performance.[7,8] However, modeling has also been used successfully in commercial environments.[9] Two difficulties with modeling that have prevented it from being used more frequently in DBMS evaluations are the degree of knowledge required about the DBMS and the analytical skills necessary to build a valid model. Many organizations are reluctant to invest the resources necessary to train personnel in more than one DBMS. Such training and in-depth knowledge of the selected DBMS may prove beneficial, especially if the analysis team is part of the DBA staff.[9]

The existence of a generalized simulation language for data base systems[10] should make simulation a more attractive evaluation tool. Such a language would remove from the evaluator the burden of developing detailed mathematical models. Instead, the evaluator would describe the DBMS activity in terms of high-level primitives provided by the simulation language. However, a good knowledge of the workings of the DBMS is still required.

Simulation is appealing as an evaluation tool because of the range of alternative situations that can be modeled. The evaluator can assess the cost or performance of the DBMS with different transaction streams or different data base sizes. However, in order to develop a model which is tractable mathematically, many simplifying assumptions must be made about the operating environment. For example, most models ignore the activity of other jobs in the system which may interact with and thus affect data base processing. Thus the more complex the DBMS and the operating environment, the more difficult it is to apply simulation as an evaluation tool.

7.3. THE DBA's ROLE

The DBA should be responsible for the evaluation of alternative DBMS packages and for a recommendation to management to acquire the package which best suits the organization's needs. Part of the evaluation task involves selection and application of an evaluation technique. However, even more important is a full specification of the organization's requirements. The "best" DBMS cannot be chosen without reference to a well-defined set of evaluation criteria. Organizations which attempt to select the best DBMS without knowing how that system will be used face an almost impossible task. The variety of features and functions offered by currently available DBMS's and their variations in performance justify the selection of any one as "best" in some regard.

A full requirements study as a prelude to DBMS evaluation followed by a systematic and quantitative analysis of the candidate systems will have several benefits. Not only will the best system be selected, but the DBA and data base users within the organization will have a clear understanding of how the DBMS will serve their needs and an informed expectation of its strengths and its weaknesses.

Part III

Data Base Design

Chapter 8

The Data Base Design Process

The objective of data base design is to produce an integrated data base which is accurate and secure and which supports application systems in an efficient manner. Each of these characteristics—integration, integrity, security, and performance—must be addressed during the design process to assure the desired outcome. Integration is the result of specifying data base content and structure in response to the needs of more than one application area. Integrity is assured through controls on application systems that prevent data loss or improper modification. The use of procedures and DBMS features that promote data sharing, while limiting access to data which are not shared, results in data base security. Finally, data base performance depends on both the efficiency of the physical realization of the data and the ability of the data base to satisfy processing requests in a timely manner.

The activities involved in data base design are not limited to one phase in the process of data base development within an organization. Rather they are continually invoked throughout the life of the data base itself. The design process is first used to create the initial data base, or initial portion of the data base. This may involve creation of a data base in an area which had little or no computer support previously, or it could represent the conversion of application data files to a data base management system. While the objective of data base design remains the same in both cases, conversion places additional constraints on the design activities. The data base designer has fewer options for data structures and physical implementations when existing non-data base applications must continue to be supported.

After the initial development of a data base, design activities are required whenever that data base is modified. Such changes may result from the development of new application systems with additional data requirements. Modifications may also be required to respond to changes in the data or processing needs of existing applications. A need to improve data base performance in general or to tune specific applications can also result in data base redesign. As with modifications to application systems, these redesign efforts must be approached as mini design efforts to ensure that the changes are not achieved at the expense of overall data base goals.

Data base design is one of the major areas of the data base administrator's responsibility. The DBA must guide and control data base design activities in such a way that the organization has ready and efficient access to the data required for its operations. Thus the DBA must be thoroughly familiar with the data base design process, the limitations on that process, and the implications of alternative design decisions.

8.1. OVERVIEW OF THE DATA BASE DESIGN PROCESS

The data base design process is divided into sets of design tasks called logical data base design and physical data base design (see Figure 8.1).[1,2] Logical data base design focuses on user requirements and the development of a system-independent description of a data base which will meet those requirements. In the terminology of the ANSI architecture,[3] user requirements are represented by a number of *external models* (views) of the data base; the *conceptual model* represents the overall view. Physical design is concerned with the actual implementation of the data base within a specific hardware/software environment. In ANSI terms, physical design results in an *internal model* of the data base. Each of these design phases is discussed in detail in the succeeding chapters, and a brief outline is provided here to serve as a basis for the discussion of trade-offs in the design process.

8.1.1. Logical Data Base Design

Logical data base design begins with an investigation of user, or application, requirements and results in a description of the data base that will support those requirements. The term *logical* is used to indicate that the description produced does not include implementation-level details, such as field lengths or file structures. The description produced by logical data base design serves as a blueprint for physical design and as a reference for later modifications to the data base.

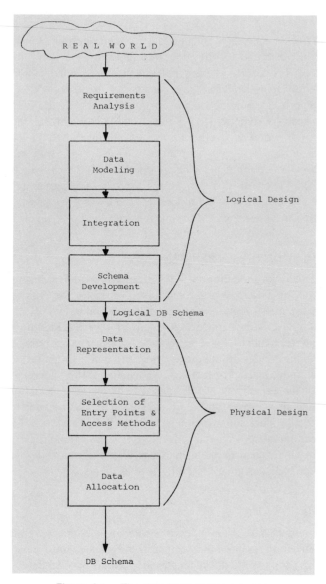

Figure 8.1.   The data base design process.

Four activities make up the logical data base design phase: requirements analysis, application modeling, integration, and schema development. These steps are generally performed in the sequence indicated. However, they may overlap or be performed in parallel.

8.1.1.1. Requirements Analysis

Requirements analysis is analogous to systems analysis. A catalogue of user needs, both for data and for the processes that must be performed using those data, must be developed. These requirements are elicited using the standard techniques of systems analysis—interviews, document collection, observation, simulated reports. Depending on the methodology used, the output of the requirements analysis step can be a strictly codified set of data and processing specifications or narrative descriptions of items of interest to the user and typical processes.

Normally the requirements analysis involves more than one user or application area. Thus alternative specifications for data and processing result. It is important that standard data definitions be used wherever possible during this step to minimize inconsistencies among the specifications developed.

8.1.1.2. Data (or Application) Modeling

During the data modeling step an attempt is made to develop an abstract representation, or data model, for each user's view of the data base. The data specified in the user's requirements are taken as indicative of the user's view. While many types of data models exist, all involve the identification of basic entities of interest to the user and the relationships that exist among those entities. For example, the entities of interest to a marketing user might be sales, products, regions, salesmen, and sales forecasts. The relationships among these entities could include the assignment of salesmen to regions, the association of each sale with a particular salesman and a product, and the association of each sales forecast with a product and a region.

The data model should represent the user's environment as realistically as possible. The closer the data model comes to a faithful model of reality, the more flexible a data base designed according to that model will be.

8.1.1.3. Integration

Since the data base is intended to serve many users, several data models may be produced by the preceding steps. These models must now be integrated into one model from which all the alternative views may be derived. Often this step is combined with the data modeling step. When this occurs, the designer resolves inconsistencies among user requirements during the data modeling process and produces an integrated model directly.

8.1.1.4. Schema Development

The schema development step marks the border between logical and physical data base design. The requirements specifications and data models of the previous steps are independent of any DBMS. However, a data base schema is a description of the data base expressed in the data description language (DDL) of a particular DBMS. The designer must choose DBMS constructs to express the entities and relationships in the data model and combine these constructs into a consistent schema. During schema development the data base designer must rely on processing specifications from the users as guides to the proper choice of DBMS constructs for the schema.

A purely logical schema can exist. Often expressed as a diagram, this type of schema simply shows the entities and relationships of the data model using DBMS-specific terminology. However, once the schema includes details of data representation and accessing, it becomes a description of the physical data base.

An additional part of schema development is the task of creating descriptions of subsets of the data base, called subschemas. These subschemas are tailored to individual user views of the data base and can be used to limit any user's access to that portion of the data base pertinent to his application.

8.1.2. Physical Data Base Design

Physical data base design involves the selection of appropriate techniques for physically realizing the content and relationships in the data base. Physical design uses the data model or logical schema as a starting point and determines how the data represented in that model are to be stored and accessed. The three major activities of physical data base design are data representation, selection of data base entry points and access paths, and allocation of data to storage devices.

8.1.2.1. Data Representation

The representation of data elements and groups involves the specification of data types, field lengths, and replication factors. Often this specification comes directly from the data definitions developed as part of the requirements analysis step, for example, when codes are defined for a data element such as Product Number. The number of replications, or occurrences, expected for a particular data group most often comes from the user's specification of data or processing requirements. For example, the number of sales that the data base must be capable of recording could be estimated by the user based on past experience or on a given maximum per salesman.

8.1.2.2. Selection of Entry Points and Access Paths

This activity can be compared with the process of file design in a typical application-oriented system. Using the user's processing requirements as a guide, the designer must select access methods for each entity in the data base and must determine how the entities are going to be linked to realize the necessary relationships among them. With commercial DBMS's the designer must select from a menu of access and linkage techniques provided by the package. Typically each technique has different characteristics of access efficiency and overhead. The designer must select techniques that will optimize the performance of the data base for the applications specified. Decisions among direct addressing, hashing, indexing, and pointer arrays are typical of this step in physical data base design.

8.1.2.3. Data Allocation

The final step in physical data base design is the allocation of the data base to physical storage devices. Techniques are available to partition the data base on the basis of activity, or some similar criteria, and to assign the partitions to different devices. Again the objective is to optimize data base performance. Techniques for clustering similar data records or creating storage hierarchies are other choices for data allocation.

8.2. TRADE-OFFS IN DATA BASE DESIGN

Often during the course of data base design the designer faces two or more ways of representing or implementing the data base. Many times the best choice depends on the designer's objective. For example, the relationship between salesmen and regions could be represented by a link (pointer) between Salesmen records and Region records (see Figure 8.2a). Or the two entities could be

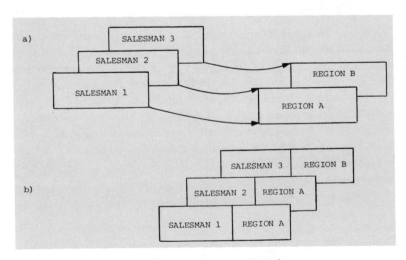

Figure 8.2. Two design alternatives.

combined, with each Salesman record including data on the salesman's region (see Figure 8.2b). The first alternative is preferable if salesmen and regions are to be processed separately as well as together. However, it has the disadvantage of the complexity and system overhead needed to create and maintain the links. The second alternative is simpler but results in redundant storage of region data. Further, region data are accessible only through salesmen.

A decision that involves this type of weighing of advantages and disadvantages between alternatives is called a trade-off. The designer is trading the advantages of one method for the more valued advantages of the other. The data base design process involves trade-offs of several types.[4,5]

8.2.1. Complexity versus Redundancy

The example in the previous section illustrates a trade-off between complexity and redundancy. Data redundancy is reduced in data base systems by introducing complex data structures to link related entities. Uncontrolled redundancy can result in costs of various types. Most obviously there is cost associated with keeping multiple copies of the same data (e.g., the region data in the example). Further, these redundant data may be inconsistent, causing a negative impact on the accuracy of processes run against the data base.

When related entities are linked, data need be recorded and stored only once. However, additional data (pointers) and processing are needed to maintain these linkages. Also the procedures that process these data must be more complex in order to take advantage of the links between the two entities.

8.2.2. Generalization versus Specialization

Traditional application systems are designed to optimize performance for a particular process. For example, a credit check application might be designed to optimize the retrieval of credit information in response to an inquiry. A system to apply charges to a customer's account, on the other hand, might favor efficient update processing. When applications such as these share the same data base, a conflict occurs. One of the two must sacrifice optimal performance. The data base can provide for generalized application support through data sharing at the expense of less than optimal performance for particular applications.

The generalization versus specialization trade-off can also occur over questions of data content and structure. Compromises over standard data definitions involve this type of trade-off. The integration of user views also occasions compromises. For example, to accommodate both credit check and charge posting applications, customer credit may be modeled as an entity separate from customer account data. As a result, the posting application must now update both types of entities rather than one that combines both types of data.

8.2.3. Control versus Efficiency

The integration of data into a common data base presents new opportunities for data control as well as new threats to that control. While the integrity of the data should be improved by reduced redundancy and centralized controls, the data are more prone to improper access and other security violations. In traditional systems much of this control was provided by physical separation of data from unrelated processes.

In a data base environment procedures can be implemented to screen all data base access and check the validity of all data stored. However, the price of this increased control is processing and storage overhead. Concern over the impact of increased processing times can minimize or even eliminate integrity and security features from data base systems.

8.2.4. Flexibility versus Efficiency

The use of data base systems to achieve data independence brings a new flexibility to the design of application systems using that data. Application program coding is simplified by the powerful commands available through the DBMS. The maintenance of such systems is reduced since programs are insulated from changes in the physical data base. This simplification represents a saving in people time and therefore costs.

However, to achieve this flexibility one must pay the price of complex data base design and complex DBMS physical support. Machine time is required for the interfaces between the application programs and the data description tables and eventually the retrieval component of the DBMS. This is additional processing that would not be required if application programs contained descriptions of the data or accessed the data directly.

The data base designer may choose to sacrifice data independence in specific situations to promote the processing efficiency of an application. However, this always means that the flexibility of changing or replacing the application will be constrained.

8.3. CONSTRAINTS OF THE DBMS

The DBMS used to implement the data base places certain constraints on both logical and physical data base design. The terminology and approach used by a particular package will certainly influence the way that the designer views the alternative designs that are feasible for the data base. Physical implementations of these designs are constrained by the way in which a DBMS represents the data and relationships in the design and by the modes of access that are provided.

Currently there are three identifiable approaches to data base management: hierarchical, network, and relational.[6] DBMS packages can be roughly classified into four groups, one for each of the three approaches and one for systems which have followed their own individual approach to data structuring or representation. If a data base designer is accustomed to working with one specific type of DBMS, the approach of that DBMS will color the designer's view of the way in which objects and relationships can be represented.

The hierarchical approach sees a hierarchy of objects as the most typical and useful data structure. Relationships between an object and several subordinate objects, e.g., between a manager and his or her employees or between suppliers and the parts they supply, are hierarchical relationships and are directly supported by the physical constructs of the DBMS. Packages following the network approach see hierarchical relationships as a special case of network relationships between objects. For example, in a manufacturing application each part may have many suppliers and each supplier may supply many parts. Each of these relationships is hierarchical; however, the overall relationship between suppliers and parts is a network relationship. Network systems assume that each object may participate in network relationships. Finally, relational systems do not distinguish between objects and relationships. The basic construct is a relation, or group of related data elements. A relation may represent an object, say a part, or a relationship, such as the relationship between parts and suppliers. Figure 8.3 illustrates these different approaches.

If the designer is not careful, the approach of a specific DBMS can constrain the data base design at an early stage. The user's data requirements can be shaped into hierarchies or networks to fit the DBMS. This early binding can eliminate other feasible alternatives and put implicit limitations on eventual system performance by building assumed modes of access into the logical design.

Even DBMS packages of the same type can have different means of data representation and access. Some associate objects with data records and represent relationships by pointers among the records. Others assign traditional data files to represent objects and relationships. Still others require unique record keys and use indexes to relate different records. Each type of representation and access has different performance implications for different applications. For example, an application that requires retrieval of objects based on several different data elements (keys) achieves better performance in a system that allows multikey indexing. The performance implications of using a system that depends on single-key accessing would be less desirable. In an existing DBMS these constraints become trade-offs in physical data base design. If no DBMS currently exists, application requirements should be matched against DBMS constraints as part of the selection process.

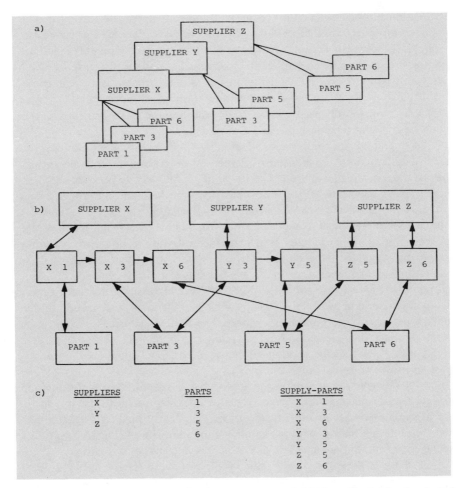

Figure 8.3. Three approaches to data base management: (a) hierarchical, (b) network, and (c) relational.

8.4. THE DBA'S ROLE

The data base administrator should play a major role in the data base design process.[7,8] The skills and the position of the DBA make this group most qualified to control and direct the design of the data base. Although many other groups within the organization must participate, the DBA serves as the link among these groups, the common point of the design process. The DBA staff also have the expertise necessary for both the logical and the physical design steps. Finally, the DBA is responsible for making all design trade-offs explicit.

8.4.1. Control the Design Process

For data to be integrated with minimum redundancy there must be a common control over data content. The DBA using the facilities of a data dictionary can merge the data needs of the various application areas and standardize the content of the data base. In the same way the DBA can have knowledge of the different data base views and processing requirements of the several areas. Thus the DBA can integrate these needs to form a common data base design and can validate the design by checking that it meets the existing requirements. The DBA can schedule data base development so that development activities in the application areas are properly supported. Whether the DBA can resolve conflicts in priorities that may arise concerning this schedule depends on the organizational characteristics of the DBA group.

8.4.2. Provide Data Base Expertise

The DBA's staff contains individuals with expertise and experience in data base–related specialties. During the design process the DBA's staff should provide guidance to the systems development staff and the users for the clear specification of their data and processing needs. The DBA's knowledge of alternative approaches to data base management and familiarity with state-of-the-art methods for data base design should be used to guide the logical design steps. Knowledge of the DBMS and its features as well as skill in the design of physical data structures are needed during physical design. Again the DBA staff is the prime source of this expertise. In fact, there is good reason to assume that the entire process of physical data base design should be assigned to the DBA's staff. If applications are to be truly data independent, the application developers should not be concerned with the physical aspects of data base design. The physical designers (on the DBA staff) will simply work to meet processing specifications set out by the applications development staffs.

8.4.3. Articulate Design Trade-Offs

The design process is fraught with trade-offs, usually between efficiency or system performance and some other desirable characteristic of the data base environment, e.g., data independence or minimum redundancy. It is reasonable to assume that the applications development staffs emphasize user needs and that the systems software and operations staff are most concerned with system performance. Thus the DBA must continually make these trade-offs explicit so that parochial views do not result in the abandonment of the data base approach. The DBA, as advocate for the data base approach, must attempt to prevent the sacrifice of long-range benefits for the entire organization to the perceived needs of individual applications.

To properly perform this role the DBA must be completely familiar with the techniques for and the implications of the process of data base design.

Chapter 9

Logical Data Base Design

The purpose of a data base is to represent objects and events of interest to the organization. Any representation of the real world is, of necessity, incomplete in that it is not the actual object but a description of that object. The characteristics described are those that are most obvious, or most interesting, or most relevant to the creator of the representation. Aspects which are not of interest are ignored. For example, the descriptive characteristics of an individual that are recorded on a driver's license include age, hair color, eye color, name, and address but not marital status or educational history.

Representations of the real world may be informal or formal descriptions. A paragraph describing the layout of a particular town can reflect the biases and interests of the author. A map of the same town must conform to conventions used in similar maps and allows less freedom of expression. A surveyor's report on the town is even more constrained.

Representations can also exhibit different levels of generality. One can describe the characteristics of books in general—title, author(s), publisher. Or one can describe a particular type of book, say textbooks. Each textbook has a particular subject, is written for a certain educational level, and may or may not contain problems for the student to solve. Most specifically, a description can refer to one particular book, such as how many copies of that book have been sold since its publication, or even to one particular copy of a book, such as who bought it, where, when, its location at the current time.

The process of logical data base design is concerned with identifying the objects and events of interest to an organization, selecting the characteristics that should be described for each, and developing a formal representation of those objects and events to guide the development of a corresponding physical data base.

9.1. THE OBJECTIVES OF LOGICAL DESIGN

The aim of logical design is to produce an accurate and complete representation of the real world as a guide to the development of a physical data base that is adequate for and flexible enough to meet the organization's information processing needs.

Accuracy is fundamental. If the representation of an object is inaccurate, any processes or decisions involving that description will not be reliable. For example, if books are represented as having only one author, a report based on that description showing the number of books written by each author will be inaccurate for individuals who have written books with colleagues.

An incomplete reresentation will fail to support certain processes or decisions involving that description. For example, if marital status is not included in the representation of students, those descriptions are useless in determining the proportion of students currently married.

Both accuracy and completeness, however, are tied to adequacy. A student description lacking marital status may be adequate where the proportion or characteristics of married students are not of interest. Even inaccurate representations, e.g., restricting a book's description to the first author, can be tolerated as long as they are explicitly acknowledged. The report in the example just discussed could clearly show that it represents the number of books that each individual has written as first author.

Questions of adequacy versus accuracy and completeness are complicated by the fact that adequacy is time dependent. What is adequate today may not be adequate tomorrow. For example, an organization may become interested in students' marital status or second authors after an initial representation of these objects, and perhaps the corresponding physical data base, has been developed. The original representation then becomes inadequate and redesign is required. If the characteristics in question had been included at the outset, the representation and its companion data base would have been more flexible. However, this flexibility is gained at the price of collecting and maintaining data which are not, initially, of interest to the organization. The logical designer plays a major role in articulating and resolving such trade-offs.

9.2. BASIC CONCEPTS

Since terminology is far from standard in this area, it is important for the reader to understand the meaning of some basic terms as used by the author.

The representations used by data base designers to guide and describe the content and structure of a data base exist at three levels: the conceptual level, the logical schema level, and the physical schema level.[1] The first two levels are of interest in logical data base design. The physical schema representation and the actual data base itself are the subject of physical data base design.

At the conceptual level the real world is represented in terms of entities and relationships. Entities can represent objects, events, or concepts. Relationships show associations between entities. For example, a catalog sales firm might be interested in two entities, customers and orders. These entities are related by the fact that customers place orders. The nature of this relationship can be made more exact by specifying that a customer may place one or more orders and that each order is placed by only one customer. This information is called the cardinality of the relationship and can be one to one (1:1), one to many (1:n), or many to many (m:n). In this example the relationship between the customer entity and the order entity is 1:n; the relationship between the order entity and the customer entity is 1:1.

The environment of interest to the organization can then be represented by assembling the entities and relationships into a data model. A data model records the entities of interest, including their names and the attributes (or descriptive characteristics) to be recorded for each, and the relationships between entities. Figure 9.1 shows a data model for the catalog sales application.

More than one data model can exist for a given environment, since the content and structure of the data model depend on how the entities and relationships are defined. Some data models have been shown to be "better" representations in that they minimize problems associated with maintaining a data base which follows the model. Such models are called normalized representations.[2-4] The process of normalization is associated with the identification of entities in that it forces attributes to be directly descriptive of the entity with which they are associated. For example, the data model shown in Figure 9.1 is unnormalized because the attributes Product Number, Description, and Price describe the product ordered, not the order itself. Figure 9.2 shows a normalized version of the data model from Figure 9.1.*

The values of the descriptive attributes corresponding to real objects or events are found not in the data model but in the physical data base. Each entity

---

*Date[3] provides definitions of the four normal forms and detailed examples of the normalization process.

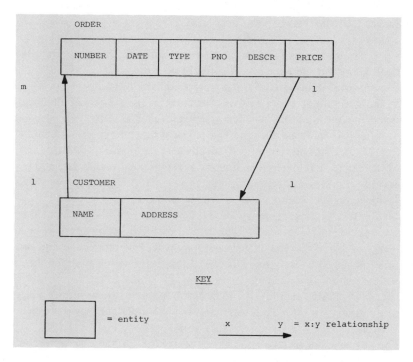

Figure 9.1. Data model for the catalog sales data base.

in the data model can represent many instances (or occurrences) of values describing different objects or events of that type. For example, the physical data base for the data model in Figure 9.2 will contain an instance of the customer entity for each customer that places an order. In physical terms each instance might be a punched card or a disk file record that contains values for each of the customer's attributes, i.e., ADAMS for Name and 111 BURNS ST. for Address. Figure 9.3 shows one possible physical realization of the catalog sales data model. In this data base, two card files have been used—one for customers and their orders and one for products.

Different instances of the same entity can be distinguished by the values that the attributes assume in each instance. The instance of the Customer entity for BROWN is different from that for ADAMS by virtue of the different value in the Name attribute. The attribute(s) that can be used to uniquely identify instances of an entity are called the key of the entity. In the example, Product Number might be a key for Product, and Name might be a key for Customer.

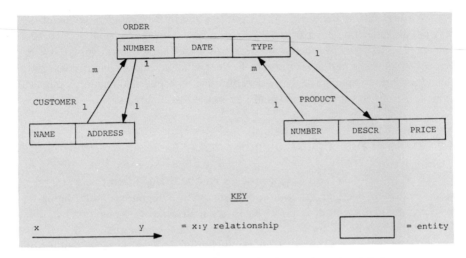

Figure 9.2. Normalized data model for the catalog sales data base.

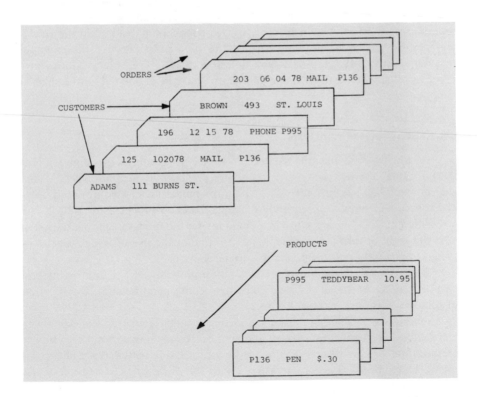

Figure 9.3. One physical realization for the catalog sales data model.

While a data model describes the entities and relationships in the data base, it is not dependent on any particular DBMS and contains no physical details, such as data element sizes. A schema is a data base description that is expressed using the constructs of a particular DBMS (a logical schema) and eventually using the data description language of the DBMS complete with physical details (a physical schema). Logical schemas are usually expressed as diagrams.[5]

9.3. STEPS IN THE LOGICAL DESIGN PROCESS

The logical data base design process can be divided into four component steps: requirements analysis, data modeling, view integration, and schema development.[6] This section describes each step in detail using a common example. Current methodologies for each step are cited where appropriate.

A simple design example is an expansion of the catalog sales application. The problem is to design a data base to support the sales and warehousing operations of a catalog sales firm. This hypothetical firm distributes catalogs to customers, receives orders for products advertised in the catalog, fills these orders using products obtained from various suppliers and stored in the firm's warehouses, and bills the customer for the products shipped. This example represents only a skeleton of a real situation of this type. Many entities and processes that would exist in a real application have been omitted for the sake of simplicity.

9.3.1. Requirements Analysis

As the name implies, the requirements analysis step is an investigation into the information and processing needs of the prospective data base user.[7] This step is much like systems analysis. It requires numerous discussions with users and the documentation of currently existing data and processes as well as the estimation of future needs. Current techniques for the requirements analysis step take the form of detailed methodologies[7,8] and/or the use of a high-level language to precisely document user requirements.[9,10]

Regardless of the methodology used, the following activities are an integral part of requirements analysis: data gathering, entity identification, specification of relationships, and process documentation.

During data gathering the logical designer interviews user representatives and collects documents from existing manual or computerized support systems. Descriptions of new reports required or new processing activities are also compiled. This process is often interactive, with the designer verifying his or her understanding of the requirements with the user by means of oral presentations or mock reports. Individuals who have had previous experience with the user's operational area are particularly valuable as designers during this step.

By the end of the data gathering the designer should have a complete and accurate picture of the user's processing environment. Relying on this understanding the designer identifies the entities of interest to the user. Each entity is assigned a name and a list of the attributes that must be recorded for the entity is compiled. Atttributes that might serve as entity keys are also identified. Physical characteristics for entities and their attributes, e.g., the number of instances anticipated for an entity or the data type and size of values for an attribute, may also be recorded at this time. These facts are not used until the physical design process, however.

Relationships between the entities identified are recorded next. The cardinality of each relationship is determined and recorded. With relationships the rationale behind the relationship is also important. For example, suppose each product is supplied by only one supplier. The nature of that relationship might be inherent in that products of that type are only made by one supplier. However, it could be that company policy prohibits ordering the same product from two suppliers. Or the fact that each product comes from a single supplier could be happenstance with no guarantee that additional suppliers might not be used in the future. These distinctions are important because the way in which the relationship is represented affects the flexibility of the data base design.

In addition to specifying data needs the designer must also document processes that will be applied against the data base. Each process should be documented in terms of the data that it requires as input and the reports and/or modifications to stored data that it produces as output. While access requirements and performance specifications for processes are not used until physical design, it may be convenient to record them at this time as well. However, characteristics such as the importance of a process and the frequency with which it is required are valuable during the schema development step of logical design.

The requirements for an integrated data base will be perceived in different ways by different data base users. Except in very simple situations the needs of these different views must be determined and recorded as separate sets of requirements. This allows each view to be analyzed in detail and verified from the user's perspective. It is the logical designer's task to integrate the several views later in the design process. Table 9.1 summarizes the entities, relationships, and processes for the sample data base, from two viewpoints: that of users concerned with the sales activities of the firm and that of users concerned with warehousing operations.

9.3.2. Data Modeling

The entities and relationships identified during the requirements analysis are next combined into a data model. If several views have been specified, a model may be developed for each view. As a basis for this step the logical designer has a choice of several different conceptual data modeling techniques.[11–14] Each

**Table 9.1.   Entities, Relationships, and Processes in the Catalog Sales
Data Base**

Entities	Relationships	Processes
	Sales View	
Customer	Customer has one account	Customer places order
Account	Customer has one or more orders	Product shipped or backordered
Order	Order by one customer	Customer billed
Product	Order for one product	
	Warehouse View	
Warehouse	Warehouse holds many products	Inventory status
Product	Products stored in many warehouses	Locate items for shipment
Model	Product has many models	Reorder product as needed
	Model for only one product	
Supplier	Model supplied by many suppliers	
	Supplier supplies many models	

technique uses its own conventions for representing entities, their keys and
attributes, and the relationships among them. For the data models in this discussion we shall use a simplified version of Chen's entity relationship diagrams
(ERD).[11]

Figure 9.4 shows the data model for the Sales view of the Catalog Sales data
base. Each box in the diagram represents an entity, and each connecting line
represents a relationship. The cardinality of the relationship is indicated on the
line itself. For example, the diagram shows that the cardinality of the relationship
between Customer and Order is $1:n$. The Warehouse view of the same data base

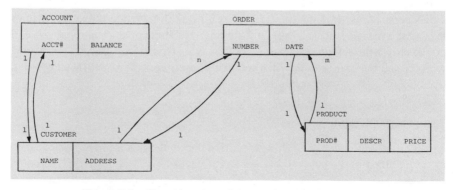

Figure 9.4.   The sales view of the catalog sales data base.

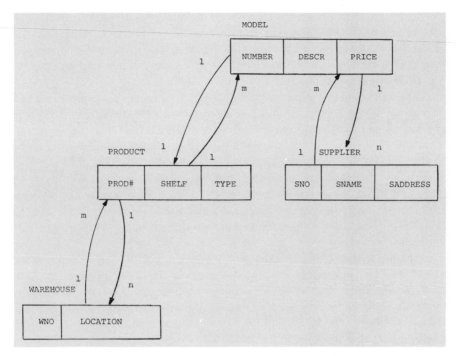

Figure 9.5. The warehouse view of the catalog sales data base.

is shown in Figure 9.5. Notice that while both the warehouse users and the sales users are interested in Products, each also needs entities that are not of interest to the other.

The data modeling process is often overlapped with the identification of entities and relationships in requirements analysis. As entities are defined, the modeling technique is used to record them. Since more than one data model may be created to represent a given situation, one can expect that a data model specified before completion of the requirements analysis will change as the designer's understanding of the situation grows. In fact, the rules that accompany each different modeling technique are designed to assist the designer in formulating a consistent and normalized representation of the data base. The formalization of a data model reduces the ambiguities that can exist in narratives and other less formal descriptions of data needs.

9.3.3. View Integration

To develop a data model that will represent a data base capable of supporting several different user areas, differing views must be integrated into one consistent view of the data base. There are two ways to approach this problem.

One is to start at the lowest level, i.e., with the attributes (or data elements) that have been identified for all views, and from them synthesize an integrated data model.[8,15,16] A top-down approach, on the other hand, requires that separate data models be developed for each view and then merged into one structure.[14] The latter approach is used here.

The integration of views requires that common entities be identified and inconsistencies in content or structure be resolved. The two views shown in Figures 9.4 and 9.5 reveal some typical inconsistencies. For example, the attribute name Number is used to describe Order in the Sales view and to describe Model in the Warehouse view. These attributes could be identical; however, it is more likely that they are homonyms, i.e., the same term used with different meanings. Also, the entity Product appears in both views but it has different attributes. Further, the entities Product (in the Sales view) and Model (in the Warehouse view) have different names but similar attributes. They may or may not be true synonyms.

Inconsistencies can also exist with respect to relationships. Suppose the Sales view had incorporated the Model entity. The Sales users might have specified the relationship between Product and Model as one-to-one. This is how the relationship appears to users in Sales since an Order can refer to only one ''product,'' i.e., a combination of Product and Model. However, this cardinality conflicts with that specified in the Warehouse view.

The detection and resolution of inconsistencies rests with the logical designer during view integration. Many naming inconsistencies can be avoided if a data dictionary is used to catalog and cross-reference entities and attributes during the requirements analysis step. Those which escape detection must be resolved during view integration. Resolution may require renaming of entities or attributes, merging or splitting entities.

Inconsistent relationship cardinalities can be resolved by assigning the more general of the two in conflict. For example, a one-to-many relationship can support a one-to-one relationship as a special case; and a many-to-many relationship can support both a one-to-many and a one-to-one relationship. Often relationship inconsistencies point out naming problems. In the example, the conflict in the Product–Model relationship was possible because the Model entity was synonymous with the Product entity (in the Sales view). The inconsistency can be resolved by renaming the Product entity in the Sales view ''Product–Model'' to indicate its true meaning.

Figure 9.6 shows an integrated view of the Catalog Sales data base with all inconsistencies resolved.

9.3.4. Schema Development

The data model of the Catalogue Sales data base shown in Figure 9.6 is a conceptual view of the data base. It is not tied to any particular DBMS, and it gives

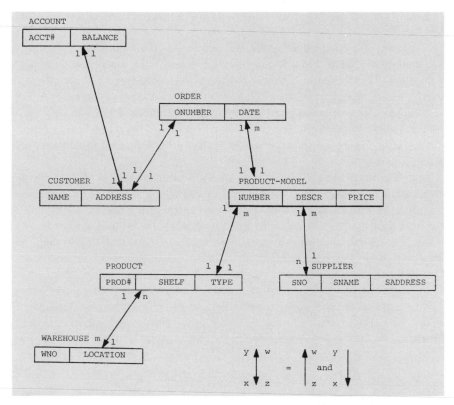

Figure 9.6. An integrated view of the catalog sales data base.

no indication of the way in which the data will be stored and accessed. This implementation-free representation is valuable for several reasons. The conceptual model can be used as a guide to implementing the data base on any DBMS in any physical environment. It is completely general. The conceptual model is also a more faithful representation of the real world than any description which must conform to the conventions of a particular system. If properly constructed, it should also remain unchanged over time. It should provide a stable frame of reference into which new entities, attributes, and relationships can be fit as the organization's data base evolves. As such, it can force design decisions that involve trade-offs to be made explicitly, thus preventing costly redesign situations that could have been avoided.

The conceptual model is not, however, directly implementable. It must be transformed into a schema for the particular DBMS to be used for implementation. It is possible when designing for a particular DBMS environment to develop a logical schema directly from requirements specifications.[15,16] However, this approach permits the implementation constraints of the DBMS to be introduced quite early in the modeling process and bypasses the construction of a conceptual model.

To convert a conceptual model into a schema, the logical designer maps each entity and relationship into constructs provided by the DBMS. For example, in a DBTG system the basic schema constructs are record types and set types.[5] Briefly, record types can be used to represent entities and set types, to represent one-to-many (1:n) relationships. The DBTG schema for a data base can be shown using a Bachman diagram where boxes represent record types and arrows represent set types. Figure 9.7 shows a DBTG schema for the Catalog Sales data model of Figure 9.6.

Schema development is not necessarily a direct mapping from the data model; some restructuring may be possible and beneficial.[17] In the example, the conceptual entities Customer and Account which exist in a one-to-one relationship have been merged into a single record type. Also, three dummy record types (LINK1, LINK2, and LINK3) have been introduced into the schema, following the DBTG convention for representing many-to-many relationships. Changes to conform to DBMS conventions are unavoidable.

Changes like the merger, however, are optional. Whether they prove beneficial depends on the processing requirements and the physical characteristics of the data base. For example, if only 1% of the firm's customers have accounts and if there are numerous and frequent processes that require only account informa-

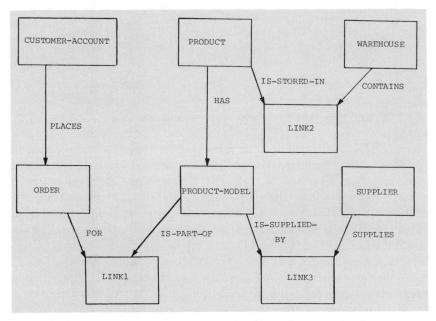

Figure 9.7. A DBTG schema diagram for the catalog sales data base.

tion, the merger of the two entities may have negative consequences in terms of storage requirements and processing time. The logical designer must rely on knowledge of processing requirements to guide the restructuring process.

9.4. THE DBA'S ROLE IN LOGICAL DESIGN

The logical designers of the DBA staff, in close cooperation with the system development staff and data base users, have full responsibility for logical data base design. The DBA staff provides expertise for data modeling and schema development, serves as a common point of reference for data definition and view integration, and is responsible for articulating the impact of design decisions throughout the logical design process.

Logical data base design is a skill founded on both knowledge and experience. Good designers must be comfortable with the terminology and conventions of a data modeling technique. They must also be expert in the DBMS schema, both its constructs and its data description language. Using this knowledge as a basis, they gain skill in identifying entities and discerning relationships through experience. Since no cookbook rules exist for producing the best design, logical designers must rely extensively on past successes and errors to improve their designs. This is a strong argument for making the logical designer a staff specialist rather than assigning logical design responsibility to existing system development staff.

Logical designers on the DBA staff bring the advantage of their perspective to the design process. All proposals for data base development and modification pass through the DBA. Data definitions are standardized through the DBA and maintained using a data dictionary under the DBA's control. Thus the DBA is in a much better position to spot and remove inconsistencies in the data base design than are the more parochial systems development staff. After all, the integrated, community view of the data base is the DBA's view.

Finally, logical designers on the DBA staff are in a better position to understand the implications of design decisions. Logical design decisions have an immediate impact on which data are collected and how those data are assembled in response to users' needs. However, over the long run these decisions can also affect the maintainability, efficiency, and flexibility of the physical data base. Questions of accuracy and completeness versus adequacy and efficiency in support of individual applications must be weighed very carefully. The risks include overdesign and underdesign. In overdesign, the expenditures on logical design and/or the design itself exceeds the needs of the firm at present and for the near future. In underdesign, logical design principles are sacrificed in a desire to meet specific, existing needs thus reducing the adequate life of the data base and requiring costly redesign within a short period of time. The DBA staff can bring objectivity as well as expertise to the evaluation of these trade-offs.

Chapter 10

Physical Data Base Design

The data described by a (logical) data base schema are not available to application programs or user inquiries until it has been realized physically, using the software and devices of the user's installation. Physical data base design includes the preparation of a plan for that realization and its accomplishment. In the terminology of traditional systems design, physical design is analogous to the selection of a file organization, preparation of file record layouts, and the creation of the file itself.

When a DBMS is used to store and access the data base, the physical designer must use the features and capabilities of that DBMS as building blocks for the physical design. The design is also influenced by the capabilities and constraints of the environment within which the data base is expected to operate.

10.1. THE OBJECTIVES OF PHYSICAL DESIGN

The aim of physical data base design is to produce a physical data base which achieves the best performance at the least cost. The physical design process assumes that the logical design has been completed and that the logical schema presented is a true and complete representation of the real world. It also assumes that a data base which follows the schema will be capable of supporting the users' needs. The physical designer tries to assure that this support is provided in the most efficient manner. Thus physical design techniques focus on factors which affect cost and/or performance.

The costs of creating and accessing a data base are related to both data storage and data processing. All other things being equal, the less storage space required for a data base, i.e., the fewer devices, the lower its cost. Similarly, the fewer the processing steps, e.g., disk accesses, required to search or modify the data base, the lower its processing costs will be.

Data base performance is also related to processing time. The faster an inquiry or transaction against the data base can be processed, the better the data base performance is rated. However, in a data base environment, performance is based on the data base's response to many different kinds of processing activities. Thus data base performance represents a kind of global optimum across all the applications supported.

Unfortunately, techniques which reduce the number of processing steps for a particular action, e.g., retrieval of a data record, often require the storage and maintenance of additional information, called overhead. Thus while processing is reduced, storage is increased. Further, techniques which improve processing of one type, say retrieval, may result in additional processing for other types, such as modification. Finally, choices that may improve performance for one application, or user, may negatively influence the performance of other applications against that same data. The physical designer must recognize these trade-offs and produce a data base which provides the best performance to all users at the least cost while meeting the minimum requirements specified for each individual application.

10.2. BASIC CONCEPTS

While terminology for file organization methods and for access methods differs from system to system, certain fundamental concepts remain unchanged regardless of what they are called. These concepts are briefly reviewed in this section before proceeding with the discussion of the physical design process.*

The smallest unit of data of concern to physical data base designers is the data element, or field. These data elements are the values of the attributes described in the logical schema. As such, data elements can be stored as various types of data, for example, alphabetic, numeric, alphanumeric. Data elements can also be of various sizes, a thirty-character name or a two-digit code.

Data elements can be grouped together into records, or groups of related data elements. For example, all data elements describing an employee can be

---

*Buchholz,[1] Dodd,[2] and Martin[3] provide excellent discussions of physical design concepts and techniques.

grouped into an Employee record. The data element(s) that can be used to uniquely identify a record are called the record key. In the example, the Employee record might contain a ten-digit numeric Employee Code that serves as the key for the Employee record. Data records may be grouped into a block of records for efficient storage on devices such as magnetic tapes and disks. Further, groups of related records or blocks can be organized into a file, or data set. In the example, Employee records might be stored in blocks of ten records each in a tape file called the Employee file.

The simplest technique is to store the records in sequence (see Figure 10.1). In a sequential file each record must be written and read in sequence. Access to individual records can be improved by storing the records on a direct-access device (e.g., a disk) and adding an index. An index is a table that associates record keys with the addresses, or disk locations, at which those records are stored (see Figure 10.2). Direct access can be achieved without an index if a hashing algorithm[4] is used to transform each record key into a corresponding disk address. See Figure 10.3. Unfortunately such transformations are rarely unique, and thus additional search techniques must be employed if the desired record is not found at the address computed.

Each of these basic storage and access methods relies to some extent on record keys. However, it is often desirable to store or access records based on a common, rather than a unique, property. For example, an organization may wish to associate all employees who are in the same department. Two techniques that allow this are linked lists and inverted lists. With linked lists, records are stored by their unique record keys, say in a direct-access file. In addition a directory is constructed which contains an entry for each property of interest, e.g., Shoe

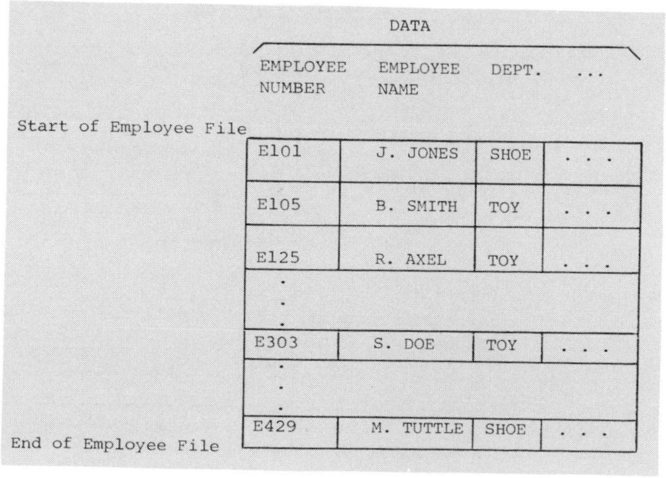

Figure 10.1.   A sequential Employee file.

Index Record key	Address			Address	Data			
E101	000			000	E101	J. JONES	SHOE	...
E105	001			001	E105	B. SMITH	TOY	...
E125	002			002	E125	R. AXEL	TOY	...
. . .						. .		
E303	152			152	E303	S. DOE	TOY	...
. . .						. .		
E429	400			400	E429	M. TUTTLE	SHOE	...

Figure 10.2.   An index sequential Employee file.

Department. The directory entry contains a pointer to the first record in the file which has the desired property, in this example, the first employee of the Shoe Department. Further, each Employee record contains a pointer to the next record with similar properties. Thus all similar records are linked together. The pointers which link the list may be either disk addresses or record keys from which addresses can be obtained. Figure 10.4 shows a linked-list organization for Employee records and their Departments.

Another organization for associating and accessing records by property is the inverted list. In this case records are stored and a directory is constructed, as in the linked-list approach. However, each directory entry contains not one

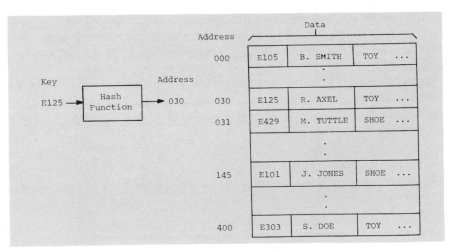

Figure 10.3.   A direct-access Employee file with hashing.

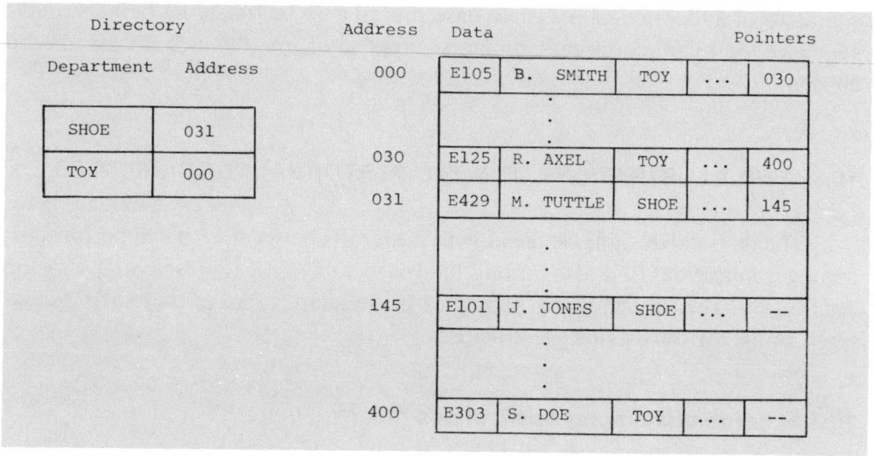

Figure 10.4.   A linked list for employees' departments.

pointer but a list of pointers, one for each record with the desired property. The records themselves are thus free of pointer fields. Figure 10.5 shows an inverted list for Departments in the Employee file.

The features and access methods used by commercial DBMS packages all employ these basic concepts of storage and accessing. For example, a TOTAL Master file is basically a direct-access file in which records are stored by means of a special hashing algorithm. Similarly, a DBTG set type is realized by a linked list which joins the owner record of that set to the members of the set. The

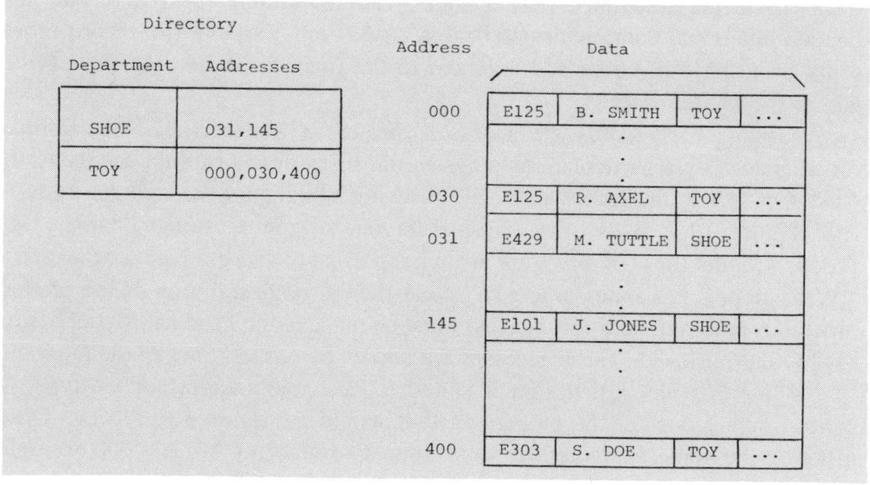

Figure 10.5.   An inverted list for employees' departments.

segments of a hierarchical IMS data base record may be linked by being stored in sequence or by direct-access pointers, depending on the IMS access method chosen.*

10.3. TWO ILLUSTRATIONS OF COST-PERFORMANCE TRADE-OFFS

The physical designer is faced with trade-offs between cost and performance among applications and also among alternative physical representations for one application. The following two examples illustrate the types of trade-offs encountered using real DBMS storage structures.

10.3.1. Trade-offs among Applications

A physical design that suits one application may not be appropriate for a second application using the same data. To illustrate this problem we shall use a physical design for the Catalog Sales data base (discussed in Chapter 9) using the TOTAL data base management system.[5]

Figure 10.6 shows a logical schema for a TOTAL implementation of the Catalog Sales data base. Reflecting the conceptual design (see Figure 9.6), the Customer, Product, Model, Supplier, and Warehouse entities have been realized using TOTAL Master files. In such files each record represents an instance of the entity described and is directly accessible using the record key. The Order entity, which is related to both Customer and Model, is represented by a TOTAL Variable file. In a Variable file, each record contains pointers which link it to related instances in the associated Master file(s). Each Variable file record can also contain additional data elements. In this case, each Variable file record represents an instance of Order and is linked to the Customer who placed the Order and to the Model ordered.

Variable file records are accessed through a Master file. For example, orders placed by a particular customer would be retrieved by first accessing the Customer Master file record and then following a linked list through the Variable file. Figure 10.7 shows the physical layout of the Customer, Order, and Product–Model files. In the figure arrows represent the access path for the query, "What models has Jones ordered?" Note that if the description of the product ordered is required, additional access must be made to the Product–Model file for each Order retrieved. These accesses are shown by dashed lines in the diagram.

While this physical design is suited to customer inquires of the type described here, consider the processing that would be required to retrieve Order instances by some characteristic other than Customer or Model. For example,

*Appendix A contains descriptions of the physical constructs used by several DBMS systems.

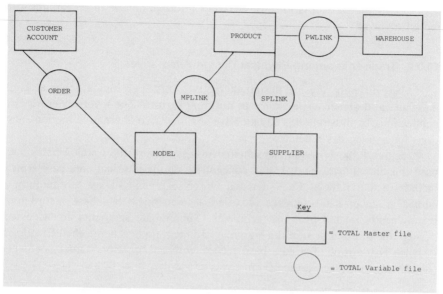

Figure 10.6. A TOTAL schema for the Catalog Sales data base.

suppose that an inquiry about a particular Order is known only by its Order Number. The data base is capable of supporting this inquiry, but the processing would involve a full search of the Order Variable file. Whether such extensive processing is justified depends on the frequency with which such queries were received. Also required is a comparison of the cost of searching the Order file with the cost of maintaining the Order entity as a Master file linked to both Customer and Product–Model. The latter design would provide better performance for Order inquiries at the price of additional data storage (i.e., a new Master file and more pointers) and additional processing for the Customer query

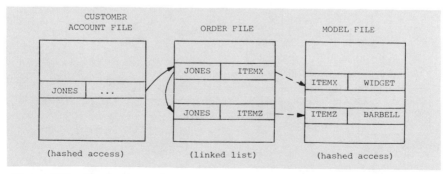

Figure 10.7. Physical layout for a portion of the Catalog Sales data base using TOTAL.

(i.e., an additional access to retrieve Order information for each Variable file record retrieved).

10.3.2. Trade-Offs among Physical Design Alternatives

Many different physical design alternatives exist for a logical schema. Thus the physical designer has a choice of different performance levels even for one application. To illustrate this situation we shall use two alternative implementations for a given IMS schema.

Figure 10.8a shows an IMS schema for a portion of the Catalog Sales data base. For this illustration we shall concentrate on the physical data base which includes a hierarchy of Customer and Order segments. In IMS terminology a named group of data elements is called a segment; a data base record is a hierarchically related group of segments. Subordinate segments are accessed through the root segment of the hierarchy. In the sample schema each Customer instance is the root of a data base record with one or more Order segments subordinate to it (see Figure 10.8b).

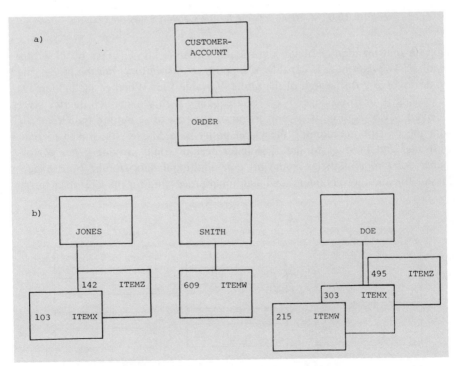

Figure 1.8. (a) An IMS schema for the Customer–Orders data base. (b) Instances of the IMS Customer–Orders Data Base Record.

IMS provides several access methods for storing and retrieving data base records.[6,7] The access method selected affects the performance characteristics of applications that use the physical data base. Figure 10.9 shows the Customer–Order data base organized using the Hierarchical Indexed Sequential Access Method (HISAM). With this method the Customer segment and possibly some Order segments for each data base record are stored in Customer key sequence in an indexed sequential data set. The remaining segments in the data base record are stored (in blocks) on another direct-access data set. Access to the Customer segments is provided by means of an index on the key of the Customer segment. The remaining segments are accessed through a linked list of blocks and a sequential search within blocks. To process the query, "What items has Jones ordered?" the block containing the proper Customer segment must be located through the index and retrieved from the main data file. Then each associated block must be located and retrieved from the overflow file.

Another possible implementation for this data base uses the Hierarchical Direct Access Method (HDAM). With this method the segments within the data base record are stored at random within one direct-access data set. A hashing alogorithm is used to assign Customer segment keys to storage locations. Within a data base record the segments are linked by pointers (see Figure 10.10).

To process the same customer query in this implementation, the Customer segment is first retrieved directly using its key. Then each Order segment related to that Customer would be retrieved using a pointer from the segment previously retrieved.

These implementation alternatives exhibit several differences with respect to performance. The HISAM implementation requires two data sets, the HDAM only one. Fewer accesses are required to retrieve a full data base record using the

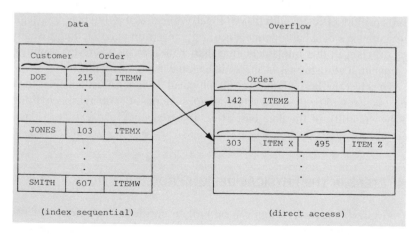

Figure 10.9. Storing the Customer–Orders data base using HISAM.

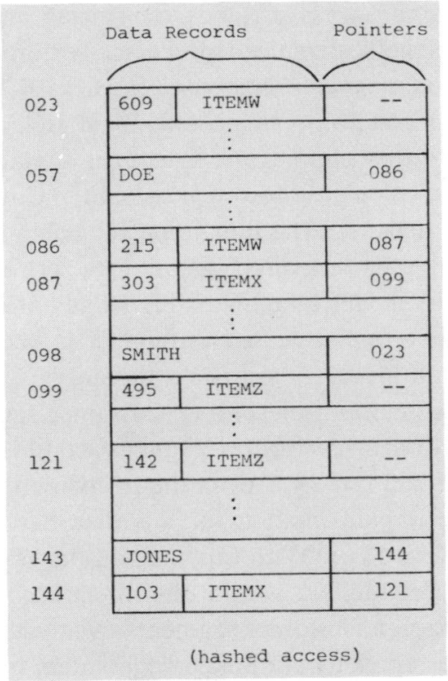

	Data Records		Pointers
023	609	ITEMW	--
	⋮		
057	DOE		086
	⋮		
086	215	ITEMW	087
087	303	ITEMX	099
	⋮		
098	SMITH		023
099	495	ITEMZ	--
	⋮		
121	142	ITEMZ	--
	⋮		
143	JONES		144
144	103	ITEMX	121

(hashed access)

Figure 10.10.   Storing the Customer–Orders data base using HDAM.

HISAM method than using the HDAM. However, using HDAM permits the physical designer to facilitate access to a specific type of segment within the data base record, i.e., the entire data base record need not be retrieved if only a particular segment type is required. Processing data base records in key sequence is more efficient with the HISAM organization, but direct access to specific data base records is more efficient with HDAM. Finally, the use of pointers to link segments in HDAM makes data base maintenance, i.e., insertion and deletion of segments, more efficient in that implementation than with HISAM, where the requirements for sequential storage makes space management more complicated.

To select the best alternative, the physical designer must consider the types of access that will be required across all applications, the operating environment, and the volatility of the data base (i.e., the frequency and extent of data base updating).

10.4. STEPS IN THE PHYSICAL DESIGN PROCESS

Physical data base design can be broken into four main steps: determining the documenting data representation, selecting and documenting access modes, allocating data to devices, and loading and reorganizing the data base as needed.

The first two steps depend on the DBMS but not on the installation or operating environment. The last two realize the physical design in a particular installation and ensure its responsiveness to user needs.

10.4.1. Determining and Documenting Data Representation

Starting with the logical schema produced by logical data design, the physical designer must determine how each data element, record, and file is to be represented. For each element, the data type and size must be determined. The size and expected number of occurrences must be determined for each record. And the size of each physical file, or data set, must also be estimated (This last task may be postponed until after the access methods are determined in the second step of physical design.)

Requirements for data types and size estimates may have been collected during the initial stage of logical design. The overhead associated with records or files in the DBMS must be added to these estimates for the computation of record and file sizes. For example, some DBMS packages require that record keys be duplicated in a record prefix. Others require fixed-length records or blocks.

The physical designers can provide feedback to systems developers and users concerning the storage implications of their data base design. The amount of storage space required for the data base and the relationship of this amount to installation constraints should be provided. Users may decide to revise data base content based on such feedback. For example, a lengthy data element might be replaced by a shorter code or abbreviation.

Once the content of the data base has stabilized, the physical designer can document representation details using the data description language (DDL) of the DBMS. Most DDL's provide a formal way of describing the names and representation details of all data elements, records, and files in the data base. This description becomes a preliminary schema for the data base.

10.4.2. Selecting and Documenting Access Methods

The choices available to the designer at this step depend on the DBMS. However, in all cases the way in which each record type in the data base will be accessed must be determined. Record types which will be entry points into the data base, i.e., they will be directly accessible by their keys, must be distinguished from those that will be accessed through pointers from other records or indexes.

Certain access constraints may be implicit in the DBMS constructs used by the logical designers. For example, dependent segments within an IMS hierarchy are normally accessed through the root segment. DBTG record types which are members of no set type must be directly accessible. Where choices remain, the designer must rely on the processing requirements specified in order to select the best alternative.

If it has not already been done as part of logical design, each process specified must be described in terms of the entry points and access paths, i.e., the sequence of records that must be located or retrieved, needed for its accomplishment. Performance estimates can then be made for each process for the various physical alternatives and cost–performance trade-offs can be evaluated. Interaction with systems development and data base users is required for this evaluation.

The number of alternatives for physical implementation of a data base and the number of factors that affect the performance of such implementations make the comparison of alternatives a difficult problem. Most researchers in this area[8-12] have addressed the problem by simulating the alternatives and attempting to optimize various cost–performance measures derived from the simulation.[13] While these efforts have provided some general heuristics to aid the physical designer, little in the way of practical tools is available.

One tool that is available is DBPrototype,[14] a package that simulates alternative implementations for IMS data bases. The physical designer provides a description of the data base and of the processing calls to be placed against the data base. The simulator produces statistics on the number and type of accesses required for the processing specified. The physical designer can simulate different structures and select the best one.

Once entry points and access methods have been selected, the physical designer revises the data base schema to reflect these selections. Some modifications may be required in record or file size estimates based on the overhead required by different DBMS access methods.

10.4.3. Allocating Data to Devices

The specification of entry points and access paths does not fully determine the physical configuration of the data base. Each record and file defined by the access method must be assigned to storage locations on physical devices, e.g., magnetic disks or tapes. This assignment completes the physical design process. During this step performance benefits can be gained by allocating the data base to physical devices in a way that gives priority to frequently used data or maximizes the likelihood that related data will be stored close together. This process is often called clustering.

Clustering can take place at three levels. Records consisting of many attributes can be divided and subsets of the attributes stored together.[15] In this way only the relevant part of a record need be retrieved, not the entire record each time. Another type of clustering associates different records that are likely to be accessed simultaneously. For example, if most accesses against an IMS data base record require a certain subset of the segments in that record, performance will be improved if those segments are stored physically close together, i.e., in the same block of storage.[16,17] Since data are transferred from disk storage in blocks, clustering increases the probability that with one disk access more than one segment of interest will be retrieved.

It is also possible to consider allocation on a higher level, i.e., allocating whole data files or parts of data files to physical devices with different performance characteristics.[18,19] The objective of this process is to assign the most frequently used portions of the data base to the faster, or more cost-effective, storage medium.

Each of these decisions depends on the designer's knowledge of the processes that will use the data base. Characteristics such as the frequencies with which attributes, records, and files will be used both individually and together are the relevant ones. If these characteristics are not known, they must be estimated for the initial allocation and then monitored so that the allocation can be modified as needed over the life of the data base.

Device assignments and other parameters of the allocation process are recorded either in the physical data base schema or through the use of an additional specification language (e.g., DBTG's Device Media Control Language) or the job control language of the host operating system.

10.4.4. Loading and Reorganizing the Data Base

In addition to developing the initial design, the physical designer is also responsible for seeing that the data base is loaded properly and for any reorganization that may be required during the life of the data base. Loading may involve the creation of a data base load program or simply the execution of a load utility provided by the DBMS vendor. Since many DBMS's place constraints on the way in which the data must be loaded, e.g., specific record sequences, it is important that someone familiar with the DBMS and the physical design of the data base be responsible for loading.

Reorganization of the data may imply changes in content, structure, access methods, or device allocation. Such changes may be required as a result of the introduction of new data elements or record types, as a result of new processing requirements, or simply to rectify the degradation in storage and processing efficiency that comes with modification of the data base. New data elements or record types will normally trigger redesign on both the logical and physical levels. New processing requirements and performance improvements can often be handled by physical redesign only. The process in any case is the same as initial physical design. However, the designer must reevaluate the physical design trade-offs using the objectives and constraints of the new requirements.

Most research on reorganization[20-22] has focused on asking when this process should be initiated. Obviously there are costs associated with both the reorganizing and the reloading of the data base and also with the continuation of suboptimal performance. One heuristic that has been proposed[22] is to reorganize when the benefit to accrue from the reorganization computed over a time period equivalent to that since the last reorganization is equal to the cost of reorganization. The physical designer must evaluate such trade-offs and initiate reorganization when it is indicated.

10.5. OTHER ISSUES IN PHYSICAL DESIGN

10.5.1. Hashing Algorithms

Some DBMS packages that provide direct access through the use of a hashing algorithm allow the package user to provide an algorithm. If that is the case, it is the physical designer's responsibility to provide such an algorithm.

To select or create an appropriate hashing algorithm, the designer must consider the nature of the record keys and the address space, or range of storage locations available to receive records. The objective is to find a transformation which preserves the unique nature of the record keys as much as possible, so that the incidence of synonyms (two record keys yielding the same storage address) is minimized. Synonyms are also minimized if the addresses generated are dispersed across the address space rather than clustered in groups within that space.

While many techniques have been proposed for manipulating keys before transformation and for the transformation itself, one simple algorithm has been shown to compare favorably with the most sophisticated.[23] Namely, the record key is treated as a numeric value and divided by a prime number close in size to the size of the address space. The remainder of this division is used as the record address. For example, in a storage space of 1,000 locations each record key could be divided by the prime 997. Thus an Employee record with Employee Number 1099 as its key would be stored at location 102 ($102 = 1,099 \bmod 997$).

10.5.2. Index Selection

When indexed or inverted-list access methods are used for physical design, the designer must specify the attribute(s) to be indexed. This selection is also necessary when a secondary access path is provided for a file organized by any method. When the attributes used to access the file are well known, their selection as indexed items is straightforward. For example, to provide access to Orders in the IMS data base shown in Figure 10.8, one could establish a secondary index to Orders using Order Number as the item indexed.

However, when the attributes of interest are very numerous or unpredictable, the choice of those indexed is more complex. To index every attribute would require a great deal of space for even a moderate number of attributes, and the increased processing required for data base maintenance would be substantial. Indexing too few attributes or attributes which are infrequently accessed would negate the performance benefits of the index by forcing extensive searches in response to most queries.

To select the proper attributes, the physical designer must know the number of possible values for each attribute (the number of index entries it would require) and the likelihood that each would be included in any query against the data base. Using these and some estimates of the activity against the data base, the designer can compute the costs of various index compositions and select the most efficient one. One method for doing this is illustrated in a case study by Schkolnick.[13]

10.5.3. Data Compression

To reduce the size of very large data bases or to offset the overhead required in indexed and inverted data bases, data compression can be used.[24] Data compression is any reversible process by which the storage space required for a string of data characters can be reduced. Methods of data compression involve eliminating frequently occurring characters (or strings) or recoding data to assign frequent characters the shortest storage codes. Either process trades increased processing time, i.e., increased time for encoding and decoding, for less storage space.

Compression methods, like hashing algorithms, can be optimized by a knowledge of the data to be compressed. One of the most powerful encoding techniques, Huffman coding,[25] uses the frequencies of occurrence for characters to guide the assignment of storage-efficient codes. The frequencies must be tabulated from the data to be compressed. Other simple procedures can achieve good results on data of unknown properties. For example, the repeated occurrence of any character can be replaced by a two-character code, the first character being a binary count field and the second being the character itself. The value of the count field indicates the number of occurrences of the character in the original data.

Compression may also be used to achieve a small measure of security in data base systems, since compressed data are not directly interpretable to an unauthorized observer.

10.6. THE DBA'S ROLE IN PHYSICAL DESIGN

Unlike logical design, in which many of the activities can be performed by system developers and merely coordinated by the DBA, physical design is entirely the province of the DBA. DBA staff members should be responsible for evaluating physical design trade-offs, selecting physical storage and access methods, and maintaining the physical description of the data base.

The physical design specialists on the DBA's staff are ideally suited to these tasks. They are experts in the DBMS and its physical implementation alternatives. They have had experience in supporting system software and are familiar with the factors that influence performance and costs. This experience also enables them to work closely and effectively with system support personnel.

The position of the DBA allows physical designers on its staff to be concerned with overall optimization of data base performance and costs. The DBA designers are not affiliated with any one application area and thus are not likely to bias the physical implementation of the data base. Requirements specified by users and systems developers can be ranked by the organization's priorities, and physical structures can be chosen accordingly. Conflicts can be referred to the DBA manager to resolve in conjunction with the managers of system development and the user departments.

One other benefit of entrusting the physical design of the data base to the DBA is the promotion of data independence. Data base users and application system developers can concentrate on the logical structure of the data base and the analysis of processing requirements. They need not be aware of any physical design considerations. Further, users and application programmers can remain insulated from the effects of hardware or DBMS modifications. The DBA physical designers can reevaluate data base requirements in the light of such modifications and redo the physical design as necessary. Only far-reaching modifications will affect data base users.

Part IV

Data Base Operation and Control

Chapter 11

Maintaining Data Base Integrity

Data base integrity refers to both the accuracy and the availability of the data base. If a data base has integrity, then it is a correct and dependable model of the organization's information processing requirements. To maintain the integrity of a data base, the DBA must be able to ensure both the quality of the data base contents and the correctness of the processing applied against that data base.

In a traditional data processing environment integrity was also required of data files. The accuracy of the data input to the file was usually checked by edit modules early in the processing of any application system. Provision was made to reject incorrect data and to allow reentry or correction at a later time. In addition, most applications provided for the retention of old master files and the transactions that were run against them, so that files could be recreated if they were lost or destroyed. Operating instructions for multistep applications also contained procedures for restarting at a previous step should an error occur during system operation.

A data base must be similarly protected. However, the threats to its integrity are more numerous, and the protection mechanisms and correction procedures are more complex. The source of this additional complexity is twofold: the high degree of data sharing in a data base environment and the predominantly on-line nature of most data base application systems. Data sharing increases the risk of inaccuracies due to improper editing or inconsistent data handling among the applications that use the same data. When a problem does occur, it is more difficult to trace its source since many application programs may have access to the incorrect data. The on-line processing environment increases both the risk of processing failures and the complexity of recovery procedures. In addition, the impact of a problem which renders the data base inaccessible is greater when users are waiting for on-line access.

Procedures and techniques for maintaining data base integrity are related to those for maintaining security. However, integrity controls are broader, since they aim to guard the data base from even friendly users. Security measures are aimed at preventing illegal or unauthorized use of the data base. A breach of security may have eventual but not immediate consequences regarding data base accuracy or availability. An integrity problem is more immediate and more substantive. Security problems are discussed in Chapter 12.

For the DBA to be effective in maintaining data base integrity, he or she must understand the nature of potential threats to that integrity, must be aware of techniques which can be used to prevent or correct integrity problems, and must be familiar with the features which are (or are not) provided by DBMS packages to meet integrity needs. With this knowledge the DBA can formulate preventive policies and can initiate responsive actions when needed to preserve the integrity of the data base.

11.1. SOURCES OF ERROR

Loss of integrity in a data base can be the result of several different types of errors.[1] The structure or content of the data base can be altered as a result of hardware failures. Similarly, incorrect data can be entered by data base users or can result from the improper actions of application programs. Finally, inaccurate operation or failure of system software can leave the data base in an inconsistent state.

11.1.1. Hardware Errors

The hardware error is the least common but most severe type of error that can affect the data base. One type of hardware failure is a head crash on a disk, in which the contents of certain tracks on that device are lost. If the damaged area contained data base records or indexes, the data base cannot maintain its integrity. The data base must be copied onto an undamaged device and the lost data replaced before the data base can be used again.

Another type of hardware failure that could affect the data base is a loss of power or CPU malfunction when the data base is being updated. If data base processing was incomplete, the data base may be inconsistent. In such a case the effects of the processing will have to be reversed (in a process called rollback or backout) and the processing restarted after the malfunction is corrected.

11.1.2. User Errors

The data base users, whether individuals or applications programs, can compromise data base integrity. In the simplest case, incorrect or inconsistent data can be entered into the data base by the user. As all programmers are aware, this represents the GIGO phenomenon—"garbage in, garbage out." Such errors can also be errors of omission, i.e., failure to verify data as it is entered.

Application programs can violate data base integrity through coding errors or through errors in logic. For example, an application program might update the wrong field in a record. Or an update program might incorrectly add an Order record for a Part that does not exist.

11.1.3. System Software Errors

Problems in the system software, or operating system, can also damage the data base. If the operating system terminates execution abnormally while the data base is being processed, an inconsistent state could result. This occurrence is identical to a system stoppage caused by a hardware failure. The data base must be returned to a state which is known to be consistent, and any unfinished processes must be restarted.

Other problems can arise depending on the way in which the operating system handles concurrent users of the data base. If two application programs are allowed to access and update the same data base record concurrently, the result may be erroneous. For example, in Figure 11.1 program A first retrieves the data base record for part X and then adds 20 to the quantity on hand (QOH) for that part. However, in the meantime program B has retrieved the original data base record for part X and made its modification. When program B stores its result, the part X record, as updated by program A, is overwritten. Thus the final state of the data base is inconsistent.

Time	Program A	Program B	Data Base: QOH for Part X
1	Get Part X	--	QOH = 10
2	QOH = QOH + 20	Get Part X	QOH = 10
3	Store Part X	QOH = QOH + 50	QOH = 30
4	--	Store Part X	QOH = 60

Figure 11.1.   Inconsistency due to concurrent processing.

11.2. TECHNIQUES FOR MAINTAINING INTEGRITY

Techniques for preventing and dealing with integrity problems in traditional systems, especially those for on-line systems, can be used equally well in a data base environment to address the types of errors described.[2–4] These techniques can be classified by the type of problem they address: validation, consistency, or concurrency.

11.2.1. Validation

Traditionally the content of a data processing system was checked for accuracy by a set of data and processing controls within the system.[1] These controls included the existence of one or more modules within the system whose function was to edit all entering data and reject any that were found unacceptable. Further, tests were often included in the processing programs to double-check computations or to verify the contents of a particular data item. For example, a payroll program might check that net pay plus deductions equalled gross pay. Finally, a number of administrative controls, external to the computer, were applied to minimize the loss or alteration of data before and after processing.

The processing and administrative controls apply equally well in the data base environment. However, the data controls become redundant if included in application systems that share the same data. The DBA can eliminate this redundancy by building an edit subsystem based on the definitions stored in the data dictionary for the data base. If each element and each record in the data base are described in the dictionary, this information can be used by the edit subsystem to verify all data as they are entered. Some dictionary systems even allow the option of automatically generating such edit software.[5]

In addition to the data element values themselves, various semantic constraints may exist in order for the data base to accurately reflect the organization's environment. Examples of semantic constraints include ''no order can be accepted for a nonexistent part'' or ''no employee can receive a higher salary than his or her manager.'' Such assertions must be true in order for the data base to be accurate.

The DBA can ensure that the data base meets these constraints in several ways. Periodic audits can be made of the data base to test for compliance, and any necessary modifications can be made. However, processes completed before the audit may be in error as a result of the inaccuracies uncovered.

Some constraints can be conveyed through structure using the data base schema. For example, orders can be made hierarchically subordinate to the part ordered. In such cases the DBMS would automatically refuse data which did not conform to the schema. In the example, to add an Order, one would have to specify the key of the parent Part. If no corresponding Part record could be found, the DBMS would not add the Order.

Assertions such as "no employee can receive a higher salary than his or her manager" depend on data base content which can change over time. Also the truth of the assertion cannot be tied to data base structure. Assertions of this type must be tested by program code. These tests can be performed in programs which update related fields, e.g., the employee's salary. Or a separate integrity subsystem[6] can be developed by the DBA to monitor compliance with user-defined constraints.

The integrity of the data base can also be compromised by incorrect or damaged structural data. For example, if the pointers that link hierarchical segments together in IMS's HDAM organization are destroyed, the segments cannot be accessed. Similarly, structural constraints, e.g., each occurrence of a DBTG set type can have exactly one owner, must not be violated if processes based on these constraints are to execute properly.

Usually each DBMS contains preprogrammed checks to verify structural constraints at data base generation. Occasionally checks can be made dynamic and context dependent. For example, DBTG systems allow the user to define certain types of set membership for a record type. When a record of the given type is added or deleted from the data base, these membership rules are applied to maintain consistency. After a system failure or as a periodic quality assurance test, the DBA can apply structural validation programs[7] to detect and correct problems. Such processing, however, can be long and extremely costly.

11.2.2. Consistency

Efforts to ensure data base consistency include both preventive measures to guard against system failures and techniques for restoring the data base to a consistent state following such failures. Procedures for data base backup and recovery fall into this category.

The objective of procedures for backup and recovery of a data base is to facilitate reconstruction of the data base after a failure in the minimum amount of time and with the minimum amount of processing overhead. The processing overhead to be considered includes the amount of additional information that must be maintained during error-free data base processing as well as the processing required to restore the data base to an error-free state after a failure has occurred. Typically backup and recovery require that periodic copies of the complete data base be made and that records be kept of modifications to the data base since it was last copied. In the event of a hardware or software failure that compromises data base integrity, the data base is restored by combining the known modifications with the last known correct state of the data base.

There are a number of ways of accomplishing this backup and recovery. These approaches differ primarily in the way in which modifications to the data base are recorded. In the simplest approach all transactions (a transaction may include the accessing and modification of several data base records) that modify the data base are recorded on a separate chronological file, sometimes called an audit trail or processing log. After a failure, the data base is reloaded from the backup copy (or dump), and these transactions are reprocessed.

Another approach, which reduces the amount of reprocessing needed, is to record modifications by keeping a separate file of the modified data base records, i.e., the "after images" of the records that were changed. Now these images can simply be merged with the backup copy to restore the data base when needed. Schemes using the differential file approach [8,9] allow these modified records to be accessed as if they were physically part of the data base. However, physical insertion is done only periodically. This technique saves processing time and provides a more ready backup copy, namely the unmodified data base itself.

When a failure occurs during on-line data base processing, recovery procedures must include the determination of where in the processing the failure occurred. Transactions completed before the failure point are captured in the normal backup routines, and their effect can be restored. However, transactions which were only partially completed must be handled differently. To avoid incorrect results or data loss such transactions must be backed out and reprocessed. Backing out means reversing the effect of any modifications already completed. For example, suppose that transaction 1 modified data base records X and Y and a failure occurs after X has been changed out before Y has been changed (see Figure 11.2). The change to X must be reversed and the entire transaction restarted. A log of before-images, copies of records before they are modified, can facilitate the backout process.

In some situations backing out the incomplete transactions may not be enough to restore data base integrity. The program executing may not be transaction oriented. Or it may compute running sums or base processing decisions on the contents of data base records accessed. In such cases the simplest procedure is to restore the data base to its state prior to the execution of the program and

Transaction 1: "Increase QTY_x and QTY_y by 50 units."			
Time	Transaction 1	QTY_x	QTY_y
1	--	10	10
2	update record X	60	10
3	------ system failure ----------------------------------		
4	--	60	10

Figure 11.2. Inconsistency due to incomplete transaction processing.

rerun the program. In an environment where only one program is executing at a time this is fairly straightforward. However, in multiprogramming environments the usual procedure is to record the state of the system at a predetermined interval by recording the contents of the registers and main memory. Processing can then be returned to this checkpoint when necessary to restart after a failure. Procedures for backing out transactions as part of data base recovery are usually coordinated with system checkpoints.[10,11]

11.2.3. Concurrency

The problem of concurrent processes modifying shared data and producing incorrect or inconsistent results has been described. The usual method for dealing with such problems is avoidance, i.e., preventing two processes from sharing data. In traditional systems this avoidance was complete since each application system had its own files. However, in a data base environment severe limits on data sharing negate one of the objectives of the data base approach. Thus an attempt is made to restrict exclusive data base access as much as possible.

The usual procedure for granting a program exclusive access to part of a data base is to require that the program lock or hold that portion of the data base before modifying it. If a particular data base record is locked by a program, no concurrently operating program can lock it until it is released. Such locking controls are usually the province of the DBMS; however, they can be implemented at the system level as well.

Techniques for locking a data base differ in the size and composition of the portion of the data base that can be locked, i.e., the granularity of the lock.[12] On the broadest level, a DBMS can require that a program be granted exclusive access to an entire file within the data base before any record in that file can be changed. Alternatively, locks may be applied to records or segments within a data base or perhaps to sets of records that fulfill requirements specified by the user (e.g., the predicate locks of Eswaran et al.[13]). If locking is handled at the system level, physical pages or blocks can be locked; for example, see the method described by Rosenkrantz, Stearns, and Lewis.[14]

One unpleasant outcome of any locking scheme is the possibility of deadlock. Deadlock occurs when two (or more) concurrent processes have certain resources (e.g., data base records) locked and each requires a resource held by the other before it can complete its processing (see Figure 11.3). If this condition is not detected and the deadlock resolved, neither process will ever come to completion. Thus any locking procedure must include procedures for detecting the occurrence of deadlock and resolving the conflict. Normally, one of the blocked transactions is backed out and restarted, and the remaining transaction is then able to obtain the resource freed by the backed-out transaction and to complete its processing.[15]

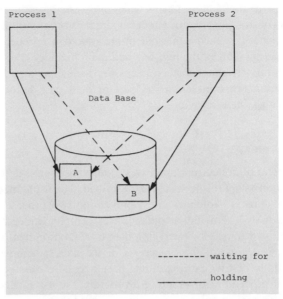

Figure 11.3. An example of deadlock.

11.3. INTEGRITY FEATURES IN DBMS PACKAGES

Most DBMS packages include features designed to promote data base integrity. These features are of four types: edit features, concurrency control features, structural maintenance features, and utility software for backup and recovery. Table 11.1 gives some examples of each of these types of features.

Edit features are normally associated with the data description langauge of the DBMS. The user describes the format (data type, size) of each data element and the layout of each data base record. The DBMS can then check data elements and records when they enter the data base and detect discrepancies from the description. Most systems also allow the user to indicate that a particular data element (a key) or record must have unique occurrences. The system can then detect and report duplicates, which represent data errors.

Some systems provide more extensive editing capability. DBTG systems allow the user to specify user-written programs which will be executed when an occurrence of a particular record type is being added to the data base. These routines can include extensive editing of the user's devising. Many relational systems allow the user to specify assertions concerning the acceptable range or set of values which a data element can assume. For example, in the SEQUEL language used with the relational System R[16] the user can state: ASSERT ON EMPLOYEE: AGE BETWEEN 15 AND 66. The system can check this assertion

Table 11.1. Examples of DBMS Integrity Features

Validation	Concurrency	Structural maintenance	Backup and recovery
MONEY, DATE datatypes (S2000)	GET HOLD logic (IMS)	Set membership (DBTG)	Checkpoint, rollback routines (Model 204)
VIRTUAL SOURCE/ RESULT items (DBTG)	TOTAL/QUEST sign-on (TOTAL)	ISRT, DLET functions (IMS)	Logging options (TOTAL)
UNIQUE, SEQUENCE fields (IMS)	AREA usage modes (DBTG)	ADDV commands (TOTAL)	Dump and restore routines (IDMS)

immediately or periodically to verify that the contents of the Age data element do not lie outside these bounds.

Some form of concurrency control is also provided by all DBMS systems. The user is required to state the nature of the access required when a portion of the data base is requested. If updating is specified, the DBMS restricts access to this portion of the data base until the user's program has been completed. Most systems allow the user to select from different levels of concurrency control. For example, in IMS the user may request exclusive access to a whole set of segment occurrences, or he may simply hold individual segments as needed during processing. If the first option is taken, no other program can access the segments until the user's program has been completed. In the second case other programs have free access to segment occurrences other than the one held by the user's program.

The structure of the data base, e.g., IMS hierarchies, DBTG set types, TOTAL Master–Variable file linkages, is also monitored by the DBMS. Additions to the data base which do not conform to the structure specified are rejected by the DBMS. In addition, the data manipulation language (DML) of the DBMS provides commands that preserve consistent data base structure during maintenance operations. For example, the IMS delete command deletes both the segment specified and all segments hierarchically subordinate to that segment. Similarly, DBTG systems provide several versions of the delete command that allow the user to control the number of records deleted depending on their relationship to the specific record being erased. DBTG systems also allow users to specify the nature of a record's participation in a particular set type. For example, suppose that Order records are members of a set owned by a Customer record. The user can make the DBMS enforce the constraint that no order may exist without a corresponding customer by declaring Order to be an automatic, mandatory member of the Customer–Order set.

Most DBMS packages provide utility software for backup and recovery of the data base. These include programs for dumping the data base, procedures for logging transactions, and programs for reloading the data base from the dump copy. In addition, the DML may include commands for transaction backout and procedures for initiating checkpoints periodically or at the user's request.

11.4. THE DBA'S ROLE IN MAINTAINING DATA BASE INTEGRITY

While the activities that must take place to ensure data base integrity may be performed by individuals other than the DBA manager or staff, the DBA is responsible for initiating and controlling these activities through the use of standards, testing, administrative procedures, and formal policies.

11.4.1. Standards

The DBA must set and enforce standards on data definition, application coding, and application system design that promote accuracy and consistency in the data base. Through centralized control over data definitions and DDL descriptions of the data base, the DBA can monitor the accuracy of data element and structural specifications and ensure consistency from application to application. DBA-written edit routines can be provided to monitor data quality. Tables of acceptable data values or codes can be maintained by the DBA and accessed as needed by application programs.

The DBA should set up guidelines for application program coding to insure that update programs make proper use of concurrency controls and structural maintenance commands. Since many DBMS packages provide the user with powerful options in these matters, the DBA must make sure that this power is not misused. For example, in many systems a program can read a data base record, even while it is being held for update. Improper use of this feature could result in serious processing errors.

The DBA should also provide formal guidelines for the consideration of integrity matters during system design. Each design effort should be required to address the questions of editing, data base structure and maintenance, concurrency controls, and backup and recovery. This is not to say that each design project will develop different procedures for these matters; rather each must indicate how existing tools and procedures will be used to ensure the integrity of any portion of the data base addressed by the new system.

11.4.2. Testing

Testing is especially crucial in a data base environment for two reasons. First, the integrated nature of the data base means that errors are more likely to be propagated from their source, affecting other programs or parts of the data base.

Second, most data base systems support on-line processing, making the verification of program correctness a more complex task. The DBA's objectives are therefore (1) to prevent errors when possible, by requiring rigorous testing of application programs before their integration into the data base environment and (2) to detect and correct data base errors that occur during and after system integration, [17] through the use of various testing tools designed specifically for that purpose.

While program testing is the province of the application development team, members of the DBA staff should be responsible for specifying test cases [18] covering the interaction between the application programs and the data base. In addition, during program testing the DBA should review each application program for conformance with DBA standards on data base access and modification as well as for proper rollback and restart provisions.

The DBA should also provide the application developers with certain aids [2] for integration testing, i.e., testing system operation before the new application system comes on-line. These tools should include utilities for simulating on-line input, for generating test data bases, for tracing DBMS calls, and for printing snapshots of the data base and related DBMS tables and pointers. The DBA may wish to assume full responsibility for integration testing by maintaining a test data base environment and requiring that all new applications be turned over to the DBA for testing before they are accepted for operation.

Final system testing, or system audit, occurs after the new system is in operation and is again the joint responsibility of the system developers and the DBA. The DBA should be able to trace all data base activity, e.g., using the log tapes, and to selectively examine and modify data base records and tables. Standard recovery routines should be used to correct major damage due to program errors.

11.4.3. Procedures

In addition to standards that govern the efforts of system developers, the DBA should develop and institute procedures for error detection and resolution during system operation. Data base users should have a formal procedure to follow to report errors as they are observed. Also, the DBA should run periodic quality assurance tests to verify data base content and structure. Such an audit might include the sampling of a number of data base records and verification of their contents and interrecord associations.

The DBA staff should include individuals who are responsible for troubleshooting, i.e., tracking down observed errors to their source. These persons will probably be physical design specialists capable of working closely with both system software personnel and data base designers and users. Once the source of the error(s) has been determined, the DBA must initiate procedures for restoring data base integrity and for preventing similar errors in the future. The latter might occasion a system modification or the creation of new edit controls.

11.4.4. Policies

The DBA is responsible for formulating policies governing the selection of techniques for and the scheduling of data base backup and recovery operations. The DBA physical design staff in consultation with the system software specialists should select or develop techniques for backup and recovery that are consistent with the DBMS and with the installation's operating environment. The DBA may adopt a set of techniques to be used by all applications or may present system developers with several techniques and provide rules for selecting the best alternative for a given system. In addition, operating instructions for the various procedures must be prepared for the computer operations staff.

The frequency with which backup is performed or checkpoints taken should also be determined by the DBA. The trade-off in this decision is the cost of frequent dumping (or checkpointing) versus the cost of reconstruction after a failure. Such operations can be scheduled by units of time, they can be associated with specific processing events, or they can be based on a count of items or events since the last operation.[19] For example, a checkpoint may be taken every n minutes, after each subtask in a process, or after m update transactions have been processed.

The DBA may wish to control data base backup and recovery centrally. In that case techniques and schedules for dumping are developed for each physical file in the data base. Application programs are required to follow specific logging procedures or to call DBA written routines. Checkpointing and transaction backout are also handled by the application systems, with the advice of the DBA.

Chapter 12

Controlling Data Base Access

Data base security can be defined as the protection of the data base from unauthorized access and/or modification.[1] This protection is not completely provided by procedures that ensure data base integrity since security violations do not necessarily compromise data base integrity. For example, the DBA may wish to restrict the operation of retrieving a record from the Employee data base to individuals who hold managerial positions. If an individual who is not a manager does manage to retrieve an Employee record, this act is a security violation but does not impair the integrity of the data base. Thus a comprehensive plan for data base security must include but also go beyond integrity measures.

In order to determine which actions against the data base are authorized and which are not, the DBA needs to do two things. First, the units or objects that need to be protected must be identified. For example, must protection be provided for data fields, records, files, programs, disk devices, the computer room, or all of these? Second, there must be a standard against which authorization policies can be measured. This standard may be formal rules of information classification within the organization, similar to the security clearance procedures within the military. Or legislative rules on privacy may serve as the standard. With these two elements the DBA can define authorization policies for all types of data base access.

As usual the imposition of security procedures, especially those technical features added to normal data base operation, presents a trade-off with system performance. The additional cost required by storage and processing for any security feature must be balanced against the risk and the cost of threats to the data base. In highly sensitive military environments data base performance may be sacrified in order to attain a high level of data base security. In many commercial environments, security features may be bypassed in the interest of performance. However, current concern within the society for individual privacy is forcing most firms in the private sector to reassess the security of data bases containing personal data.

The creation of a system or a data base which is 100% secure is highly unlikely and perhaps impossible to attain. Thus the objective in selecting security measures is to make security violations difficult and costly to perpetrate. A high cost of penetration and great risk of discovery will discourage most potential violators.

12.1. THREATS TO DATA BASE SECURITY

The first step in formulating a data base security program is to determine the types of threats which exist. The likelihood of each type of threat, i.e., the risk associated with it, can then be determined and the cost of an occurrence of each can be estimated. Threats to data security can be broadly classified into three categories: disclosure, modification, or destruction of data.[2]

12.1.1. Disclosure of Data

Data disclosure means that the contents of the data base are divulged to individuals other than those for whom it is intended. This can occur when an unauthorized person obtains a report or inquiry response from the data base. Or a legitimate data base user may gain access to some portion of the data base which he is not authorized to see, for example, his co-worker's salary. Data can also be obtained by eavesdropping or intercepting data transmissions to or from the data base.

Theft is an extreme version of data disclosure. A disk pack containing data base directories or records may be physically removed. Or a backup copy of the data base can be removed from the tape library.

The motivation for data disclosure may be personal advantage or gain. For example, an employee might use the knowledge of a co-worker's salary in his own salary negotiations. Or he might sell the contents of a customer information data base to another organization. Unauthorized disclosure can also be the first step in more extensive penetration or manipulation of the system. For example, the stolen data might include account numbers or transaction codes that would enable the perpetrator to masquerade as a legitimate user in later data base operations. Finally, disclosure can affect the firm's competitive abilities. For example, data on a planned acquisition or on a new product might be disclosed to a competitor.

12.1.2. Modification of Data

Unauthorized modification of the data base is a less obvious but equally damaging possibility. An individual may change a data field for personal benefit. For example, he might increase his salary or change the rate of commission that he is paid on sales. Another type of modification involves entering false transactions that modify the data base. The phony transactions may be used to cover up fraud or embezzlement, or they may be used as an aid in discovering the meaning of data codes. For example, in a system that encrypts sensitive data a perpetrator might introduce a false transaction in order to obtain an example of plain and encrypted data.

12.1.3. Destruction of Data

Data may be destroyed in several ways. Damage to the data storage device is perhaps the most obvious. However, data may also be lost through improper modification of the data base, e.g., deletion of data records. Damage to the data base directories or to the DBMS itself can destroy the data base. In fact, any act which renders the data base inaccessible, e.g., a system crash, is effectively data destruction. Depending on the integrity features in place, the difficulty and cost of recovery from such data loss may vary.

An individual may destroy data out of malice or in retaliation for some perceived wrong, say being fired. Data destruction may also hide fraud or facilitate other criminal acts. For example, if an on-line credit inquiry system is down, the criminal may overdraw a credit account without detection. Also, a system or data base failure may allow the perpetrator access to system directories or other sensitive data during the crisis or the recovery period.

12.2. METHODS FOR ENSURING DATA SECURITY

The threats to data base security have two things in common: improper access to the data base and improper use of the data accessed. Thus methods for ensuring security focus on controlling access to the data base and controlling the way in which data may be used. Given that control may be less than total, methods are also employed to limit the usefulness of data which is successfully obtained through unauthorized means. Finally, some methods are directed at detecting and reporting violations and attempted violations.

12.2.1. User Identification and Authentication

A first-level control on data base access is to require that all legitimate users be identified and that they authenticate their identity when they access the data base.[3,4] Normally this identification is accomplished by assigning each user an identification number. When the user accesses the system, he provides his identification and the system checks to determine whether that identification number is valid. In addition to security checking, identifiers can be used to track data base usage or for system accounting.

Once a user has been properly identified, he may be asked for a password to authenticate that he is who he says he is. The password should be a code known only to the individual and should be masked or not printed when it is entered. If the password agrees with the password on file with the system for that user, access is permitted. Passwords may be user selected or system selected. The latter is preferable since user selected passwords may be easy to guess; many people choose their own initials.

Alternatively, authentication can be provided by a procedure.[3] In the example in Figure 12.1, the system generates a random number, the user performs a calculation on it (e.g., adds the date to it and selects the second and fifth digit) and sends the result back to the system. The system also performs the calculation and verifies the result. Other means of authentication include magnetically coded badges or cataloging of physical features, such as hand geometry or voiceprints.

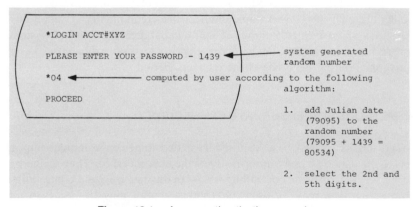

Figure 12.1. A user authentication procedure.

In any scheme security depends on the secret nature of the identifiers and the secret or unique nature of the authentication mechanism. Thus administrative procedures are necessary to control the assignment of identifiers and the distribution of passwords or badges.

12.2.2. Usage Authorization

In identification and authentication, protection is provided to the system or the DBMS facilities as a whole. Authorization, on the other hand, provides protection for objects within the data base, i.e., files, records, or actual fields. The philosophy is that even legitimate data base users should have access only to those portions of the data base that are necessary for their jobs.[5]

Most authorization schemes define different types of access, and users are granted access by type to objects in the data base.[5-7] For example, in the method described by Griffiths and Wade[6] users may be granted read only, write only, or read and write access to a data base relation (or flat file). When a user attempts to access the relation, the access control list of all authorized users for that relation is checked before access is granted.

The authority granting procedure varies. In most time-sharing environments[5] and in the relational system described by Griffiths and Wade[6] the creator of each file or relation has authority to grant and revoke access privileges to other users regarding that file. In INGRES, another relational system,[8] one central user, the DBA, has sole authority for granting and revoking access privileges on shared data.

Authorization procedures can be invoked at various levels. Permission to access a given portion of the data base may be checked at compile time, at the time the data base file is opened for processing, or with every transaction that accesses the data base. The time at which authorization takes place affects the level of security attainable and also the overhead required to implement the authorization mechanism.

A more subtle problem with data usage arises in the manipulation of statistical data bases.[9] Statistical data bases are those that maintain data on individuals or items but are intended to provide only summary data, i.e., statistics, on groups of items to the user. Census data provide a good example of a statistical data base. Queries or report requests from such data bases are normally honored only if they apply to two or more items or individuals. However, even with such restrictions security can be compromised. For example,[10] to obtain the bank balance of customer A, the perpetrator requests the sum of the balances of customers A, B, and C; then he requests the sum of the balances of customers B and C; taking the difference in these two results gives him the balance of customer A. Most strategies to deal with this problem set a minimum on the number of cases allowed for a query or report request.[11]

12.2.3. Privacy Transformations

To counter the threat of wiretapping or reduce the value of data which fall into the hands of unauthorized users, the primary technique used is encryption, or privacy transformations.[1,3,4,12] The data, or plain text, is transformed by some encryption method into code, or cipher text, before transmission or storage. When a coded message is received or a coded record retrieved, it must be decoded by an inverse of the encryption method. Thus if the message is intercepted or the stored data disclosed to an unauthorized user, that user must be able to break the code before the data are useful.

Traditionally encryption methods relied on the secrecy of the transformation for security. Now, however, most methods use a known algorithm that depends on a secret key datum.[13,14] For example, the algorithm might be to perform an exclusive OR between the bits of the message and a secret key bit string (see Figure 12.2). The result of this transformation is transmitted or stored. To decode the encrypted data the operation is reversed. Thus authorized users or programs must have knowledge of the key.

Public key methods have also been proposed.[15,16] In these methods even the set of keys, or methods for deriving possible keys, can be public knowledge. However, which key is actually being used for any given message is known only to authorized users. An interloper is forced to search a very large space of possible keys before he can decode any data that he intercepts. Since the key being used can easily be changed, public key methods are very flexible. The key can be replaced immediately after the occurrence of a security leak. Or the key can be changed at random time intervals to confound eavesdroppers.

	A	B	A EXOR B
a)			
	0	0	0
	0	1	1
	1	0	1
	1	1	0

b)	Data (or Message):	00111010	11001111	01010101
	(Secret) Key:	11011011	01110101	10101110
	Coded Message:	11100001	10111010	11111011

Figure 12.2. (a) The exclusive OR operation. (b) Data encryption using a secret key.

12.2.4. Security Audits

Audits or monitoring of data base usage, are an integral part of the data base integrity subsystem. Security audits can in a similar way enable the DBA to detect and perhaps track security violations when they occur. Security auditing has two aspects: monitoring of successful and unsuccessful access to the data base and periodic tests of security features.

Logging of access, especially denied access requests, is often called threat monitoring. Loss of data base activity may enable the DBA to isolate a particular user who has attempted to gain unauthorized access or a particular terminal location which has been the source of frequent unsuccessful access attempts. These logs also facilitate tracking of data base activity to reconstruct and analyze a situation in which a security violation has occurred.

Tests of security features may include attempts at penetration by the DBA staff or confirmation of currently valid user identifiers or authorization lists. Such tests should be performed without the knowledge of user or system personnel. As with financial audits, the random and unanticipated nature of these tests increases their ability to detect violations.

12.3. DBMS SECURITY FEATURES

The DBMS is a natural vehicle for applying controls on data base security.[17] The architecture of the DBMS requires that all access to the data base be channeled through that system. Thus it is reasonable to place access controls at this same interface. Most DBMS packages provide some degree of security over data base and use, but the sophistication and dynamic nature of these features varies widely.

The features provided by DBMS packages are of three types: view mechanisms, identification and authentication procedures, and usage authorization procedures.

12.3.1. View Mechanisms

One of the simplest ways to prevent a data base user from accessing data other than his own is to keep him unaware that other data exist. That is, a user (an individual or a program) is allowed to see only the data which he is authorized to access (see Figure 12.3). This capability is provided by most DBMS packages. For example, in a DBTG data base the DBA prepares a schema for the entire data base. However, each user is provided with a subschema containing only a portion of the full schema. Similarly, in IMS each application program has a Program Control Block (PCB) which indicates the segments that the program is allowed to access.[18] Some systems, like TOTAL,[19] go further. Only requested data fields

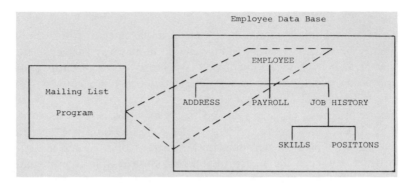

Figure 12.3. Security via a data base view.

are made available to an application program, rather than the entire record retrieved. Relational systems such as System R[18] define views as transformations of existing base relations. An application program can then access a view while being unaware of the underlying relations.

12.3.2. Identification and Authentication Procedures

Most DBMS packages assume that they are operating within a secure system environment. Thus user account numbers and passwords to access the system per se are assumed. However, many DBMS's provide additional identification and authentication procedures. These procedures may govern the execution of programs, the opening of data base files, or the performance of specific data manipulation commands.

In IMS the DBA can assign passwords to programs or to data files within the data base. Further, in an on-line environment, the execution of a particular application program can be restricted to one terminal or to a class of terminals. DBTG systems use an extensive system of locks and keys to limit access. Locks may be defined in schemas or subschemas to protect data base areas or even DML operations on specific record types. An application program must then supply the proper key to be granted access. This lock and key system is also used to control access to and operations on the schemas and subschemas themselves.

12.3.3. Authorization Procedures

Authorization procedures control the type of access or use that a data base user or application program may invoke against the data base. IMS combines authorization with the PCB view mechanism by requiring that the PCB for each application program contain a list of processing options (PROCOPT) for which the program is authorized. In DBTG systems authorization is handled by an extension of the lock and key procedures. Locks may be defined on DML operations on particular record and set types. Thus any application program wishing to exercise the LOCKED operation on that record type or set must supply the appropriate key.

Relational systems, such as System R and INGRES, have the most sophisticated and dynamic authorization mechanisms.[6,8] In these systems authorization for different types of access, e.g., READ, INSERT, DELETE, UPDATE, are granted on a user-by-user basis and checked dynamically when a user attempts to access a particular relation.

12.4. COMPONENTS OF DATA BASE SECURITY POLICY

In order to establish a comprehensive and consistent data base security policy, the DBA must first identify and analyze the threats to security which exist in the organization's environment. The probability that each threat will result in a security violation must be estimated. In addition, the cost of the potential violation and its impact on the firm's operations must be evaluated. With this information the DBA can select the type and extent of security procedures required to protect the data base (see Table 12.1).

In addition to technical safeguards within the data base system, a data base security system must contain polices on authorization, internal control, personnel, and other issues.[2]

12.4.1. Authorization Policies and Procedures

Identification, authentication, and authorization mechanisms within the data base system are worthless unless they are accompanied by policies and procedures governing the granting of access privileges. Policies must be formulated in conjunction with data base user management and company management to guide

Table 12.1. Methods for Data Base Security

Method	Threat addressed	Procedures	Policies
Identification, authorization	All	Identification assignment Password assignment	Definition of legitimate DB user
Authorization	All	Grant, revoke privileges	Definition of "need to know, use"
Encryption	Disclosure	Select algorithm	Definition of sensitive data, processing
Audit	Modification	Verify selected data Verify DB structure	Determine time and scope of audit

decisions on who may access the data base and in what manner. Procedures are needed for the submission of authorization requests and for the modification or revocation of access privileges.

The DBA should administer the authorization procedures and be responsible for any secret data required by the security methods in use. For example, the DBA should assign passwords and data base keys as necessary and be responsible for protecting those data within the system. In addition, the DBA staff should contain an individual who can act as a "locksmith" [5] should damage to system tables of keys or passwords render the data base inaccessible. This role might be assigned to two individuals acting in concert in order to minimize the vulnerability of the locksmith.

Requests for access should be reviewed and coordinated by the DBA. However, the DBA's decisions on authorization are not arbitrary but based on existing policy. Requests in conformance with the policy are granted pro forma. Thus, in the formulation of authorization policy, user and company management share the responsibility for data base security.

12.4.2. Internal Controls

The DBA should review, and augment where necessary, existing internal controls within the organization. Internal controls include procedures for preventing, detecting, and responding to security violations. Many of these procedures are directed at maintaining data base integrity, e.g., data verification, audit trails, and processing controls. To these may be added identification procedures for data base users and authorization schemes for application programs.

The probability of detecting violations can be increased by planning and executing tests of the security system. Violations can be attempted or operation of the controls verified with known test data. Careful analysis of audit trail information can also uncover violations. Finally, samples of data base content and processing output should be checked against expected values.

The response to a security violation may involve simple notification of the users involved. Or a change in passwords or security procedures may be required. If the integrity of the data base has been compromised, data base recovery may also be required. A full audit of the data base may be needed to ascertain the extent of the problem.

12.4.3. Personnel and Other Control Procedures

Security violations are the result of the actions of individuals. In most cases the individual responsible is within the organization, perhaps even an authorized data base user. Violations can be avoided if the circumstances which encourage illegal or destructive behavior are limited. For example, if the organization is security conscious and employees are aware that violations will be detected and severely dealt with, many will be dissuaded from improper data access or use. This attitude should also prevail when hiring people for sensitive positions, e.g., DBA staff responsible for data base security measures. In personnel assignment the principle of separation of duties should be applied to prevent a single individual from having inordinate power over any portion of the data base or any specific application system. Finally, procedures for revoking an individual's access rights and for secure transfer of authority at the time of that person's termination or resignation from the firm must be in place.

Other control procedures that are part of any security system include controls on physical access to terminals and storage media and plans for legal action and insurance coverage in the event of security violations. These issues are relevant to the entire data processing system and should exist in any well-managed installation. The DBA should review existing safeguards of this type and evaluate their adequacy with respect to data base security. If weaknesses are found, recommendations should be made to data processing management for modifications or additional controls.

12.4.4. Guidelines for the Development of a Security System

The consistency of the techniques selected and the procedures developed to ensure data base security can be enhanced if the DBA follows a conscious philosophy in making these decisions. An excellent framework for such decisions is provided by Saltzer,[5] who describes the design principles used in the development of the security system for the Multics time-sharing system. These principles can be restated as guidelines for the DBA as follows:

1. Be conservative in usage authorization. Access privileges should be denied unless specifically granted, and each user should be granted the minimum privileges required by the job. This conservative strategy allows error to be on the side of increased security. Legitimate users who are denied appropriate authorization are more likely to be recognized than illegitimate users who are granted privileges to which they are not entitled.

2. Restrict the amount of secret information to a minimum. This reduces the risk of compromising the entire system due to an indiscretion on the part of someone privy to that secret. Wherever possible, public algorithms and procedures should be used which depend only on a few secret passwords or key values. This approach also allows independent review and verification of the security system without exposing the system to additional threats.

3. Security actions on the part of users should be easy and commensurate with the value of the data that they are designed to protect. If procedures

are cumbersome or difficult, users will be inclined to bypass these controls. Or, if extensive security procedures are imposed on data or actions which have little value, users may perceive this as security overkill and pay less attention to security of more valuable data.

4. Recognize the dynamic nature of authorization. Security procedures must anticipate and be prepared to cope with changes in the individuals allowed to access the data base and in the types of usage authorized. It must be possible to revoke privileges as easily as they are granted. If this is not the case, then time and habit will aid security violators.

12.5. THE IMPLICATIONS OF PRIVACY

The advent of the data base approach has caused concern among those interested in preserving the privacy of individuals.[20,21] The ease of storing and retrieving information in a data base system has expanded the types and the uses of personal recordkeeping within both government and private organizations. Check processing systems, mail order and billing systems, telephone call routing systems, and credit card authorization systems all result in records of individuals' actions. In addition to their primary uses, these records can easily be used in other ways with or without the knowledge of the individuals involved. For example, records of an individual's calls can be used to trace their whereabouts. Or address information from a billing system can be sold to another firm or a fund-raising organization.

Technological advances in data collection procedures and the accessing capabilities of DBMS software have also had an effect. Text-scanning and high-volume storage devices have made obscure coding systems less necessary. Complex storage structures have made it easier to correlate and integrate data. Data correlated from several sources can be combined into an extensive dossier on an individual. The danger is that government agencies, private firms, or unauthorized individuals might compile these records without the subject's knowledge or consent. Examples of such abuses in the credit industry have been cited.[22]

In response to abuses that have occurred and in anticipation of increased risk in the future, the U.S. government has become concerned with privacy legislation. Some measures have already been passed and others are being considered. The DBA should be aware of this legislation and the impact of compliance on a data base environment.

12.5.1. Privacy Legislation

The first attempt to control access to personal data and to limit abuses was the Fair Credit Reporting Act of 1970. The objective of this act was to define and prevent unfair uses of personal data by credit organizations. Its main provisions were to limit those authorized to receive credit data and to allow consumers to see and challenge the contents of their own records.

The Privacy Act of 1974 set standards for the collection and use of personal data within the public sector. Private sector firms were excluded from the act before it was passed. Briefly, public agencies were required to

1. Keep personal data accurate, complete, timely and pertinent.
2. Permit individuals to examine and possibly correct records of data on themselves.
3. Restrict usage of personal data to routine use only.
4. Keep records of all disclosures of personal data outside routine use for five years or the life of the record, whichever is longer.

Difficulties with the 1974 Privacy Act revolve around the definition of the terms used in the legislation. For example, how does an organization determine what is meant by "routine use" or "life of the record" with respect to its operations? Also, what constitutes adequate compliance to the act can be determined only through judicial rulings on test cases. As a result, government agencies have had to develop procedures and techniques that meet their own standards for compliance.[23]

After the passage of the 1974 act the Privacy Protection Study Commission was set up to assess the impact of similar legislation for the private sector. Other issues considered were the interstate transfer of data and the use of universal identifiers, e.g., Social Security numbers. The final report of the commission was completed in July 1977. Among the needs identified by this group were procedures for bringing new and revised recordkeeping systems under scrutiny, methods for evaluating their safeguards and impact, and measures for compliance with privacy laws. The findings of the commission will be used in congressional debate over the Comprehensive Right to Privacy Act (HR 1984) which is still pending.

12.5.2. Implications for the DBA

The content of existing and proposed privacy legislation is of importance to the DBA for several reasons. Its provisions may affect data base content and design, data base security and integrity measures, and the selection and responsibilities of DBA personnel.

The simplest way to avoid misuse of personal information is not to collect it. The content of personal data bases should be reviewed at design time, and only necessary items should be maintained. Also, data base structure should not rely heavily on the use of individual identifiers such as Social Security numbers.

Concern for privacy reemphasizes the need for a conservative authorization strategy. Data base users should be allowed to access the minimum data required for their authorized functions. Consistent with this is the use of data-dependent controls. For example, a manager should be authorized to see the records of just his or her employees rather than all employees. Data encryption should be considered to protect particularly sensitive personal data. The cost of encryption may well be offset by the possibility of penalties should private data be disclosed.

Requirements that the firm maintain records of unusual disclosures may be satisfied through skillful use of audit trails in the data base integrity subsystem. The processing log could be used to generate notices to individuals affected by a transaction as well as the necessary archival files. The log could also provide accountability if full details were recorded on all affected transactions. Denied access requests could also be recorded.

DBA personnel must be selected and assigned in a way that preserves data privacy and limits liability should data be improperly disclosed. For example, individuals selected for the DBA's staff should be aware of privacy requirements so that a concern for privacy is reflected in their decisions and actions. Further, responsibility for personal data bases should be divided in such a way that an abuse of data privacy would require the combined actions of several individuals.

The future of privacy legislation is uncertain. However, it behooves the DBA to follow the progress of congressional debate on the subject so that compliance to proposed measures may be evaluated and anticipated.

Chapter 13

Monitoring Data Base Performance

In selecting the logical structure and physical implementation for a data base the DBA must strike a delicate balance. For each application different structures and storage methods yield different cost-performance results. A configuration favorable to one application may be unfavorable, even untenable, to one or more of the others. The DBA must weigh these trade-offs and select the configuration that produces the best overall performance for the least cost.

Over time the factors involved in this decision will almost certainly change. These changes may be in the data base environment, in the data base itself, or in the use of the data base. New or updated hardware or system software may affect data base performance. The data base itself may grow or require other modifications. Or the priorities of the data base applications or frequencies of certain access requests may change. Any of these changes could upset the cost-performance balance of the data base configuration, resulting in degradation of system performance.

The DBA must be constantly aware of data base performance and alert to signs of imbalance. In order to do this the DBA must be familiar with the causes of imbalance and their effects on performance. Measures must be developed and used regularly to detect performance problems and to guide the DBA in tuning, i.e., improving the performance of, the data base. If simple tuning is not enough, a reorganization or even a redesign of the data base may be required.[1]

13.1. CAUSES OF IMBALANCE

Data base performance can deteriorate as a result of four factors:[2,3] hardware changes or contention, problems with system software, problems in application design or coding, and changes in the data base itself. The first two types of problems affect the operation of the system as a whole. As a result, the DBA must work in cooperation with the system support personnel to detect and resolve them. The latter two center on the content and use of the data base. The DBA must anticipate these problems during data base design and be ready to respond to them during data base operation.

13.1.1. Hardware

The cost–performance balance of a data base environment can be upset if the hardware configuration is inadequate or underutilized. Inadequate or heavily loaded secondary storage devices such as tapes and disks can bog down system throughput by requiring extensive searches for free space. Inadequate primary memory can increase the rate at which multiprogramming or virtual systems must move active tasks in and out of memory, again delaying processing. Underutilization does not affect performance but increases the cost of the processing performed. It can indicate that some existing hardware is unnecessary or being used improperly.

Sometimes inadequate hardware and underutilization show up simultaneously as a contention for system resources. For example, the central processing unit (CPU) may be underutilized while the data channels connecting the CPU to secondary storage devices are overloaded. In such a case, programs may be competing for use of the data channels, and tasks that are denied access must simply wait until a channel is free. Resolution may require the addition of channels or a change of schedule so that data base accessing programs are run with programs that require less input/output processing and more CPU processing.

Hardware changes can also result in problems. Data base access methods may involve blocking factors and addressing techniques related to the characteristics of a specific device. For example, block size may be related to track size on a disk. Should that track size change, e.g., in a new disk model, the parameters of the access method must also be changed. Resolution of this problem may require a dump and reload of the entire data base.

13.1.2. System Software

Performance problems can also be the result of factors related to system software including the DBMS itself. Improper memory management on the part of the operating system can cause excessive input/output activity. The size of system input/output buffers can affect the number of secondary storage accesses required. The algorithms for resource management, i.e., handling queues, scheduling, CPU allocation schemes, and servicing I/O requests, are all critical. Normally, these aspects of performance are monitored by the systems support staff and affect all users equally. However, some problems like buffering can be exacerbated by interaction with the DBMS.

A DBMS, especially those designed to handle multiple data base users simultaneously, can act like an operating system. In these cases the DBMS can suffer from similar weaknesses in memory or resource management. Even when restricted to a single user the DBMS can create performance problems because of improper buffer sizes, poor search techniques, or inefficient handling of overflow. Buffer sizes which are too large can increase contention for main memory. Small buffers may result in more data base faults, i.e., requests for data not currently in the buffer. If the requested data are not in the system buffer either, a secondary storage access is required.

DBMS code that is vendor written should be of high quality. Poor coding or choice of algorithms, whether by users or vendors, can have a negative impact on performance. For example, a hashing algorithm that results in numerous synonyms can cause extensive searches on data base access and storage operations. An overflow method that requires access to more than one disk cylinder or data set increases the time necessary to handle any operation that involves overflow.

13.1.3. Data Base Applications

Poor design or inefficient coding of data base applications can result in performance problems. For example, a retrieval program should be designed to search for records according to the most exclusive criteria first. If an employee data base contains 1,000 records on female employees and only 45 records on employees in department X, a request for all female employees in department X should be fulfilled by first selecting the employees in department X and then checking the employee's sex.

Similarly, the use of a fully inverted data base to support applications where the access is primarily by record keys reflects a poor design choice. Performance of this design is no better than a direct organization, yet costs are higher because the inverted directory must be maintained.

Excess processing and poor performance can also be the result of incorrect use of the DBMS. Some DBMS languages include a command that finds and retrieves a data base record. Should an application programmer use this command when locating the record is sufficient, unnecessary processing results. For example, to compute the total number of current employees an application program could simply locate each occurrence of an employee record and maintain a count of those found. Since no data from the records themselves are required, retrieval is unncessary.

13.1.4. Data Base Content, Structure, and Use

The data base is responsive to the applications that use it only if it accurately reflects the organization's information environment. To be accurate the content and structure of the data base must conform to the applications' requirements, and the physical implementation must reflect the priorities among applications. In any organization these requirements and priorities change over time.[4]

Normal modification of the contents of the data base, e.g., adding new orders for a customer and deleting old ones, do not affect its logical structure. However, these changes have a physical impact. Insertion and deletion can leave the storage area of the data base fragmented and can fill the overflow areas. Thus performance deteriorates.

Modifications which add new objects of interest to the logical schema or result in new relationships should trigger both logical and physical redesign. Accomodating the modifications within the existing structure, even if possible, could have undesirable implications for performance. For example, additional data fields could be added to an existing customer data base by creating a new set of data base records linked to the original customer records by key value, i.e., Customer Number (see Figure 13.1). This allows the addition of these new items without substantial change in the existing data base structure. However, the applications using the new data require additional accesses in any operation that retrieves or updates the customer records.

Physical data base design choices rely on application priorities and expected usage patterns. When these priorities or patterns change, the data base no longer performs optimally. For example, in a hierarchical data base, records that are expected to be used frequently are stored as root segments. Those used less frequently are stored at the leaves of the hierarchy. If data base activity reverses

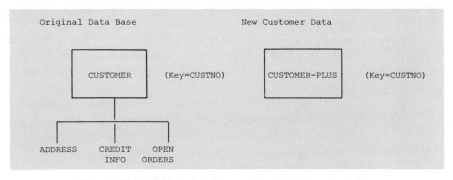

Figure 13.1.   Adding data items without data base redesign.

this expected pattern, the records used most frequently require the most processing to retrieve. Similarly, suppose that an indexed sequential access method is selected over a direct or list method because of the high priority of an application that requires sequential access. If that application becomes less crucial or is no longer needed, the physical implementation becomes inappropriate. The sequential order is maintained at a cost but never used.

13.2. MEASURES OF PERFORMANCE

To determine whether the data base is performing as expected, the DBA must gather statistics on the performance of the operational system.[2,5] To make the best use of this data the DBA should know which indicators should be measured and how to analyze the data collected to pinpoint the source of the performance problem. Since performance is relative, i.e., better or worse than some standard, data should always be collected with some comparison in mind. The point of comparison may be previously observed performance or an ideal model of performance.[4] The statistics to be collected fall into four categories: time, resource utilization, memory management, and data base activity. Table 13.1 shows representative statistics for each of these categories.

13.2.1. Time

The first indication of performance problems is most likely to be related to time. The DBA or a data base user may observe that a specific program or transaction is not being processed as fast as it should. The turnaround time for a program or transaction is measured from the moment that it enters the system

Table 13.1. Representative Performance Indicators

Time	Resource utilization	Memory management	Activity
Turnaround	CPU state (supervisor, problem, wait)	Amount of free space	Distribution of access
Throughput		Size of application programs	Distribution of structures
Access	Data channel	Overflow	Functions performed
	Disks	Paging rates	Deadlock
	Memory		Errors
	Job mix		
	Queue sizes		

until processing related to it is completed. If turnaround increases, then some portion of the processing is taking longer than it previously did.

The DBA or system support staff may also observe a decrease in system throughput, the number of jobs or transactions processed in a given time period. If throughput decreases, one of two problems can exist. A job (or transaction) in the stream may be taking longer than it formerly did. Or a bottleneck may be occuring, with several jobs (or transactions) competing for the same resources. Since both turnaround and throughput can be measured external to system operations, these data are easy to record. However, they are gross measures. For example, if turnaround on a particular transaction type increases, it is not possible to say whether that increase is caused by the DBMS, the application program processing the transaction, or some other system software function.

A finer measure of time with respect to the data base is the access time required for a given transaction or series of DBMS operations. Access time can be measured dynamically[6] or computed based on known access paths, search strategies, and device times.[7] If access times exceed those expected for a transaction the DBA can conclude that more disk accesses are being required, perhaps because of long overflow chains.

13.2.2. Resource Utilization

The DBA can get an idea of how efficiently system resources are being used by measuring the percentage of time that a resource, e.g., a data channel, is in use during a given time period. Utilization figures can be used to determine whether the system is balanced in its use of available resources. For example, a high utilizaation of data channels may indicate the need for an additional channel. Utilization can also be tied to cost of the resource,[8] so that less expensive resources are not optimized at the expense of more costly components. A cost–utilization chart (see Figure 13.2) can be used by the DBA to get an unbiased picture of system utilization.

A comparison of utilization data for the CPU and the data channels can be used to spot imbalances in job mix. Job mix refers to the amount of time spent on CPU activity versus that spent on I/O activity. If these amounts are roughly equal, the system is balanced. If CPU exceeds I/O activity, the job mix is CPU bound. If I/O activity exceeds CPU activity, the job mix is I/O bound. An imbalance in either direction is undesirable since it implies that a system resource is not being utilized to its fullest potential.

Utilization of CPU cycles, memory space, or input/output devices can also be used to locate inefficient program coding or improper data base access strategies. Or programs or sections of code that have the most significant performance implications can be identified for tuning.

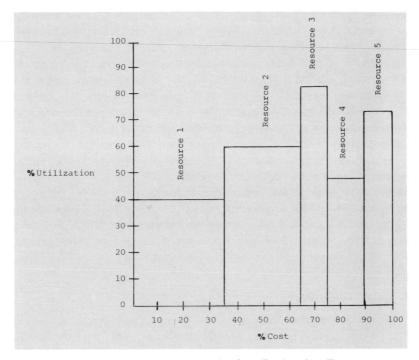

Figure 13.2. An example of a utilization chart.[8]

Another indicator of the quality of resource management being provided by the system software is the size of system queues. When different jobs or transactions require the same services, e.g., printing or CPU processing cycles, the operating system queues these requests and fills them as the resource becomes free. Average queue lengths over a period of time indicate how efficiently this allocation is being performed. Large average queue lengths indicate a bottleneck. Uncorrected, the bottleneck decreases throughput, increases turnaround time, and increases the amount of overhead processing that the operating system must expend to manage the queue and the allocation scheme.

13.2.3. Memory Management

Accesses to secondary memory are much more time-consuming than internal CPU processing. Thus in a high-performance system these accesses should be minimized. Access to secondary memory is triggered either by a data base access or by the system's need to move pages of data or program code in and out of main memory to facilitate multiprogramming or virtual memory. To minimize the need to retrieve pages, areas of temporary storage called buffers are set aside in internal memory. Access is required only when the desired page is not in memory or the buffer. This occurrence is called a page fault.

The number of page faults in a given time period can be called the paging rate of the system and can be used an an indicator of system performance. If the DBMS maintains its own buffering system, a similar rate of data base faults can also be recorded.[9, 10] Page rates and thus system performance can be affected by buffer sizes, by the strategy used to replace the contents of main memory, and by the management of the buffers. For example, if two buffers are kept for input and two for output, the likelihood that a needed record will be present in the buffer is greater than if only one buffer is kept for each.

High paging rates can indicate contention for system resources or improper program coding. Large application programs that transfer control back and forth throughout the code result in more paging than shorter programs with localized references. High rates of data base faults could indicate improper data base structures or inefficient coding of data base programs.

13.2.4. Data Base Activity

Statistics on data base activity can be used in two ways. First, they can allow the DBA to identify frequently used DBMS functions and frequently traversed access paths. Performance can then be optimized by streamlining the process of those functions and shortening those access paths. Monitoring of activity can also provide an early indication of performance problems and a guide to locating the source or cause of an observed problem.

The kinds of statistics that are indicative of data base activity include the frequency of occurrence of each type of data base operation, by program. For example, program A may involve almost 100% access by hashed record keys, while program B may show the pattern of hashed access to a single record followed by sequential access to related records. As a result, a compact data base with related records stored physically close together is much more important to the performance of program B than to program A.

Activity can also be viewed from the data base side in terms of the distribution of record types or even of key values accessed. These distributions allow the DBA to compare actual activity against the type of activity that was predicted at data base design time. If actual activity varies from predicted, the physical structure of the data base may no longer be optimal. For example, if inquiries are expected by Customer Account Number and by Account Type, an inverted directory may be built for these keys. If, however, data base activity shows that many inquiries are by Branch Code, this attribute should also be indexed. Systems which provide an ad hoc inquiry capability benefit from this type of tuning.

Many DBMS systems include a provision for storing related data base records physically close together. The insertion and deletion of records in data base activity can upset this plan and impair the performance of applications which rely on the proximity characteristic. Statistics on the distribution of data base structures across data storage devices enable the DBA to observe the scattering process and to initiate a reorganization to consolidate the structures as needed.

The DBA should also be informed of error conditions that arise during normal data base operation. The occurrence of deadlock can indicate contention for specific portions of the data base which could be resolved through redesign of the contending programs or through rescheduling. A summary of DBMS or system-reported errors by type and by program or by transaction can point out incorrect use of the DBMS, conflicts between data base programs and the operating system, and possible hardware problems (e.g., errors on a particular disk cylinder or data channel).

13.3. PERFORMANCE TOOLS

The DBA has four basic tools with which to gather and analyze data base performance measures: observation of system activity, hardware and software monitors, benchmarks, and simulation or modeling of the data base system.[5, 11, 12]

13.3.1. Observation

Many statistics of interest in monitoring data base performance can be gathered from normal system output. Most installations have job accounting systems in place which associate resource usage figures with programs run on the system. These figures include turnaround time, CPU time, number of I/O accesses, amount of main memory used, and the time of day at which the job was run. System error messages are also a part of normal output.

In addition, system access methods and the DBMS itself may have automatic or optional reporting of data base storage statistics. Statistics such as the length of overflow chains, the amount of free space remaining (or the amount of storage space filled), and the number and type of records accessed may be produced when any application program modifies the stored data base.

The DBA may also require application programs to contain code that compiles additional data on data base use. For example, an inquiry processing application might be required to record the number of requests for each record type and or each key field.

A certain amount of performance monitoring is done by the data base users themselves. They should be encouraged and given formal procedures and guidelines for reporting problems, e.g., unusual terminal response time or increasing cost per transaction processed.

13.3.2. Hardware and Software Monitors

Monitors are systems or devices capable of detecting and reporting various types of system activity. Hardware monitors consist of a set of electronic probes plus a device to record the data collected by the probes. The probes may be attached to any of a number of circuits within the CPU itself or within system-peripheral devices. Activity of these devices can be detected and recorded over a prespecified time interval. Distributions of resource utilization statistics can then be compiled from the data recorded. Some monitors provide programs which can be used to summarize and analyze the data collected.

The advantage of hardware monitors is that their operation does not interfere with the operation of the system. They observe the system without disturbing it. However, expertise is required for their use since attachment locations must be determined and the probes physically connected. Also, measurements by hardware probes cannot be identified with specific software components of the system. With the possible exception of the operating system nucleus which is usually assigned to a fixed portion of internal memory, memory locations are not associated with any particular application or system program. Thus, for example, to observe the activity of the DBMS or certain data base applications, hardware monitors alone will not suffice.

In such cases the monitoring function is assigned to software monitors. The software monitor is a program that can be called as needed to gather data on the state of the system. For example, a software monitor could check system tables and record which programs are active and how much memory they are occupying. Or a software monitor could record system time for a particular data base function by being called before and after the function is performed. [12] Since the monitor can be coded by the DBA, it is very flexible and can be tailored to the needs of the installation.

The major difficulty with software monitors is that since they must be stored and executed in the system, their very presence adds an additional factor to system operation. So if the monitor is measuring page faults, for example, it may not be possible to subtract the effect of the monitor itself on memory availability and thus on the paging rate.

13.3.3. Benchmarks and Synthetic Code

Performance measurements can be made on program code of known characteristics. This code can be a program typical of the jobs that are run on the system, i.e., a benchmark. Or synthetic code can be created artificially to embody a function or series of functions known to be prevalant in or critical to the work loads. These techniques are most valuable during the evaluation and selection of a system or as a performance standard during operation of the system. For example, if a full set of optimal statistics is known for a benchmark program or synthetic code sequence, the benchmark can be run and corresponding measurements made when operational problems are encountered. A comparison of the two sets of measurements may help pinpoint the source of the performance problem.

13.3.4. Simulation and Modeling

The DBA can simulate, or model, the performance of the data base system using a mathematical model that describes the processing characteristics of the DBMS and its hardware/software environment. The results of the simulation can be used as a performance standard or to assess the impact of changes in hardware/software configuration on data base performance.

For some DBMS systems, packaged simulation models are available. [13] In other cases the DBA staff must develop a model based on the characteristics of the DBMS in use. [14] Since DBMS modeling is a complex, mathematical task and requires an intimate knowledge of the DBMS and the system software, not many DBA's are willing to undertake this task. If a high-level simulation language [15] were available, the use of modeling to predict and assess data base performance would be used more frequently.

13.4. RESOLUTION OF PERFORMANCE PROBLEMS

The DBA must be able to resolve as well as detect data base performance problems. The actions necessary may be outside the scope of the DBA's operational responsibilities. However, the responsibility for initiating such actions lies with the DBA. Depending on the nature of the problem, resolution may require reconfiguration of the system, data base reorganization, or data base redesign. Table 13.2 summarizes these alternatives.

System reconfiguration refers to changes in system software or hardware, such as the addition of new data channels or disk storage devices. These decisions lie within the scope of the data processing computer operations staff. However, the DBA must be able to state and support the case for such changes when they affect data base performance. Similar action may be required for changes in system software or processing schedules.

Data base reorganization is the operation of consolidating the stored records of the data base so that they conform to the physical constraints of the initial

Table 13.2. Resolution of Performance Problems

Problem	Relevant statistics	Resolution
Contention for disk access	Channel utilization Queue sizes Distribution of accesses	System reconfiguration
Increased response time for fixed access to data base	Amount of free space Length of overflow chains Distribution of data base structures (across data sets)	Data base reorganization
Application throughput below desirable level	CPU state Job mix Distribution of access	Physical data base redesign

physical design (see Chapter 10). Lack of conformance is usually the result of insertion or deletion resulting in fragmented physical storage and excess overflow. Reorganization requires copying currently active data base records onto an auxiliary storage device, perhaps as a part of regular backup procedures. Then additional space must be allocated and the data base reloaded in proper sequence with minimal overflow. The frequency with which this operation is performed depends on the volume of insert/delete activity, the cost of the reorganization process, and the amount of performance deterioration which is tolerable.

Data base redesign may be required on one or both of two levels. The simplest is a physical redesign in which the factors involved in selecting a physical implementation are reevaluated and the access method or indexing procedures are changed accordingly. This process should follow the steps and procedures of the initial physical design and should not affect the application programs which access the data base. It is this type of change that the objective of data independence is designed to facilitate.

If through error or change in the organization's requirements, the logical structure of the data base must be changed, the redesign is more extensive and its effects are more far-reaching. In such a case a full data base design must be initiated, perhaps resulting in major changes to both the logical and the physical structure of the data base. All application programs which use the revised schema will have to be recompiled, at a minimum, and possibly redesigned as well. The objectives of initial data base design is to avoid the need for this if at all possible.

Part V

Managing the User Interface

Chapter 14

Data Administration

The data base approach presumes the integration of formerly separate stores of data. While this integration may or may not involve centralization of the physical data, it certainly implies an increase in data sharing among user applications and a decrease in redundant storage of identical data items. To facilitate sharing and minimize redundancy requires central control of the content of the data base. Such control addresses the form and meaning of the data items and structures in the data base rather than the actual values of the data items themselves. The management function which exercises control over the form and content of the data base is called data administration.

Control over data base content is maintained through the collection and maintenance of accurate and complete information about the data. Such data about the data base, often called metadata,[1] include descriptions of the meanings of data items, the ways in which the data are used, their sources, their physical characteristics, and other rules or restrictions on their forms or uses. This information provides a ready resource for the analysis of new data requirements, the design and programming of new applications systems, the maintenance of existing systems, and the documentation of all phases of data base activities. The metadata is a resource for the DBA in the same way that the data base itself serves the organization. To fully exploit this resource the DBA must understand the types of metadata that exist and their uses.

14.1. TYPES OF METADATA

Data about the data base, or metadata, can be classified into three types: semantic information, physical characteristics, and usage information. In short, the metadata required by the DBA is the data necessary to document the form and content of the data base as well as the data which describe the way in which the data base is used.

All components of a data base are worthy of description. These components include both elementary-level data elements and more complex data groupings and structures. The actual components described vary with the type of DBMS used. However, most often the components include data elements, records or segments, files, and data bases as well as data base users and the application systems that process the data base.

14.1.1. Semantic Information

Semantic information is information which describes the meaning of each data base component. This information is used to relate the entities of the organization and its business functions to the elements and structures used to represent them in the data base.

A basic type of semantic information is the name(s) of the component. A unique identifier should be assigned to each component in the data base to allow unambiguous reference to that object. However, each component may have additional names by which it is known in different contexts. For example, a data element may be referred to by different names depending on the source language of the program which references it. Or a file in a data base may be identified by one name to the DBMS and by another to the operating system. These alternative names, called aliases, promote sharing of common data among diverse applications.

The most typical means of expressing meaning in human communication is the definition. A good definition is clear and precise and expresses the meaning of the component in terms of other objects which are already known or defined. For example, the definition ''The Salesman–Customer set represents the relationship between a Salesman and the Customer(s) on whom the Salesman calls'' presumes that a reader knows the meaning of the terms *Salesman, Customer,* and the action *calls on.* To be complete, a definition must address all those characteristics of importance to the object being defined. For example, the characteristics of a DBTG set include an owner record type, a member record type, and a membership class for insertion and deletion of the member records. Thus the definition of the Salesman–Customer set should be expanded to include a description of all these characteristics for the set in question.

The exact form of the definitions for various data base components varies.

Each requires recording a number of elements or facts which are characteristic of that component type. These characteristics must be well specified before the task of assembling definitions begins if full and unambiguous definitions are to be produced. While definitions can be free narrative in form, a structured format highlighting each of the characteristics that must be described yields clearer, more consistent results.

The meaning of a data base component can also be conveyed by a description of any constraints or exceptions which affect it. For example, a data element may be constrained to take its values from a standard set of code values. Or a data file may contain records relating to a specific time period, e.g., employees hired since 1975. The expression of these conditions as constraints or exceptions eliminates the risk that they will be incorrectly, included as fundamental characteristics of the components they describe. For example, the time constraint could also be conveyed by restricting the Date-Hired data element in employee records to have values greater than 1975. However, this restriction becomes unnecessary if the data file is properly described.

14.1.2. Physical Characteristics

The physical characteristics of a data base component are those related to the system-dependent representation of that component. This information provides the exact specification for the representation of the component in the physical data base. For data elements, the physical characteristics include size (number of storage bytes required), data type (alpha, numeric, or alphanumeric), and length (fixed or variable). Operational data, such as the volume of occurrences for a data element or record in the data base, are also of interest.

Physical information is also contained in the relationships within the data base and in the relationships among systems and programs which use the data base. The fact that a specific data element may be found in records X, Y, and Z and is referenced by programs A and B in system C describes the physical structure of the data base and of the processing environment as well.

As with definitional characteristics, the physical descriptors of a data base component depend on the type of component being described. To be complete, the physical description must supply enough information for a user to access and/or manipulate the component described.

14.1.3. Usage Information

In addition to knowing which data are in the data base and in what form those data are stored, it is valuable to know how and by whom those data are used. Information on usage enables the DBA to trace the source of errors in the data base, to assess the impact of changes in data base content or structure, and to monitor and control access to the data base.

When the scope of metadata includes usage information, the data base components of interest must include users and processes as well as data components. Users can be represented as organizational units or as individuals. Processes are typically represented by hierarchical structures of systems, programs, transactions, and reports.

Information on users should contain the identity of the user and the reason that the user has access to the data base. The processing functions over which the user has control should be listed. Responsibility for data-base-related tasks, e.g., source of a particular transaction or responsibility for updating a particular data element, should be assigned. Authorization for data base access should also be recorded, either in terms of the data base view permitted or a password protection scheme.

The extent of process-oriented information collected depends on the DBA's intended use of metadata. Full documentation requires semantic and physical information on each processing component as well as relationships to users, to other processing components, and, of course, to the data base.

14.2. USES OF METADATA

Just as the data base is a valuable resource for the organization, the metadata is a resource for the DBA.[2] Data about the data base can be used in every phase of data base application development. For most organizations the primary, or at least initial, use of metadata is for data base and application system documentation. However, the collection and maintenance of metadata can augment requirements analysis, data base design, application programming, and application maintenance as well.

14.2.1. Requirements Analysis

When a study is undertaken to determine the need for system support in a new organizational unit or for a new application, much of the effort is devoted to recording the functional components and operational statistics of the existing system. The study team records which processes are being performed and which data classes are being used. Similar information must be recorded for new processes desired and new data required. Once this information has been captured, it can be correlated to search for new opportunities for data sharing, to identify redundant processing requirements, and to locate opportunities for modifying or expanding existing systems rather than developing a new system from scratch.

During the course of a requirements study, the team's understanding of the needs change and thus modifications must be made to the recorded metadata. If cross-references are maintained, they can be used to prevent inconsistencies in the requirements as the modifications occur. At the conclusion of the study the metadata provides a thorough documentation of user data and processing needs, a starting point for system and data base design.

14.2.2. Data Base Design

In logical data base design the DBA aims to develop a sound conceptual model of the organization's data needs. At the logical level this consists of identifying the necessary data entities and the nature of the relationships among entities. The attributes, or data elements, necessary to describe each entity must also be identified. In an organization of any complexity this information rapidly becomes too voluminous to be expressed in the graphical terms of most data models. Instead, the information is recorded for each component of the data model in turn, e.g., entities, attributes, and relationships.

As with analysis, cross-referencing among the items described is valuable to discover inconsistencies or redundancies. Additional facilities for manipulating this metadata, e.g., the analysis of descriptive words in context, are valuable for the identification of synonyms or homonyms and thus for the integration of logical views.

Metadata on the physical characteristics of the data base becomes important in the physical design task. Data on the size and structure of data items can be used to estimate record and file sizes or to define clusters of data items for storage. Other quantitative information on volumes and frequency of use for data items or records can be used to select access paths for the physical data base. Physical data base descriptions can be kept accurate and up-to-date by referencing the physical characteristics recorded as metadata.

14.2.3. Programming

Metadata on the physical entities of the data base—items, records, files, data sets, and various DBMS constructs—can be used as a reference by application programmers as they code programs which access or manipulate these entities. In fact, installation procedures can require that data descriptions used in application programs be maintained centrally and shared by any and all programs that use the data described. This practice promotes consistency in data item naming and reduces the likelihood of program bugs due to inaccurate data or file descriptions.

Constraints on data base contents or usage may also be applied more effectively if they are recorded centrally and referenced by application programmers or the programs themselves. Edit criteria, such as the type or range of data values legitimate for a particular data element, if recorded centrally can be used consistently by all programs that require that data element. Authorization data, on which users or programs can use certain portions of the data base, can also be a part of the metadata. If so, the DBA can develop an authorization subsystem which uses this information as a basis for granting or denying access to potential data base users.

14.2.4. Maintenance

System maintenance implies the accommodation of changes in existing programs or data bases. These changes may be required to correct errors in the original systems or programs or to reflect changes in system objectives. The central risk of changing existing systems is introducing new errors or inconsistencies. For example, if the size of a data element is changed from 8 bytes to 12 bytes, that change must be reflected in every program that uses that data element. Or if a new code value is added to those previously acceptable, this change must be made in all programs that accept and validate the data element. In either case if a program is overlooked it may not work, or it may work incorrectly, after the change occurs.

A central store of metadata can aid system maintenance by providing the cross-referencing capability necessary to trace the potential impact of changes. Information about the usage of an element (e.g., the data records and files in which it appears, the programs which supply or access it) is precisely that needed to assure that any change to that element is thorough and consistent. The impact of physical changes can also be assessed more easily if information on physical data base characteristics is collected and maintained centrally. For example, what is the overall impact if record X is expanded by 50 bytes? Finally, information on usage can be used to assess the impact of changes in usage patterns. One might wish to determine, for example, the impact of processing 1,000 more transactions per day than the current work load.

Organizations using a DBMS face a complex maintenance task with respect to the DBMS data descriptions. These elements define both data base content and data base structure in a preformatted way. Normally, such descriptions are maintained centrally and accessed by the DBMS during compilation and execution of all programs that access the data base. Examples of DBMS data descriptions include IMS Data Base Descriptions (DBD's) and Program Specification Blocks (PSB's) and DBTG schema and subschema descriptions. Since this descriptive information corresponds to metadata, the latter can serve as a central source from which the required data descriptions can be generated. As with traditional application programming, centralizing the source of the descriptions used instead of recreating them as needed promotes consistency and minimizes errors.

14.2.5. Documentation

Historically, those charged with the development and maintenance of information systems have been less than successful in keeping the documentation of those systems accurate and up-to-date. A major problem has been timing. If documentation is compiled as a system is being designed, it must be changed constantly as the system evolves, producing an additional burden for system designers and programmers. If documentation is postponed until after the system has been implemented, motivation for its completion is often lacking and the result is superficial or incomplete. Even in the latter case good procedures must be in place to capture any postimplementation modifications.

Metadata is documentation. The facts and descriptions related to the content and usage of the data base are precisely those that would be needed in any document describing an application system that uses the data base. If proper cross-references are maintained, e.g., among systems, programs, data bases, files, records, elements, and users, system documentation can easily be extracted and assembled from metadata. Documentation created in this way is dynamic, always reflecting the most current state of the system.

14.3. THE ROLE OF DATA DICTIONARY/DIRECTORY SYSTEMS

The DBA has a valuable tool for assisting generally in the collection and management of data about the data base. This tool, called a data dictionary/ directory (DD/D) system, consists of a data base and a set of programs designed to perform some of the common processing tasks associated with the maintenance and use of metadata. Without such a tool the DBA must rely on traditional methods of manual documentation and cross-referencing. These methods are cumbersome and ill-suited to the dynamic nature of metadata. Their use requires extensive clerical support to maintain the cross-references and to modify the metadata as needed. Replacing this function with an automated data dictionary system places such routine processing tasks in the dictionary system and frees the DBA staff to make productive use of the contents of the dictionary.

A number of software vendors, especially those already offering a data base management system, offer data dictionary/directory systems. (See Appendix B for feature summaries of several DD/D systems.) These DD/D systems vary in the structure and complexity of the data base they support as well as in the extent of the processing functions that they provide. However, they all follow the same general architecture.

14.3.1. General Architecture of DD/D Systems

The major objective of a DD/D system is to support the integration of metadata in much the same way that a DBMS supports the integration of an organization's data. The benefits achieved are also comparable: minimum redundancy, consistency, standardization, and metadata sharing. In addition, the integration of data describing the data base allows the DBA to monitor data base content and to effectively enforce security and integrity policies.

The architecture of a data dictionary/directory system is shown in Figure 14.1. The central feature is a repository of metadata, called the DD/D data base in the diagram. Facilities are provided to support both management and computer uses of this data base.[3,4] Programs to support management use provide for data capture, indexing, and reporting for documentation purposes. The facilities to interface directly with application programs and/or with a DBMS support the computer use of the dictionary. Generally the term *dictionary* refers to support for management usage, and the term *directory* refers to support for computer usage.

From a management perspective the DD/D system is merely an automated means of storing and retrieving data about the data base. Management users (including the DBA staff, application programmers, systems analysts, and others) are concerned with the content of the dictionary and the relationships documented there, not with the workings of the DD/D system itself. Features that enable easy and direct user access to dictionary contents are of most importance

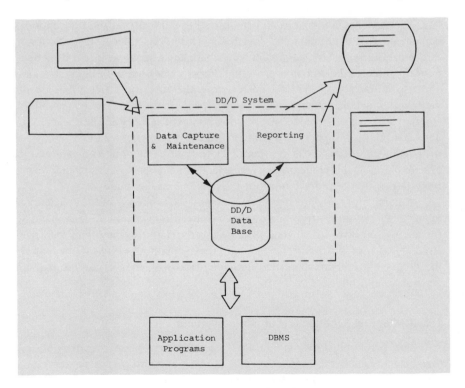

Figure 14.1. Architecture of a DD/D system.

to management users. Also, the variety and the flexibility of reports available from the DD/D system contribute to the system's value as a management tool.

Computer users of DD/D systems are most concerned with the interfaces provided between the DD/D system and other software systems. An installation using a DBMS wants the DD/D system to be able to generate descriptive data in a format acceptable to their DBMS. They may also wish the contents of the dictionary to be easily and efficiently accessible to application programs. This facility extends the reporting capability of the dictionary beyond that provided by the DD/D system vendor and makes the metadata in the dictionary available for use in integrity and security checking.

In selecting a DD/D system for his or her environment, the DBA's primary concern is that the dictionary be capable of supporting descriptions of that environment as directly as possible. The DBA must have a clear understanding of the uses of metadata in the organization and must match the features provided by the DD/D to planned uses. As with any software selection, anticipation of future requirements is also beneficial. For example, the organization may initially wish to use the DD/D system only to maintain DBMS data descriptions. However, in the future they may wish to expand its function to include data base design support or documentation. Not all DD/D systems are capable of effectively meeting these expanded requirements.

14.3.2. Features and Functions of DD/D Systems

All data dictionary/directory systems provide the basic functions necessary to capture and maintain metadata and to generate reports from that store of metadata.[5] In addition, some DD/D systems include the ability to generate data descriptions and program code and to support test environments.

Data capture implies the initial loading of the dictionary with metadata of all types. This capability may be provided through fixed- or free-format transactions in either batch or on-line mode. If fixed format is required the DD/D system often includes predefined forms for coding input data. Since the startup of a DD/D system may require a high volume of input, the option of a mass, batch load is very desirable. For modification, however, the ability to interrogate and modify the dictionary on-line is very convenient.

One feature that allows additional streamlining of data capture is the ability to generate all or part of a dictionary entry directly from source program data descriptions. Thus the DBA may use existing COBOL or PL/I data descriptions or those of a particular DBMS to initally load the dictionary. After that, additional information may be added to complete each entry and to establish relationships. Some DD/D systems even capture preliminary relationship data from program source code, e.g., which programs use which files and records.

The ability to generate and maintain data descriptions for a particular language or DBMS is provided by many DD/D systems. The format and the structure of these data descriptions are built into the DD/D system, and certain system specific functions, such as computing IMS segment lengths from component field sizes, are also provided. These features substantially aid the DBA with the task of generating and controlling data descriptions.

Reporting is a primary function of any DD/D system. Basically two types of reports are provided. Dictionary reports list dictionary entries in much the same way that a language dictionary lists words. The user controls the order of the entries, e.g., alphabetically or by entry type, and also the selectivity of the listing, e.g., all entries of a given type or only those matching some criterion of selection. In a dictionary listing, or glossary, the data recorded on each entry are provided. Some DD/D systems allow selectivity at this level also, e.g., list only the name and physical characteristics of each element, not all the data in the entry.

The second type of report provided is usually a cross-reference report. In this type of report entries in the dictionary are associated by the relationships in which they participate. Since these relationships are bidirectional, the cross-reference may be either top-down or bottom-up. For example, one may ask to see a top-down listing of entries associated with a particular application system (see Figure 14.2). Or one might ask for a trace of all entries with which a particular element is associated, a bottom-up view (see Figure 14.3). Again some selectivity may be allowed with regard to the entries displayed. For example, one may wish to see only those programs associated with an application system, not data bases or elements. Selectivity may also be applied to the scope of information

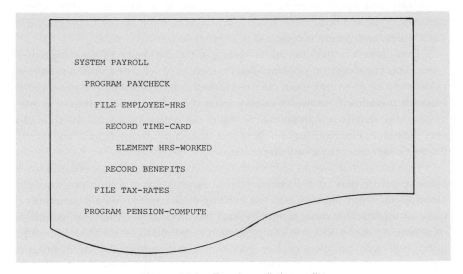

```
        SYSTEM PAYROLL

          PROGRAM PAYCHECK

            FILE EMPLOYEE-HRS

               RECORD TIME-CARD

                  ELEMENT HRS-WORKED

               RECORD BENEFITS

            FILE TAX-RATES

          PROGRAM PENSION-COMPUTE
```

Figure 14.2. Top-down dictionary list.

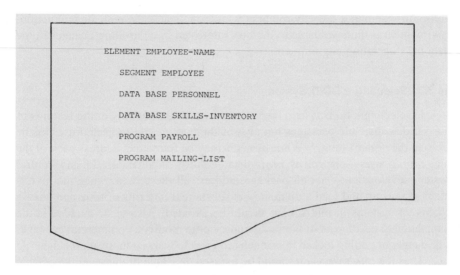

```
ELEMENT EMPLOYEE-NAME

SEGMENT EMPLOYEE

DATA BASE PERSONNEL

DATA BASE SKILLS-INVENTORY

PROGRAM PAYROLL

PROGRAM MAILING-LIST
```

Figure 14.3. Bottom-up dictionary list.

displayed for each entry. For example, one may wish to see only the names of those entries associated with element X, not the full information on each.

Most DD/D systems provide a selection of preset reports that can be executed by the user directly. Some also provide a query language so that users may formulate reports of their own choosing. If the dictionary data base is maintained in a standard DBMS format, the reporting features are normally extended to include the report generator or query language facility available with that DBMS.

A feature that is found less frequently is program code generation or direct program support. The production of source language or DBMS data descriptions is a type of code generation. However, the creation of code for data editing or data base usage authorization is less common. Since edit criteria may be captured as part of metadata, it is certainly possible to supply edit criteria to source language programs during execution. MSP's DATAMANAGER (see Appendix B) is an example of a DD/D system that provides this feature.

The directory function of a DD/D system makes it the point of contact between application programs and the data base. In such environments it is valuable to be able to define a number of statuses or conditions under which the objects defined will be used. For example, if a file is being modified, the directory should reference the old version of the file until changes are complete and have been verified. Then the new version of the file should be referenced. If the DD/D does not allow differences in status, e.g., old and new, the two definitions cannot exist simultaneously. Another use for this type of classification is the maintenance of archival definitions so that the evolution of a dictionary entry can be traced from its historical version to its present and even projected form. The ability to maintain a test environment which duplicates the real, or production, environment is quite valuable to the DBA interested in controlling changes in the data base operating environment.

14.3.3. Selecting a DD/D System

In selecting a DD/D system the DBA must be aware not only of the features of the various available packages but also of the current and projected uses of the DD/D in the organization.[6] While systems may be found that address each of the major DD/D uses—control of DBMS data, control of all data, aid and control system development—not all packages address all these uses. Since the investment to start up and load a dictionary is substantial in terms of time and cost, a change of systems in mid-stream should be avoided. Also to be avoided is the temptation to develop an in-house dictionary or to modify a commercial package. The danger of getting locked in is much too great to warrant these approaches.[6]

Thus the DBA's decision should be focused on which of the several available DD/D system packages best suits the needs of the environment. A first step in the evaluation should consider three characteristics that differentiate these systems from one another: the types of objects supported by entries in the DD/D data base, the DD/D system's dependence on, or compatibility with, a specific DBMS, and the accessibility of the DD/D data base to non-DD/D system languages and processing programs.

The types of objects supported directly by entries in the DD/D data base give an indication of the flexibility of the DD/D system. Are these objects limited to a specific DBMS terminology? Are they limited to systems, programs, and records, or do they admit non-EDP objects such as users or forms or procedures? A good test is for the DBA to attempt to describe a major system or application area in the terms provided by the DD/D system. Even when additional objects may be defined, those primarily supported will be most efficiently supported. The types of interrelationships supported are also of interest. May files be associated only with records or systems, or may they be related to other files and/or other objects that the user chooses? Reporting on relationships maintained by the DD/D system will be most efficient, while even routine maintenance of relationships not directly supported may be quite a burden for the DBA.

Some DD/D systems are intended to operate as an adjunct to a specific DBMS. Thus the DD/D data base is described and maintained by the DBMS, and all programming and access features available through the DBMS may be applied to the DD/D data base. This approach is most sensible for users of the DBMS in question. However, often such DBMS-oriented DD/D systems have DBMS data description maintenance as their main objective and are less capable of handling non-DBMS definitions or system development information.

The architecture of some DD/D systems is DBMS independent; however, interfaces may be provided for selected DBMS systems. A system of this type may

Table 14.1.   Feature Checklist for DD/D Systems

General Characteristics
  Number and types of objects directly supported (elements, records, etc.)
  Type of relationships supported (hierarchical or network)
  Form of DD/D database (DBMS dependent?)
  Facility for high-volume input
Features for Management Use
  Facility for on-line, ad hoc inquiry
  Reporting capabilities
    On-line or batch
    Number and types of reports
    Selectivity of reports
  Facility for assuring security of DD/D data base
  Generation of user-defined documentation or reports
Features for Computer Use
  Compatibility with DBMS systems
  Accessibility of DD/D data base to application programs, or teleprocessing (TP) monitors
  Facility for deriving dictionary entries (on objects or relationships) directly from source
    language code
  Direct access of dictionary data via program calls
  Generation of test data

be the best choice in an environment where a DBMS has not yet been selected or where more than one DBMS is in use. If data description maintenance for a DBMS is a main objective, the DD/D system selected must have an interface available for this DBMS.

For proper control, access to DD/D data must be restricted. In particular, only DD/D-controlled routines should be capable of updating the contents of the DD/D data base. However, for maximum flexibility in reporting DD/D data base contents it may be desirable to access the DD/D data base with application programs or a report generator or query language. Thus the ideal mix of features is that in which such application program access is provided but where this external access is monitored by the DD/D to prevent unauthorized modification of the dictionary contents.

A first-level analysis based on these three aspects should enable the DBA to limit the alternative DD/D systems being considered to two or three. At this point a more detailed analysis of the features of each system can be made. The checklist in Table 14.1 can serve as a guide for this analysis.

14.3.3. Getting Started

To be maximally effective the DD/D data base should contain all metadata of interest to the organization. Even if the scope of the DD/D data base is limited to DBMS-supported data and systems, the amount of information is sizable. Its collection and recording in the DD/D will not be an overnight task. However, until the amount of data in the DD/D system reaches a "critical mass," the DD/D will not be very effective.

Thus the DBA must develop a strategy for getting started. One approach is to initially restrict the DD/D content to DBMS-related data and to gradually build up the dictionary data base as new DBMS-based application systems are developed. Another possibility is to focus on one application area and initially load the DD/D system with data descriptions from programs related to that application. Procedures developed in the process can then be applied to other application areas as they are added. Finally, the DBA can take a strictly logical approach and first use the dictionary to document information requirements and processes without regard for supporting systems. Then existing systems can be added as they are documented and related to the logical model. Similarly, new systems can be added as they are developed.

Once procedures are in place to capture the necessary metadata as systems are developed and modified, the maintenance of the DD/D data base can proceed smoothly and with minimal effort. Then the DBA may begin to reap the promised benefits of improved control, in terms of shorter system development times and a reduction in design errors and inconsistencies.

Chapter 15

Data Base Standards

Standards are rules and procedures established by an authority in an attempt to measure the quantity or quality of some object or process. In data processing, standards are promulgated by EDP management to measure the quality of data processing systems and their operation. The variety of standards that may be developed for a data processing installation cover the full range of systems activities.[1] Standards may exist for system development (including project management and the specification of system components, such as backup and recovery procedures), for data and file definition, for program coding, for all aspects of system documentation (including manual procedures and user training), for system test and conversion, and finally for system operation (including the specification of the hardware/software environment of the installation itself).

The benefits associated with the development and use of data processing standard are four types: improved communications, easier maintenance, transferability of programs and personnel, and quality control.[2] If programs and systems are developed and documented in standard ways, it is easier for users to become familiar with the mode of documentation and thus to understand and contribute to the system development process. It is also easier for system developers to communicate unambiguously with the staff who operate systems after their installation. Computer operators do not have to deal with the idiosyncratic documentation of individual system developers.

System and program maintenance is easier if the impact of prospective changes can be traced and assessed before they are made. Standard forms of coding, the choice of standard programming languages, and the existence of standardized documentation facilitate these types of changes. Understanding the function and operation of a program or system no longer depends on consultation with the originators.

Requirements for standard system software, hardware, and programming languages allow EDP management maximum flexibility in transferring systems and programs from one installation to another within their organization. This transfer may be desirable to minimize redundant system development or to balance the development or processing load among available installation resources. Standard procedures and documentation also facilitate the transfer of EDP personnel from project to project.

Finally, the existence of a set of standards provides a training base for data processing personnel and a standard for quality against which all data processing products and efforts can be measured. Thus a prescribed level of quality and conformability is assured, regardless of individual differences in skill and experience.

In spite of these benefits many data processing organizations do not have complete sets of installation standards or full compliance with existing standards. This is because effective standards are costly. The cost of standards includes their initial development and continuing modification, the investment in personnel education and training in standard practices, and the cost of obtaining compliance.

The initial development of standards includes the selection of elements to be covered and the formulation of rules to be followed for each. For example, is program coding to be subject to standards, and if so, of what sort? What about choice of language? internal program structure? mandatory subprograms? Resources must be allocated for the development of a manual or handbook setting forth the standards for the installation. Resources must also be devoted to revising standards as operating practices and environments change and to publishing and distributing these revisions to all concerned.

For standards to be effective, installation personnel must be trained in their use. New personnel should receive training according to installation standards as part of their orientation to the organization. As standards change or new areas are covered under standards, affected employees must be brought up to date by special workshops or courses.

An organization may choose to obtain compliance with standards through a program of motivation or through the application of enforcement procedures. The first approach requires that all employees be trained in standards and encouraged in their use through a reward system. The second approach exacts compliance by reviewing all objects (e.g., programs, data file layouts) and refusing acceptance (e.g., for production status or project completion) until all standards are met. These two approaches normally coexist, with the stricter procedure applying to items or elements judged to be critical to the operation of the installation. For example, an organization may enforce strict compliance with standards regarding the form and documentation of programs accepted into production status, yet may only encourage the use of structured programming techniques in program coding.

Data base standards share both the benefits and the problems of data processing standards in general. In fact, many of the standards required in a data base environment are identical to those required in a traditional data processing installation. Four areas, however, deserve special mention for their importance in a data base environment: data element naming, application coding, data base documentation, and the development process for data base applications.

15.1. CONVENTIONS FOR DATA ELEMENT NAMING

The centralization of data into an integrated shared data base promises to reduce redundancy and improve data consistency. To achieve these benefits requires that the content of the data base be clear and unambiguous to all those who interact with it. Standards that govern the naming of data elements can improve communication among data base users and can catch redundancy or inconsistency before it becomes part of the data base.

Data element names can be divided into three types: descriptive names, primary data names, and aliases. The descriptive name is a brief English-like phrase which should convey the meaning of the element to any data base user. The primary data name is a name formed according to specific rules and under which all information in the data dictionary on this element is filed. Aliases are other data names for this same element necessary to conform to the requirements of specific programming languages or software systems. As an example, consider a data element in a banking data base SAVINGS ACCOUNT NUMBER. This three-word phrase is its descriptive name. If the primary source language used at this bank is PL/I, the primary data name may be its PL/I identifier: SAV—ACCT—NBR. If the element is also used by programs in other languages it may have aliases, e.g., SAN for BAL programs, or SAVNBR for FORTRAN programs.

As the example implies, the rules for forming the primary data name may be governed by the language of choice (or the standard) for the organization. Users may be further guided in their choice of names by the DBA's suggestion of standard abbreviations or acronyms.[3] These standard abbreviations can be chosen in such a way that they minimize the risk of ambiguity; e.g., NBR can mean only "number", not "name" or "north."

Another valuable technique is to define standard data types or classes and to require that all elements be assigned descriptors indicative of the class(es) to which they belong.[4] The descriptors may be either part of the primary data name

Table 15.1. Examples of Data Element Classes

Class	Definition	Examples
Name	Alphabetic data that identifies specific entity	Customer name Product name
Code	Alphanumeric data that represents classification of entities	Container code Tax code
Amount	Quantity of money	Price Balance
Count	Quantity (except money)	Stock-on-hand Quantity ordered
Date	Calendar date	Date billed Birth date

Source: Muehl. [4]

or part of the description of the data element. Table 15.1 shows some examples of classes that may be useful. If such a classification is made, the searcher can look for like data elements without knowing the primary data names of the elements involved.

15.2. STANDARDS FOR DATA BASE APPLICATION PROGRAMS

The intent of standards for data base application programs is to make such programs easier to code initially and easier to comprehend and thus maintain. A by-product of the use of programming standards is the reduction of program bugs and failures through the use of standard well-tested components (e.g., subprograms or standard processing formats) in place of code freely composed by application programmers.

Many of the programming conventions useful in a data base environment are identical to those currently in use for software development in general. Techniques such as structured programming, restricted module lengths, mandatory commentary, chief-programmer teams, and structured walkthroughs have been found to contribute to the production of better-quality program code. Certainly these standards should be in place regardless of the existence of a data base environment.

The shared nature of a data base, however, raises increased concern for those portions of application program code that reflect or affect the data base. Errors or inefficiencies in this code affect not only the application at fault but perhaps other data base users as well. Thus standards should be in place to control the way in which application programs describe the data base, manipulate data base content, edit or authorize the use of data base information, and to assure proper operation for each program accepted into production status.

To prevent redundancy, data definitions and data base descriptions (e.g., schema and subschema) should be centrally recorded and controlled. Application programmers should be required to use these standard definitions in any program that accesses the data base. Most data dictionary/directory packages allow data definitions to be copied into program libraries, and some provide the capability of maintaining DBMS-specific data descriptions which are then called by name into any program that requires them. This capability is a simple extension of the COPYLIB facility already in use by most installations for shared use of file definitions. Programmers should also be required to call existing data elements by their standard name and to register new elements and their names with the data base administrator as they arise.

Applications programmers should also be required to manipulate the data base in standard, predefined ways. For example, most DBMS data manipulation languages use parameters in a subroutine call to communicate with the application program. Commands and names of variables and storage areas are sent to the DBMS as parameters; retrieved data and status codes are returned to the program in a similar fashion. An installation benefits from developing standard protocols for this interaction. Common processing functions, such as reading a record based on a key value or writing a record as the next in some specified sequence, could be translated into the proper DBMS calls with symbolic arguments for the application-specific data required. Then a programmer need only consult the standards to develop the code for a given application. In addition, the DBMS may require special command words or other parameters. These words could be predefined, in the data dictionary or in a common storage area, and programmers required to use them. For example, IMS requires the use of specially formatted segment search arguments when the data base is scanned for specific records. The coding for these arguments could be predefined by data base for each application.

Another source of variation, and thus error, which can occur in application programs is the verification that they perform on data in the data base. This may be verification in the form of editing a data field to conform to a required set of values or in the form of authorization of users or transactions to manipulate or display the data. Improper verification impairs the integrity of the data base. Standards can thus be developed that require the application programmer to access the data dictionary to retrieve proper edit and authorization criteria. Or standard verification modules could be coded for each data base and programmers could be required to call these modules rather than write their own. This technique is especially convenient with a DBTG system in which procedures can be invoked automatically as a result of ON conditions.

A final control point in application program development is testing. Standards can be developed for proper testing procedures and applied to all application programs before they are accepted into production status. Indeed, the DBA may wish to maintain a test data base environment, which reflects but is separate from the actual data base(s). Programmers could then be required to turn their programs over to the DBA for final testing to assure that they operate without error in the data base environment. This is especially valuable to test the effects of multiuser data base access and contention for data base resources.

15.3. DATA BASE DOCUMENTATION

Documentation is the recording of facts about objects or events of concern to facilitate communication and to provide a permanent record. Systems documentation traditionally addresses the several components of a data processing system: general information about the purpose and structure of the system, information on the programs that make up the system, information on the data files created and maintained, and information on the external procedures required for operating or interacting with the system. This information is compiled for several classes of users—systems analysts, programmers, end users, and system operators. Each user of the documentation is concerned primarily with a certain portion of the information recorded. For example, end users are interested in general information and the external procedures for use but not in program documentation or operational procedures.

In a data base environment the emphasis on systems is replaced by an emphasis on the data base itself, its content and its structure. Systems and programs are still of interest but more from the point of view of how they interact with the data base. All the traditional facets of system documentation can be captured, say in a data dictionary. However, data base documentation focuses primarily on data-related components, e.g., data elements, data groups (records or segments), data structures, and data bases per se.

As with traditional systems documentation, data base documentation covers several types of information and is intended to support the needs of several classes of users. Figure 15.1 depicts the relationships between data base documentation and its users. Seven types of documentation can be compiled for each component of the data base environment (e.g., element, system, segment):

Name/Meaning. A unique identifier and descriptive information that conveys the full meaning of the component. The name is used for reference and retrieval purposes, while the description is valuable to managers and users.

Physical Description. The physical characteristics of the component, e.g., the size of a data element or the length of a data record.

Edit/Authorization Criteria. Criteria to be used to test the validity of instances of the component, e.g., acceptable range of values for a data element. Or

Types of Data Base Documentation

Class of Data Base Documentation Users	Name/Meaning	Physical Description	Edit/Authorization Criteria	Usage	Logical Description	Procedures	Responsibility
General Management	X						
Auditors	X		X	X			
End Users	X		X			X	
EDP Management	X						X
DBA	X	X	X	X	X	X	X
Systems Analysts	X		X	X	X		
Programmers	X	X	X				
Operators	X					X	

Figure 15.1.   Users of data base documentation.

criteria to determine who is authorized to use the component, e.g., password for update of a data base.

Usage. Information on where and by whom or by what a component is used; for example, the programs within a system or the system(s) that reference a given data element.

Logical Description. The characteristics and structure of each user view of the data base; for example, logical relationships among data records or the characteristics of a data base structure such as automatic deletion rules or sequencing.

Procedures. Guidelines for human interaction with the data base components. These include operational procedures, such as those for backup, recovery, and system restart; and user procedures, such as guidelines for terminal access or output distribution lists.

Responsibility. A record of the individual or organizational unit(s) responsible for the generation and maintenance of the component. For example, one could record the name of the user group responsible for generating a particular data base transaction or the name of the systems analyst responsible for maintaining a data base application system.

As described in Chapter 14, a data dictionary/directory system provides a dynamic repository for data about the data base and, as such, is an excellent source of data base documentation.

15.4. THE DEVELOPMENT OF DATA BASE APPLICATIONS

The need for a more systematic method of system development has long been recognized.[5] The system development process is a cooperative one involving diverse groups, each with different skills and a different interest in the process as a whole. A systematic methodology for this process can be relied on to document consensus among these groups as the development process proceeds and to ensure that no vital step or consideration is overlooked.

In the past decade a number of methodologies have been developed and adopted by organizations as standards for system development.[6-10] Most of these methodologies use aids such as standardized forms or special charting techniques to assist designers in documenting their ideas and in communicating these ideas and plans to the end users of the system. They also include a number of well-defined phases, each with its component tasks and required documentation.

The advent of the data base approach has influenced the more modern methodologies in two ways. First, it has forced system developers to recognize that all application systems developed for an organization are based on the underlying information and processing requirements of that organization. By recognizing this context at the outset, system developers can plan applications that will be more flexible and more responsive to changes in the business environment than those developed in isolation. Second, the system analysis and development process now reflects the importance of both information and processing requirements, not just the latter. The flow of information among interconnected activities and the use of a shared data resource are presumed.

Thus the development of data base applications varies very little from the development of systems in general using a structured methodology. As Figure 15.2 shows, the development cycle for a data base application follows the usual pattern of analysis, design, programming, testing, conversion, and operation. However, four issues relate specifically to development in a data base environment: the division of tasks between systems developers and the DBA, the impor-

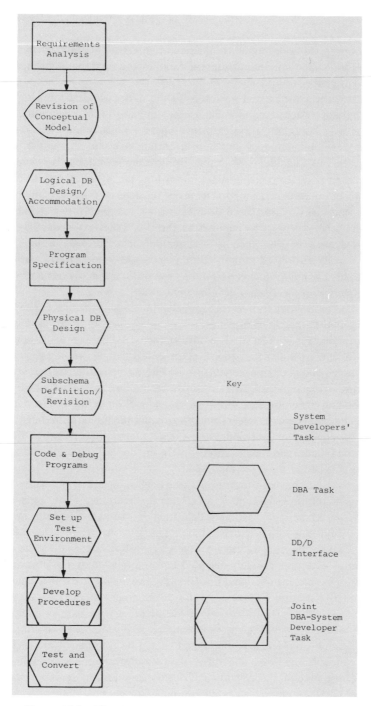

Figure 15.2. The development process for data base applications.

tance of conceptual data modeling, the accommodation of the data base to the new application, and continuing support for the data dictionary throughout the development process.

Probably the most radical departure of the data base development process from traditional system development is the division of responsibility for development tasks between the systems developers (analysts) and the DBA.[11] The ceding of development tasks and thus a certain amount of control over the process to the DBA encounters resistance in most organizations. However, if the DBA is to be given the responsibility for controlling the accuracy and accessibility of the data base, certain development tasks must be within DBA authority. In particular, the tasks of data base design, quality assurance, and standards for backup and recovery must be handled by the DBA. The DBA should work with system developers on tasks such as the development of data definitions and the planning and execution of system testing and conversion. Responsibility for problem analysis, requirements definition, program specification, and program coding remain with the system development group.

The data base should reflect the information needs of the organization that it supports. Often these data needs are discovered piecemeal as the need for data processing support is addressed. The development of a conceptual data model is an effective way to guide data base development so that conflicting requirements can be resolved and diverse needs integrated into a consistent architecture before the data base is implemented. The information structure can then be mapped into a corresponding data base structure for implementation.[12] If, at the start of the system development cycle, the information requirements identified can be used to update the conceptual data model, e.g., using the facilities of a data dictionary to record the objects and interrelationships in the model, the maintenance of an up-to-date conceptual model is facilitated.

Data base design, both logical and physical, is a task which assumes new importance in the development of data base applications. Traditional systems certainly required the specification of data files and formats. However, with data base applications this step is expanded to include a search for required data in the existing data base, the construction of a data base subschema to meet the application's requirements, and, possibly, the physical modification of the data base itself.

To promote the accuracy and timeliness of the metadata captured and stored in a data dictionary/directory system, the development process for a data base application should feed information to the dictionary as it is collected. This collection should start during the requirements analysis phase, where revisions and modifications to the conceptual model should be captured. Next, definitions for data elements, records, and other data base structures should be added. Finally, information on the system itself, component programs, reports, transactions, etc., could be entered to provide a basis for documentation.

15.5. THE DBA AND DATA BASE STANDARDS

Standards are a difficult organizational problem for the DBA. They are essential to the effectiveness of the DBA function and to the control over data base quality that the DBA must exercise. Yet many of the standards crucial to data base systems, e.g., data naming, application coding, and system development procedures, are imposed on individuals and organizational units outside the DBA's management control.

Thus the DBA must attempt to achieve compliance through a balance of education, motivation, and enforcement. Those affected by data base standards must be educated to the purpose for such rules and the benefits forthcoming to them as well as to the DBA. Motivation can be provided through well-defined standards which are easy to understand and for which compliance is facilitated, perhaps through aids such as predefined data definition forms provided by the DBA. On system testing and standard procedures for backup and recovery, strict enforcement may be the only method of guaranteeing compliance. In such cases standards should be enforced consistently and equally for all applications. Exceptions will only weaken the DBA's position.

The discussion of standards brings us full circle to the issue of organizational dynamics discussed in Part I. The existence of a data base environment implies a centralization of control which is vested in the DBA. Resistance to this necessary centralization can only be countered by the support of data processing and general management. Users and systems developers must perceive the necessary changes in traditional procedures and the DBA's role in the new environment as being in the interest of the organization and strongly supported by management. This perception allows a transition to a working environment in which cooperation, not competition, governs the interactions between DBA and other organizational units. In a data base environment the success of the data base administration function is synonymous with the success of system support for the organization.

Part VI

Case Histories

Chapter 16

The DBA in Practice

The discussions of DBA roles and responsibilities in the previous chapters may give the impression that DBA is a formal and well-structured function in all organizations where it exists. In actuality, this is not so. The broad and detailed view presented so far is meant to touch on the many aspects of the DBA function. However, one must realize that the full DBA function is seldom if ever encountered in practice.

To illustrate this fact this chapter contains case studies of the data base administration function in three different firms.* Each case addresses the development of a DBA function since its inception and its current position and set of responsibilities within the organization. These studies are not intended to represent correct or incorrect approaches to DBA. They are meant to convey the variety of ways in which organizations have instituted successful DBA functions.

16.1. COMPANY X: GETTING STARTED

Company X is in the retail sales distribution business. It operates stores throughout the country, which are stocked from a central warehouse in Chicago. The chain sells a wide variety of merchandise, although the largest part of their

*These cases are based on interviews conducted by the author[1] and by Francis M. Lowell.[2]

sales is in household goods and appliances. Customers select the items they want from a catalogue and then go to a distribution center to pick up the merchandise. If there are no distribution centers within a certain number of miles of the customer, orders can be mailed directly to the company to be filled.

The company has about 6,500 employees, but the EDP area is quite small, with 35 employees. Three of these 35 are in the data base administration group; thus the ratio between EDP and DBA is approximately 12 to 1. At present, the DBA staff consists of Mr. Smith, who is the manager of data base administration, and two assistants.

The data base administration function was established four years ago when the data base management system TOTAL was acquired from CINCOM Systems. Although the DBA function came into being at the same time, Mr. Smith feels that in a philosophical sense DBA was established before the DBMS was installed. To date, the company has not truly adopted the data base approach. This is because at present TOTAL is being used exclusively as an access method. TOTAL was selected by a member of a project design team responsible for an on-line order entry system. The existing IBM access methods were not considered suitable for the system, and so an investigation into available packages was started. TOTAL was the simplest, least sophisticated package that met the system's needs. It was not acquired as a DBMS.

The order entry system is still the only major system at Company X that uses TOTAL. One other system, a simple batch application, uses TOTAL. The individual who programmed this application decided on his own initiative to use TOTAL. By the time management realized that he was using it, the system had progressed too far to justify removing its dependence on TOTAL. The application was not harmed by the use of the package, but it was not helped either.

Although TOTAL has yet to be used as a true data base management tool, Mr. Smith is not satisfied with it. He sees its simplicity as an advantage, but he has encountered problems with it. Mr. Smith has not been satisfied with vendor support and feels the package has limitations in regard to complex data base structures and data security features. As a result, Company X plans to replace TOTAL with IMS. Mr. Smith has carefully investigated many data base packages in the last few years, and it is his determination that IMS will best suit the needs of his organization. Contrary to their current practice, Company X will use IMS as a data base management system and not simply as a new access method.

Once IMS is installed, Mr. Smith plans to select a small, noncritical system for initial implementation. This system will serve as a vehicle for learning how to use IMS: it need not promise any other tangible benefits to the organization. After the data base staff feels comfortable with IMS, work will begin on implementing some major systems.

Because of the retail sales nature of the business, many files have been created to process the large number of products sold by the firm. Since the company does not manufacture its own products, everything must be purchased from outside manufacturers, stored in the warehouse in Chicago, and shipped to distribution centers around the country. The files created to handle all this processing are known loosely as the commodity files. Thus the first important IMS application will be the consolidation of all these files into a data base which will then be used to expedite the processing of the goods.

Following the installation of the commodity data base, a general ledger system will be implemented on IMS. This system will have its own data base. It will not be integrated into the commodity data base, simply because the two data bases are completely independent of each other. Mr. Smith expects, however, that a third system (possibly sales reporting) will then be developed to integrate the two data bases (as shown in Figure 16.1).

As manager of data base administration, Mr. Smith reports directly to the Assistant Vice-President of Information Services. The DBA area is on an equal level with the application and operations areas, namely financial systems, administrative systems, distribution systems, and operations, as shown in Figure 16.2.

Mr. Smith's staff consists of a standards control analyst and a project manager. The standards control analyst reviews programs before they achieve production status. He checks to see that libraries are being called correctly and that, in general, the programming standards are observed. The project manager is the person who according to Mr. Smith "does everything that needs doing." She maintains the data dictionary, the data base management system package, and some COBOL programs used as data base utilities. The project manager is solely responsible for entering data into the data dictionary.

Because of the small size of the Information Services department, the DBA

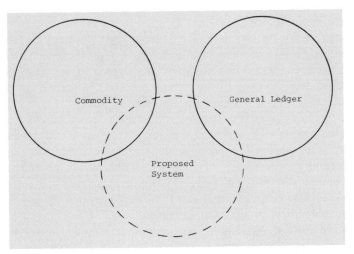

Figure 16.1.   Integration of data bases at Company X.

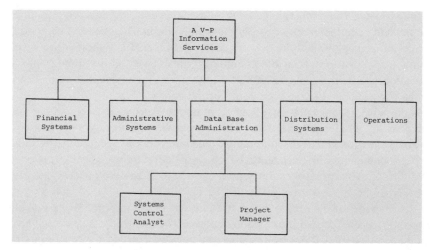

Figure 16.2. EDP organization at Company X.

tends to use a lot of very informal procedures. In many larger EDP departments, there are, by necessity, established channels of communication which must be followed whenever a new system is being developed. This is because the different EDP areas, such as applications, data base administration, and operations, are too large for each to know what the other areas are doing. At Company X, however, Mr. Smith can easily keep abreast of what is happening in each EDP area. Thus, if one of the applications areas is planning a new system, they may come to Mr. Smith to discuss the feasibility of using the DBMS. If they do not, however, and Mr. Smith feels the system will be helped by DBMS support, he will go to them to discuss it.

At present this method works fairly well. There have not been any critical breakdowns of communication among the areas. Nonetheless, it is not a completely reliable approach. This is particularly evident in the system discussed earlier which was developed using TOTAL without the knowledge of the DBA staff.

Mr. Smith recognizes that there are serious limitations to the informal approach currently in use, and he is working to develop more formalized procedures for the development of new systems which will be put onto the data base. Once IMS is fully implemented, these methods will be absolutely necessary, since IMS will be used with the goal of developing true data bases. If this is to be done successfully, close control of the data will be necessary and the informal method of hearing about new systems will be inadequate.

Toward this end, Mr. Smith is working on developing a three-phase system design procedure. The first phase, conceptual design, is done by the application area developing the system along with the end user of the system. This phase is concerned mainly with defining precisely what the system is expected to do.

The second phase is the logical design. It is at this point that data base administration becomes involved. The logical design is developed by the application area and the DBA area working together and is concerned with how the system will do what it is expected to do. From the DBA standpoint, this phase will focus on how the system will tie into the data base.

The final phase is physical design, which is done solely by the data base administration area. This phase deals with the details of implementing the logical design of phase 2 as a physical data base. Through a formal procedure such as this, the development of data base applications will be much smoother than with the rather haphazard, informal procedures currently being used.

True data base administration is still in its infancy at Company X. However, with a firm commitment to the data base approach and the introduction of the system development procedure, the organization should be able to progress toward a true data base environment fairly smoothly. Mr. Smith has carefully planned Company X's transition to the data base approach. This planning should be a major step toward the ultimate goal of an integrated data base.

16.2. COMPANY Y: BALANCING TECHNICAL AND COMMUNICATIONS SKILLS

Company Y is a division of a major financial institution. This division is a large worldwide firm whose main function is to process traveler's checks. It employs about 250 people in the EDP area. Of these, 11 are on the data base administration staff. DBA was established four years ago along with the introduction of the data base management system, The company uses IMS and has been satisfied with its performance.

The DBA function has experienced a number of growing pains since its inception. DBMS support was originally part of the operations area, and DBA was treated solely as a technical function. The first DBA was a very technically oriented person with little experience in communicating with users. However, over time it became more important for the DBA staff to establish succesful lines of communication between themselves and their users. The users in this company include staff from a fairly large number of different areas, including applications development, operations, technical support, quality assurance, and EDP auditing.

The DBA position went through several technically oriented persons without much success. Finally, management sought someone with both technical skills and communication skills. Ms. Jones, the current director, was hired to fill that role. She came to Company Y with several years of experience as a data base consultant, which gave her the required combination of interpersonal and technical skills.

As the DBA function developed, it was moved out of the operations area and into the systems development area. The function is still undergoing change. Ms.

Jones' position is evolving from data base administrator to data administrator, with most of the functions of data base administration being handled by a sub-group under her direction. Ms. Jones was involved in the GUIDE project, which established guidelines for the data administration function, and many of these guidelines are now being established at Company Y. Therefore she and her staff, as presented in the organization chart in Figure 16.3., will be referred to as the data administration (DA) area through the remainder of this study.

The DA staff is broken into three components, with Ms. Jones at the head as Director of Data Administration. The data base development group now handles most of the traditional data base administration functions such as data base design, the preparation of feasibility studies on proposed projects, and the generation of data base descriptions. In addition, they do simulation and modeling of new systems in a pseudoproduction environment. This task may involve program coding, but the DBA staff do not get involved in the coding of programs for the production system itself. At present, this group consists of six people: three senior programmers, two senior systems analysts, and one junior analyst.

The second group, data integrity and security control, has responsibility for maintaining the data dictionary and for all data security and standards. This group consists of an IMS programmer and a clerical position.

The final group is DBMS support, which is responsible for the maintenance of the IMS package. This group also consists of two people, both systems programmers. One is at a senior level, while the other is a junior programmer. No significant increase in staffing is planned for the near future.

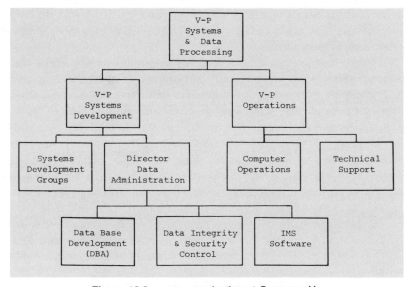

Figure 16.3.   EDP organization at Company Y.

In her search for qualified personnel, Ms. Jones tries to find people who have both the technical experience necessary for the job and interpersonal skills. She finds this to be one of her most difficult problems. While a great many people have one or the other skill, not many have both. At one point, it took her a full year to find two people who had the requisite skills.

A serious communications problem exists between the DA area and the applications development areas. The applications groups view data administration as a threat, since the control which they formerly had over the data is being surrendered to DA. In the old systems development methodology each application owned its own data. Each development group was responsible for designing the files and collecting the data required to successfully implement the system. Under the approach promulgated by data administration, however, data are viewed as a corporate resource and, as such, must be centrally controlled. The applications developers do not adequately understand how the new DA approach helps them meet their goals through such means as standardizing data requirements. They see only that power they formerly held has been transferred to another area.

Ms. Jones acknowledges that her function is indeed a real threat to applications development. Quite simply, the application areas cannot proceed with the accessing of data without the approval of data administration. In addition, all new systems must go through a feasibility study to determine how they will fit into the data base. Once they have passed this study, DA develops a data collection and storage methodology to enable the system to meet its goals. Finally, all data needs identified during systems development must be entered into the data dictionary. All these requirements only add to the feeling that DA is threatening the position of the applications development group.

In discussing this situation, Ms. Jones commented:

> With a staff versed only in technical skills, the problem is made worse, since the DA staff simply tells the applications areas what they must do with little attempt made to soothe the ruffled feelings or change the belief that DA will take over virtually all power in EDP.

> With a staff properly trained in interpersonal skills, a feeling of working together on projects can be developed. It is important that each area recognize the role it plays in systems development, both in terms of responsibilities *and* limitations. The DA function must be careful, however, that it does not simply pacify the applications areas by assuring them that everything is fine and then go ahead and strip as much authority from them as possible.

Right now, the procedures in the data administration area are relatively informal, but this situation will not last much longer. Since the EDP staff is quite large, formalized procedures are very important. Otherwise each area will be relatively ignorant of what the other areas are doing. This informality at least partially accounts for the feelings of the application groups. They simply do not have an adequate understanding of how they fit into the overall systems development picture. More formal procedures are currently being developed and it is expected that the shop will be highly formalized within the next six to eight months.

Two operational systems are now supported by the DBMS. One system handles inventory management of the traveler's checks; the other is a settlement processing system which reconciles the checks against money in accounts. There is some sharing of data between these two systems, but the company is still some distance from a fully integrated data base. More systems are planned which will be tied into the data base, so that Ms. Jones anticipates that the company will have an integrated data base within two years.

The biggest factor in the success of the DA function at Company Y has been management commitment to it. Despite the problems faced in getting the function started and properly staffed, top management has continued to be deeply committed to the success of data administration. Nevertheless, there is a need to maintain and enhance the credibility of DA throughout the company. Since users are assigned on a full-time basis to a project development team, there is plenty of opportunity to observe the functioning of the DA staff. Thus Ms. Jones' commitment to interpersonal skills among her staff becomes even more understandable.

She is also committed to increasing the visibility of data administration. In the sense described, they are already very visible, since they interact directly with many diverse users. However, like all of EDP, they are a support function. They do not make any money for the company directly, and so their performance can often go unnoticed by top management unless there are problems. As a result, Ms. Jones must work hard to see that the good work they do is recognized at the top, thereby maintaining management commitment to the function.

All evidence shows that Ms. Jones is indeed correct in her belief that good communications skills among her staff are as essential to success as technical ability. Under her direction, data administration has improved from a function beset with problems to one that is healthy and growing.

16.3. COMPANY Z: DBA AS "STORAGE COP"

Company Z is a very large insurance firm which specializes in health insurance. Their operations are centered in New York, although they have branch offices throughout the United States. The EDP personnel number about 500, and their data bases are loaded onto nearly 150 disk packs, each of which can store approximately 300 million bytes of data. This gives a total capacity of over 40 billion bytes of disk storage.

The data base administration function was started five years ago along with the acquisition of the TOTAL data base package. TOTAL was selected by Mr. Brown, the current DBA at Company Z. At that time, however, Mr. Brown was a team leader in one of the application development groups. He was involved in a project for which a data base philosophy was well suited, and so he was given the responsibility for the selection of the DBMS.

The position of DBA was first given to one of the application programmers. This person had no real authority and initially had no staff under him. In addition, he had no prior supervisory or managerial experience. His job was to bring up TOTAL, maintain it, and control its use. Unfortunately, he was not very successful at this. Concerned, Mr. Brown advised his superior of this fact. His superior agreed and replaced the original DBA with Mr. Brown himself. The position then began to develop into a true data base administration function.

Shortly thereafter, the EDP organization was expanded through the creation of an area called resource planning and control. Now data base administration, systems programming, and technical support all report to this area. Originally they reported directly to the manager of resource planning and control, but later a new position was created to act as liaison to the manager and to perform the technical functions of coordinating the three areas. This is shown in the organization chart in Figure 16.4.

The DBA staff itself is divided into two areas of responsibility: data base integrity and data base distribution. Data base distribution controls the data. They determine where the data are to be loaded and in what format. Their objective is to achieve optimum data placement on the disks, in terms of both the efficient use of space and the efficiency of access times. They also keep track of the growth of the data base in order to determine when new disk storage must be obtained.

Once data base distribution determines the physical requirements for the storage of data, the data base integrity group takes over to actually load the data. As their name implies, they are responsible for keeping the data base in working order. They maintain, purge, and reorganize the data base as necessary in order to ensure that all users have access to their data at all times. Included in this is the responsibility for the loading and maintenance of Company Z's data dictionary.

Because of the huge size of the data base, highly formalized procedures are essential. Whenever a new application is planned, the project leader comes to data base administration to discuss how best to store and access the required data. DBA then offers its suggestions on how to proceed. The DBA area has a great deal of influence in this regard, and its suggestions are essentially the final word. If there is a real conflict between DBA and the applications group, the matter is brought to the vice-president of data processing who then makes a final decision. This is unusual, however.

Data base administration developed standards for the control and accessing of data, and it has the responsibility and authority for enforcing them. Systems

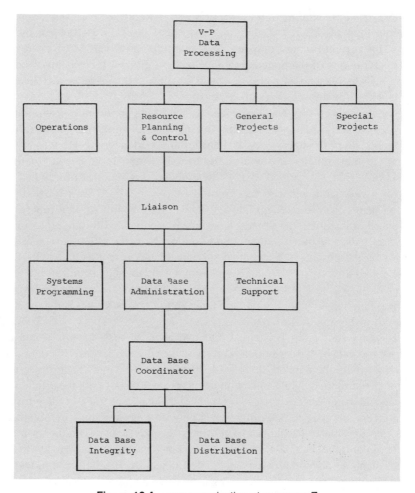

Figure 16.4. EDP organization at company Z.

must adhere strictly to these standards as they exist as any given time, but the standards are always subject to change as new conditions and situations arise. Again, however, it is DBA that authorizes any changes to the standards. In an environment as large as Company Z, such strict control of standards is deemed a necessity.

As in other firms, at Company Z the applications areas often view the data base administration area as a threat to their own authority. The applications people feel they are losing their identity in the organization and that DBA is controlling them. Mr. Brown acknowledges this and feels that this in fact is his job:

> Since data base administration *is* a control area, I must establish myself as a "storage cop"! I have no sympathy for complaints from applications people

that their creativity is being stifled, since such "creativity" usually results in inefficient, poorly designed systems and data. Since the company is a profit-making organization and since EDP is there to enhance the operations of the company, the proper approach is the simplest and most straightforward one. Creativity and experimentation may have a place in a research and development type of environment, but not in this type of environment. Of course, this does not mean that new developments and techniques should not be employed. It simply means that they must be controlled.

Through his administration of the data base function, Mr. Brown feels that his area has achieved a high level of respectability. His superiors have given him the responsibility for coordinating all data base users, and the data base is viewed as a corporate resource. That is, the data belong to the corporation and not to the individual applications. Company Z, however, does not have a data administrator per se. Mr. Brown, in fact, was not familiar with the concept of a high-level, non-EDP corporate official having control over the data resource while the data base administrator carried out the technical functions of maintaining the data base. When the concept was explained to him, he felt that he would find such an arrangement unworkable, since it would strip him of much of his authority. "Responsibility without authority is useless," he said, "and a DA–DBA relationship would put me in that situation." He sees his current position as including the duties of both DA and DBA.

Mr. Brown has had considerable success in getting systems loaded onto the data base. Almost all major applications systems are now tied into it. He estimates that they are approximately 90% of the way toward a fully integrated data base. This is a very high percentage for a function that came into being only five years ago. Brown feels that TOTAL was partially responsible for the success of the data base philosophy at Company Z. Brown himself selected it, and he has been quite satisfied with its performance. IMS was rejected because he felt it was too complicated and came with too many frills that were not necessary in his environment. ADABAS was also considered, but its inverted list structure was thought to be unsuitable for such a large data base because the size of the lists would become unwieldy. TOTAL suited their needs better than any other available package. Brown feels that IDMS has now developed some new features which would be quite helpful to him, but he has no intention of replacing TOTAL at this time.

The biggest problem faced by Mr. Brown is the size of the data base. Currently, the company has almost 200 spindles, counting both data base and system packs, and this number is growing. As a result, the problems of managing the data base are also growing. While they have an adequate system for purging, recovering, reorganizing, and archiving the data base, improvements in these procedures become more important each time the size of the data base is increased. In addition, the physical placement of data becomes increasingly important with growth, in order to minimize bottlenecks arising from contention. Data must be placed to minimize arm movement and improve throughput. This is a problem that cannot really be solved, since as long as the company continues to enjoy success, the data base will probably continue to grow. The only course of action is to devise new methods of coping with the problem.

Mr. Brown's other major problem is finding qualified personnel. The data processing field is filled with job applicants, but finding someone very good is a major problem. Brown gave the analogy, ''There are auto mechanics on practically every corner, yet most people never find one thay can truly rely on and trust.'' In his search for personnel Brown concentrates on technical skills. While it is an added benefit to find someone with good interpersonal skills, he views this strictly as a bonus. His only real criterion for selecting an applicant is whether or not he feels the person can do the job. Since his area does not deal with the end users at all but only with other areas within EDP, he feels that good communications skills are not a necessity. DBA at Company Z is a technical function and as long as a person can perform the required tasks, Brown is satisfied. Nonetheless, the problem of finding qualified people is still a major one.

The data base administration function at Company Z is a highly technical and specialized one. This is due in part to the very large size of Company Z, in which each area has its own very clearly defined areas of responsibility. Mr. Brown has brought his function a long way with his own technical skills and the skills of his staff.

16.4. OBSERVATIONS

The organizations on which the three case studies are based take quite different approaches to the data base administration function. Yet each DBA is essentially successful in carrying out his or her responsibilities.

The differences among them can be attributed to a combination of four factors: size, maturity, orientation, and personality. The size of the EDP function, in terms of staff and in terms of data base size, will influence the degree of formality and control required of the DBA. The maturity of the DBA group will influence the types of tasks which dominate the DBA activity. Task content, on the other hand, will largely determine the orientation—i.e., technical versus administrative—of the DBA staff. Finally, the personality and the background of the DBA manager and of the organization itself have shaped the function, through philosophy and practices.

In forming a DBA function it is essential that an organization be familiar with the full potential of the DBA role and responsibilities. Existing literature and established DBA groups can serve as valuable guidelines in this task. However, more important are the requirements and characteristics of the firm itself. It is only by addressing these needs that a truly successful DBA function can be forged.

Data Base Management System Packages

NAME: ADABAS

Vendor: Software Ag. of North America
11800 Sunrise Valley Drive
Reston, Va, 22091

Logical Data Structure(s):   The basic unit of data in an ADABAS data base is the field. Fields are grouped into records and stored in files of homogeneous records. Files may be logically related, or coupled, through any common field(s). Using the coupling feature, ADABAS can support both hierarchical and network structures. Though ADABAS is not a relational system, its flat files are quite similar to relations.

Physical Data Structure(s):   ADABAS uses a partially inverted file structure for data storage. The records in each file are stored in a direct-access file and assigned a unique Internal Storage Number (ISN). The correspondence between an ISN and the physical block on which it is stored is recorded in the Address Converter portion of an ADABAS file called the Associator. This technique preserves independence of storage placement.

Each field designated as a descriptor is indexed through inverted lists for each of its values. These lists are also kept in the ADABAS Associator, in a section called the Association Network. Lists of ISNs in the Associator are also used to support coupling between files.

To bring the combined size of the Data and Associator files within the range of the initial data base size, ADABAS uses data compression. Records entered into the data storage area are compressed before they are stored and then expanded when retrieved.

Data Definition: ADABAS files and their contents must be described before the file can be loaded into the data base. This description consists primarily of describing each field in the file. These descriptions are processed by ADABAS to form Field Description Tables which are stored in the Associator for later reference. One of the several characteristics that must be described for each field is whether or not the field is to be a descriptor. File coupling must be defined after a file is loaded using a special ADABAS utility.

Data Manipulation: ADABAS data bases may be manipulated from host-language programs (i.e., COBOL, PL/I, FORTRAN, or Assembler) using a CALL to a standard subroutine called ADABAS. Command codes, search arguments, storage areas and formats for the data retrieved are all specified as parameters of the CALL. A macro facility, called ADAMINT, is also available to allow the use of high-level DML commands in the application program. A preprocessor converts these commands to the corresponding CALLS before program compilation.

Options also exist for natural language inquiry and for generalized report formatting.

Operating Environment: ADABAS may be used in single- or multiple-user fashion (i.e., with several user programs sharing one copy of ADABAS). Interface modules are also available to allow on-line use of ADABAS with any of several teleprocessing monitors.

Utilities: ADABAS provides utility programs for the following functions; loading and deleting files, coupling/uncoupling files, changing file definitions or ordering, saving/restoring the data base, expansion of the physical data base storage area, entering and maintaining information required by the ADABAS security feature (i.e., passwords for files and fields for each data base user), and reporting the contents of the Associator (i.e., file descriptions, file coupling information, storage management data).

Related Products

ADASCRIPT. The ADABAS query language.

ADAWRITER. The ADABAS report generator.

ADABAS Dictionary. To store and generate ADABAS file definitions
(see Appendix B for more details).

ADAMINT. A high-level data manipulation language for ADABAS.

References

Tsichritzis, D., and F. Lochovsky. *Data Base Management Systems,* Chapter 15, Academic Press, New York, 1977.
ADABAS Introduction, Software Ag., IMO3 (undated).

NAME: DMS 1100

Vendor: Sperry UNIVAC Computer Systems
P.O. Box 500
Blue Bell, Pa. 19422

Logical Data Structure(s): DMS 1100 is an implementation of the CODASYL Data Base Task Group (DBTG) specifications. As a result, it uses a network data model whose basic components are fields, record types, and set types. Set types describe a one-to-many relationship between an owner record type and one or more member record types. Two set types sharing a common member record type describe a many-to-many relationship between the owner record types of the two sets.

Physical Data Structures(s): Instances of record types are stored in pages of direct-access data files. A page represents a unit of physical storage. Records may be grouped into logical groupings called areas which are in turn mapped into the available physical pages.

The placement of each record type is specified by the user to be one of three types: DIRECT, CALC, or VIA SET. With DIRECT placement a record is stored on the page and record location specified in its data base key. This option allows the user the greatest control over record placement. CALC records are stored using a hashing technique on the value of the record key fields(s). The user must supply the key values in order to retrieve CALC records. Records stored VIA SET are stored on the page closest to the owner record of the set specified.

Data Definition: DMS 1100 provides a data description language with which the user must describe the data base before loading. The DDL is used to describe all fields, records, sets, and areas in the data base. This source schema description is processed by the DDL Translator to produce an object schema. The object schema is used later by the DML Preprocessor and the Data Management Routine (DMR) of DMS 1100.

DMS 1100 does not have a separate device media control language (DMCL). Logical-to-physical mappings normally handled by a DMCL are divided between the schema DDL and the system job control language.

Data Manipulation: The data manipulation language for DMS 1100 is an extended version of ANSI COBOL. Additional commands are used in the data division (to invoke a predefined schema) and in the procedure division (to access and modify the data base). A DML Preprocessor is provided by DMS 1100 to convert the extended COBOL source code to standard COBOL. The preprocessor replaces the extended commands with descriptive information from the schema (in the data division) and with subroutine CALLS (in the procedure division). The CALLS link the user program to the DMS 1100 Data Management Routine (DMR).

Utilities: DMS 1100 provides utilities for transaction logging and recovery, rollback, page compaction/expansion, area initialization, data base patching, data printing, and set verification.

References

UNIVAC 1100 Series Data Management System (DMS 1100), Schema Definition (UP-7909), Data Manipulation (UP-7908), System Support Functions (UP-7909), Sperry UNIVAC Corporation.

NAME: IMS

Vendor: IBM Corporation
Data Processing Division
1133 Westchester Avenue
White Plains, N.Y. 10604

Logical Data Structure(s): IMS presents the user with hierarchically structured views of the data base. Data fields are grouped into segments, and segments are related in a parent–child fashion. That is, each parent segment may have one or more child segments related to it. Many-to-many relationships are accommodated through interconnection of the physical data bases, but user programs and processing deal only with hierarchical structures.

Physical Data Structures(s): The physical representations of segments are records stored in physical data bases. A physical data base may comprise all or part of a logical hierarchy. Logical connections are maintained through the use of physical pointers linking the several physical data bases.

IMS users may select from four different access methods to configure each physical data base. The HSAM and HISAM access methods store data base segments in sequence, with HISAM providing indexed access to the root (or highest-level segment) of each tree. The HDAM and HIDAM access methods store segments directly and provide hashed and indexed access to root segments, respectively. Within each tree, segments are related by pointers.

Data Definition: IMS data bases must be described in two ways. First, a data base description (DBD) is prepared that names and describes each segment in the data base, each field in the segment, and the parent–child relationships between segments. A DBD must exist for all data bases, whether they are physical data bases or logical data bases (i.e., built through interconnection of other physical data bases). The second type of data description is the Program Control Block (PCB). The PCB defines a user view by naming the segments of the data base which the user is authorized to access and by specifying the type of access allowed. Each user program that accesses an IMS data base must have associated with it a Program Specification Block (PSB) containing PCBs for every data base to be accessed. Processors are provided to build the necessary control blocks from DBDS and PCBS.

Data Manipulation: The IMS data manipulation language, DL/I, is invoked from host-language programs using subroutine calls. The user passes the DL/I command and its associated arguments to DL/I as parameters. Different DL/I interfaces are provided for COBOL, PL/I, and Assembler.

Operating Environment: The basic IMS system provides for batch access to the data bases. An option for data communications support, IMS DB/DC, is also available.

Utilities: IMS provides utilities for generating several different kinds of control blocks: system definition, DBDS, PCBS, security, message, and devices. Also provided are utilities for analysis of system logs, to load/reorganize the data base, for data base recovery, and to dump/restore the data base.

Related Products

> Interactive Query Facility (IQF). An on-line retrieval language for accessing IMS data bases.
> IMS DB/DC Data Dictionary. A dictionary specially tailored to handling IMS data definitions. (See Appendix B for more details.)

References

Date, C. J. *An Introduction to Database Systems,* second edition, Chapters 12–18, Addison-Wesley, Reading, Mass., 1977.
IBM Corporation, IMS/VS General Information Manual, GH20-1260-6, July 1977.

NAME: IDMS

Vendor: Cullinane Corporation
20 William Street
Wellesley, Mass. 02181

Logical Data Structures(s):   IDMS is a CODASYL-type data base managment system. As such its basic data structures are named data fields, data records, and sets. One-to-many relationships are represented by sets, which have one owner record and one or more member records. Many-to-many relationships are represented by two sets which share a common member record type.

Physical Data Structure(s):   Data records are stored within physical blocks called pages. Each record is assigned a unique data base key which corresponds to the page and the position within the page where it is located. The user may group pages of equal size together into an area. Each area is named and may be referenced in data manipulation commands. Data base pages are stored as blocks of a direct-access data file(s). The data base may comprise one or many files.

Records within the data base may be stored and accessed by one of three location modes: CALC, DIRECT, and VIA SET. CALC records are stored on the basis of their key values using a hashing technique. DIRECT mode allows the user to specify the physical page on which a record is to be stored. Records stored VIA SET are stored as close as possible to the owner record of the set occurrence to which they belong.

Data Definition: IDMS provides a data description language (DDL) for describing the schema and subschema(s) of the data base. The schema describes the areas, files, records and sets for the entire data base. It is compiled by an IDMS utility and stored in an IDMS directory file for later reference. Each subschema describes a particular user view of the database, i.e., those records and sets of interest to the user program. Subschema DDL is compiled by an IDMS utility which enters descriptive information on the subschema into the directory and creates a link-edited load module for use during program execution.

A device media control language (DMCL) is also provided for describing the relationship between logical data base structures and their physical counterparts. For example, the DMCL is used to describe how areas are mapped into files and to describe the buffer storage required. Like the subschema DDL, the DMCL is compiled and link-edited into a load module for later use.

Data Maniuplation: The data base can be manipulated from host language programs through CALLS to IDMS routines or through a data manipulation language (DML) tailored to the host language. Taking the latter option, the user employs high-level commands, such as FIND or STORE, in the host language program. An IDMS preprocessor is then used to convert these commands into low-level CALL statements before the program is submitted to the host-language compiler. Currently DMLS exist for COBOL and PL/I.

Operating Environment: IDMS can be run in one of three modes: local, central, or communications. In local mode operation the DBMS is dedicated to one data base application program. In central mode, IDMS provides a central monitor (CAMP) that queues requests from one or more application programs(s). Each program may use its own subschema, but all share the same DMCL. In communications mode requests for IDMS services are sent to the IDMS monitor through a special communications interface tailored to the communications monitor in use (e.g., CICS). Batch programs can use IDMS concurrently with communications programs. Again, all programs share the same DMCL for the database.

Utilities: IDMS provides utility routines for the following functions: to dump and reload the data base, create and process journal files of data base transactions, initialize and maintain the Data Directory file, generate reports of Data Directory contents, load the data base, and for data base restructuring (correction, changes in record or set formats).

Related Products

IDMS/CULPRIT. A report generator package that may be used for IDMS databases and/or conventional files.

Integrated Data Dictionary. An expanded version of the Data Directory. (See Appendix B for a full description.)

On-Line Query Facility. A facility for on-line inquiry into IDMS data bases using the equivalent of IDMS DML retrieval commands.

Sequential Processing Facility. A somewhat misnamed facility that allows indexing by secondary (generic) keys of records stored in physical sequence or by one of the IDMS-supported location modes.

Reference

IDMS Concepts and Facilities, Cullinane Corporation, 1977.

NAME: Model 204

Vendor: Computer Corporation of America
575 Technology Square
Cambridge, Mass, 02139

Logical Data Structure(s):   Model 204 data bases consist of fields, records, files, and file groups. Each field has both a name and one or more values known to Model 204. Fields may be grouped into records of fixed or variable length. Files are collections of records which may be logically connected based on fields in the records. File groups are collections of files which Model 204 can treat as single files. Through proper definition using these structures the user can define hierarchical, network, or relational structures.

Physical Data Structure(s):   Model 204 uses a proprietary access method called the Inverted File Access Method (IFAM). Records may be stored and accessed in sequence, using hashing, or as entered. Alternative access paths are provided by inverting on fields designated as retrieval keys. The inversion tables are encoded (compressed) to save storage space.

Data Definition: Files in a Model 204 data base must be defined before they are created. The descriptive information on them is retained in two tables: the File Control Table and the Dictionary. The File Control Table contains status information on the file and information for mapping the file to physical data sets. The Dictionary contains descriptions for each of the fields in the file.

Data Manipulation: Model 204 has a self-contained English-like User Language which can be used in batch or on-line mode. Facilities are also provided for creating, modifying, and storing User Language requests.

A Host-Language Interface allows access to Model 204 data bases from programs written in COBOL, PL/I, FORTRAN, or Assembler. The user program must include certain descriptive information and storage areas. The program CALLS on several Model 204 subroutines to execute Model 204 commands.

Operating Environment: Model 204 can be used in single-user batch environments with host-language or User-Language programs. A multi-user capability is also provided through the Model 204 Cross Region Access Method (CRAM). Teleprocessing support is provided by the Model 204 monitor, TP204, or through interfaces to several standard TP monitors.

Utilities: Utilities are provided for data base loading, system security, accounting, checkpoint/restart, and dump/restore operations.

Related Products

Model 204 Data Dictionary. Stores data about Model 204 files and conventional files using a Model 204 data base. (See Appendix B for more details.)

TP204. The Model 204 teleprocessing monitor.

References

Model 204, System Features, Nos. 2–9, Computer Corporation of America, 1977.

Datapro 70, Model 204, Portfolio No. 70E-174-01a, Datapro Research Corporation (Delran, N.J. 08075), November 1978.

NAME: SYSTEM 2000

Vendor: INTEL Systems Corporation
12675 Research Boulevard
P.O. Box 9968
Austin, Tex. 78766

Logical Data Structure(s):   System 2000 provides the user with a hierarchical logical structure of data elements (also called components) and repeating groups of elements. The latter are comparable to CODASYL record types or IMS segments. One-to-many relationships are represented by levels in the hierarchy, i.e., a group of elements at level 1 may be related to many instances of a group of elements at level 2.

Physical Data Structure(s):   System 2000 users an inverted file structure to store its data bases. Each component defined is indexed (i.e., inverted) unless the user specifically exempts it. Logically related repeating groups are physically linked through pointers; however, access to any level may be accomplished using the inverted file feature.

Data Definition: Two types of data definition languages and processors are provided by System 2000. The components and groups in a data base are defined and the definition is compiled into a data base schema using the DEFINE processor. A second processor, called CONTROL, is used to define subschemas (i.e., portions of the data base available to specific users), to set user passwords, and to limit user authorization privileges. The output of both processors is maintained by System 2000 and used during data base processing.

Data Manipulation: System 2000 provides a self-contained Natural Language for data base access. The user may use this language in Immediate- or Queued-Access mode. In the former, each command issued is executed immediately. In the latter, commands are scanned and then collected until the user signals that processing should begin. The Natural Language is high-level and nonprocedural.

Users may also access System 2000 data bases from host-language programs. System 2000 commands are included in the host-language (COBOL, PL/I, or Assembler) and then converted into CALLS to S2000 routines by a preprocessor.

Operating Environment: The basic System 2000 package operates in a single-user, batch environment. Options are available to provide for mulitple users of one copy of System 2000, concurrent processing of multiple System 2000 commands, and teleprocessing support.

Utilities: System 2000 provides a report writer, for highly structured retrievals; utilities for transaction logging and SAVE/RESTORE processing; an optional rollback facility; and additional DBA facilities, for data base restructuring, statistical analyses, user accounting, and system tuning.

Related Products

TP 2000. A generalized teleprocessing monitor for an IBM processing environment.

CONTROL 2000. A data dictionary system. (See Appendix B for details.)

References

System 2000, MRI Systems Corporation, PR78-06-012, 1978.
Cardenas, A. F., *Data Base Management Systems*, Chapter 8, Allyn and Bacon Boston, Mass, 1979.

NAME: TOTAL

Vendor: CINCOM Systems, Inc.
2300 Montana Avenue
Cincinnati, Ohio 45211

Logical Data Structure(s):   The logical data structure of a TOTAL data base is virtually the same as the physical structure which supports it. Data fields are grouped into records. Records are divided into two types and stored in two different kinds of files. Master files are used for records of basic data, which are generally fixed in size and static in existence. Variable files are used either for records of data that are less predictable or to represent associations among the Master file records. One-to-many relationships are represented by a Master file linked to a Variable file. Many-to-many relationships are represented by two Master files linked by a common Variable file. These linkages are quite flexible, and thus TOTAL can support both hierarchical and network data structures.

Physical Data Structures(s):   TOTAL Master files are stored as direct-acess data sets, with the records placed based on key values using a hashing technique. Variable files are also direct access, with records stored in the next available location rather than by key. Pointers are used to link Master file records with associated Variable file records and to link related Variable file records together.

Data Definition: Each data file and record in the TOTAL data base must be described using a fixed-format data description language. This description is processed by a TOTAL routine and used to generate a Data Base Module (DBMOD). The DBMOD is used to initially format the data base and is referenced by all programs which load and/or access the data base. Similar descriptive information must be included in the data description portion of the application program.

The newest version of TOTAL also allows the user to define Logical Views which describe data fields required by specific applications.

Data Manipulation: A TOTAL data base may be accessed from programs written in host languages, such as COBOL, PL/I, FORTRAN, and Assembler, through the use of a CALL to a TOTAL routine. Data manipulation commands, such as READ MASTER or ADD VARIABLE, are passed as parameters of the call, along with record keys, data field names, and status information. The result of the operation, e.g., retrieved data or a status flag, is also returned as one of the parameters.

Operating Environment: The basic version of TOTAL operates in a batch mode, with one or more users sharing a single copy of the DBMS routines. Application specific data is kept in a control file. CINCOM provides a teleprocessing monitor for use with TOTAL, or an optional interface to one of the other standard TP monitors.

Utilities: TOTAL provides utilities for data base load, for journaling of data base transactions, for integrity checks (e.g., verifying record keys), and for handling of abnormal conditions (e.g., abends or other processing errors).

Related Products

ENVIRON/1. A teleprocessing monitor tailored for use with TOTAL.

SOCRATES. A generalized report generator package.

CINCOM Data Dictionary. A data dictionary with the capability of generating and maintaining TOTAL data descriptions. (See Appendix B for more details.)

References

Total Information System, The Next Generation of Software, CINCOM Systems Inc., 1978.

CINCOM Systems OS/TOTAL Application Programmer's Guide, Publication No. PO2-1236-00, 1976.

NAME: SEED

Vendor: International Data Base Systems, Inc.
2300 Walnut Street, Seventh Floor
Philadelphia, Pa. 19103

Logical Data Structure(s): SEED is a network DBMS which follows the CODASYL DBTG Report specifications. Named and typed data items are grouped into records, which may be related through the use of DBTG sets. Each set type connects an owner record type with one or more member record types. Many-to-many relationships are supported by two set types sharing a common member record type.

Physical Data Structure(s): Record instances are stored in physical pages, grouped into one or more named Areas. An area corresponds to a physical data file. Records may be stored using DIRECT, CALC, or VIA SET placement. With the first, storage is by page number within Area. CALC is a hashed access method and VIA SET is used to cluster records that are part of the same set type. Within a set, access from the owner to the member records may be through a linked list or a pointer array (inversion).

Data Definition: The SEED DDL is used to describe the data base schema and its component areas, record types, data items, and set types. A subschema DDL is also available which allows the user to define different views of the data base for different application programs. A DDL processor is used to build a data base structure dictionary from the users' DDL. Subschema descriptions are part of application programs and preprocessors are available for COBOL or FORTRAN to convert these into the necessary file description tables.

Data Manipulation: SEED may be used with the host languages COBOL or FORTRAN. For COBOL the SEED DML is in the form of additional COBOL verbs, e.g., FIND or STORE. For FORTRAN the SEED DML is a selection of CALL statements, one for each DML command. An interactive DML, called DBLOOK, is also available and can be used to retrieve information from the dictionary as well as the data base itself.

Operating Environment: SEED is implemented as a FORTRAN program and thus can run under a standard operating system. As a result it is available on a large number of different CPUs and operating systems, including many microcomputers. The DBLOOK feature requires interactive terminal support from the operating system.

Utilities: Utilities are provided for data base dumps, initialization of data bases and schemas, and for monitoring usage statistics. Standard file backup and recovery procedures are used. A journaling option with before and after images is in development.

Related Products

HARVEST Query Language. A relational-like interface to SEED data bases.

REAP Report Writer. A nonprocedural report specification language.

GARDEN. An on-line DML with facilities for interactive update and retrieval.

SPROUT. A transaction processor which can be used for data file to data base conversion.

DESIGNER. An automated logical design aid.

Automatic Program Generator (APG). Generates application programs from non-procedural descriptions.

DBD–DSS. A physical data base design decision support system.

References

International Data Base Systems, Inc., *SEED*, 1978.
International Data Base Systems, Inc., *HARVEST Query Language/Report Writer*, 1979.

Data Dictionary/Directory Packages

NAME: ADABAS Data Dictionary

Vendor: Software Ag. of North America Inc.
11800 Sunrise Valley Drive
Reston, Virginia 22091

Description: The ADABAS Dictionary is used to record information on data, personnel, processing entities, and the relationships among them. The dictionary includes facilities for its own maintenance, for report generation, and for other functions in conjunction with the ADABAS data base management system.

Entities: The ADABAS Dictionary supports two types of entities: data entities and usage entities. The former include data bases, fields, files, relationships between files, and verification procedures. Usage entities include systems, programs, modules, reports, and owner/users.

Input: A utility is provided to initialize the data dictionary with entries that describe the dictionary itself. An update facility is also provided so that the user may add, change, and delete entries. ADABAS file definitions may also be used as input to a conversion utility that generates dictionary entries for these files and fields.

Data Base: The dictionary is a file in an ADABAS data base.

Reports: The dictionary system produces two types of standard reports: data reports and usage reports. Data reports include lists of the dictionary entries for entities of a particular type or for fields within specified files. Usage reports are lists of dictionary usage entities of a given type. Also provided are top-down reports of system components and bottom-up lists of field and file usage (i.e., where used). Systems, programs, modules, etc., can also be listed by owner/ users.

Application Program Access: Since the dictionary data is maintained as an ADABAS file, it may be accessed by the ADABAS report writer (ADAWRITER), the ADABAS query language (ADASCRIPT), or any application program using the ADABAS DBMS facilities.

Other Features: The dictionary can be used for various functions related to the maintenance and processing of ADABAS files. It can produce input for the ADABAS loader for any files described in the dictionary. It can also generate file and field name information for the query facility. Finally, it can produce input for the ADABAS preprocessing facility (for transforming file and field names into ADABAS form).

References

ADABAS Data Dictionary Overview, ADD-110-010, Software Ag.

NAME: CINCOM Data Dictionary

Vendor: CINCOM Systems, Inc.
             2300 Montana Avenue
             Cincinnati, Ohio 45211

Description: The Data Dictionary includes a series of interrelated files containing data on the various components of a user's data processing environment. Also provided are utilities to load and maintain these data, plus facilities for reporting and generating data descriptions for the TOTAL data base management system.

Entities: Information is maintained on users, systems, data bases, elements, transactions, source documents, files, reports, programs, and physical data elements. Relationships among these entities are also maintained.

Input: An initial load facility is provided to allow for the loading of a large volume of entity descriptions using preformatted transactions. Modifications and new entity definitions can be added after initial load using the maintenance facility provided. Utility programs are also provided to (1) establish relationships between element definitions and physical elements using data initially loaded into the dictionary DICT file, (2) scan TOTAL DDL statements to load the dictionary, and (3) scan COBOL source programs to determine relationships between programs and elements.

Data Base: The dictionary data base is a TOTAL data base consisting of five Master and four Variable files.

Reports: The Data Dictionary Reporting Facility allows the generation of 25 different standard reports. Each report is requested using a one-statement, fixed-format command. Two types of reports are possible: category reports and relationship reports. Category reports produce detailed information on entities of a given type. Relationship reports describe the relationships that exist between entities of a given type and other entities in the dictionary. If the user does not wish to see all entities in a given type, he may restrict the scope of the report by using a trigger file (containing the names of those entities desired).

Application Program Access: The Data Dictionary data base should be available to any host-language program using the facilities of the TOTAL data base management system.

Other Features: The user may define default values for specific types of entities, establish required attribute fields, or assign password protection to entities in the Data Dictionary.

The user may generate the TOTAL DDL statements required for the generation of a TOTAL data base from the data dictionary.

Source code for the dictionary is provided so that users may customize it to their needs.

Reference

CINCOM Systems, Inc., Data Dictionary Technical Overview, Publication No. G06-0001, 1978.

NAME: CONTROL 2000

Vendor: INTEL Systems Corporation
12675 Research Boulevard
P.O. Box 9968
Austin, Texas 78766

Description: Control 2000 is a dictionary/directory system designed for users of the System 2000 data base management system. It includes a dictionary data base of data about the organization's data and processing applications plus a variety of reports for displaying these data.

Entities: Control 2000 has, as standard entities, applications, programs, data bases, files, records, data elements, and users. Relationships among these entities are also supported.

Input: Currently data are entered into the Control 2000 data dictionary using predefined transactions. Future releases of this product will contain the facility for loading the dictionary from System 2000 data descriptions or from source program data descriptions.

Data Base: The Control 2000 dictionary is maintained as a System 2000 data base.

Reports: A variety of reports are provided for displaying entity descriptions. Relationships may be traced using the directory report or the impact report. The directory report displays the relationships among two types of entities, e.g., all the programs in a given application. The impact report traces the relationships for a specific entity, e.g., all applications, programs and reports related to a specific data base.

Application Program Access: It appears that the Control 2000 data base is accessible to an application program using the System 2000 commands. It may also be accessed by the System 2000 query language and report writer.

Other Features: All the facilities of System 2000 including backup and recovery features, security features, and a multi-user capability are available in Control 2000.

Reference

Control 2000 Data Dictionary/Directory System, PR78-09-016, MRI Systems Corporation, 1978.

NAME: Data Catalogue 2

Vendor: Synergetics Corporation
One DeAngelo Drive
Bedford, Mass. 01730

Description: Data Catalogue 2 records data on any of a number of entities. Specific characteristics of these entities, called attributes, can be used to categorize and index the dictionary contents.

Entities: Entities supported by Data Catalogue 2 include elements, groups, records, segments, files, sets, data sets, data bases, modules, forms, reports, systems, and users. In addition the user may define new entities that are meaningful in his environment.

Input: Data are entered in either batch or on-line mode using free format, data forms, or structured codes. A utility is also available to pick up data from existing source program data divisions.

Data Base: The dictionary data base does not depend on any DBMS.

Reports: The standard reports produced by Data Catalogue 2 include indexes, a name analysis, a catalogue, a hierarchy report, a usage report, and a relational report. The indexes list entities by attribute, e.g., all modules coded in COBOL. The name analysis report compares all names of a given type, e.g., data set names, and groups them based on common names or parts of names. For example, the name analysis report would group all names that include the term STUDENT. The catalogue report is a master list of attributes defined for all or selected entities. The hierarchy report produces a top-down list of hierarchically related entities. The usage report produces attributes of a specified entity and all other entities which use it. Finally, the relational report is a summarized cross-reference between entites of a given type and all those which reference it.

Application Program Access: The data in the catalogue are indirectly available to application programs through a data extraction facility or through calls to a Data Catalogue application module.

Other Features: The user can define keywords that describe an entity and thus build in additional cross-referencing among entities.

A simple query language is provided that can produce ad hoc lists of counts of entities with specified characteristics.

Reference

Data Catalogue 2 System Overview, Synergetics Corp., February 1979.

NAME: DATAMANAGER

Vendor: MSP Inc.
21 Worthen Road
Lexington, Massachusetts 02173

Description: DATAMANAGER includes a data dictionary, to hold information on various entities of interest to the user; a data definition language to create and maintain the dictionary; and a command language to display and generate reports concerning the contents of the dictionary.

Entities: DATAMANAGER supports eight member types, i.e., entities. The standard entities are systems, programs, modules, data bases, files, segments, groups, and items. The user may redefine these members as desired. Relationships among entities are also maintained, including hierarchical and network associations. Further a distinction is made between the association *contains* and the association *refers to*.

Input: Entity descriptions are entered into a DATAMANAGER dictionary using free-format English language keyword statements. The user may also use a DATAMANAGER facility for deriving dictionary input from COBOL or PL/I source code.

Data Base: The DATAMANAGER dictionary may be generated as a basic direct access method (BDAM) or virtual storage access method (VSAM) file.

Reports: The DATAMANAGER command language allows interactive access to the dictionary for display and reporting purposes. Commands are included to generate lists and glossaries, as well as to interrogate the dictionary on a more specific basis, e.g., "Which file uses element X?"

Application Program Access: User application programs can access the DATAMANAGER dictionary in three ways. First, a teleprocessing interface exists for several TP monitors that allows on-line programs to interface with DATAMAN-AGER. Second, DATAMANAGER can be used to generate a specially formatted output file to be used as input to the application program. Finally, a CALL facility is provided so that the application program can call on DATAMANAGER directly.

Other Features: DATAMANAGER allows dummy entity descriptions so that the user can build the dictionary in a top-down manner. When actual entities with the same names are added, the dummy is replaced by the actual definition.

Password protection is provided to allow the restriction of dictionary users to specific commands and/or specific entities.

Locking is provided to prevent simultaneous update of the dictionary, and backup and recovery routines are provided.

Users may define a variety of status codes to separate identical entities by time (past, present, future) or by usage (test, production).

DATAMANAGER can be used to generate data description code for COBOL, PL/I, Assembler, MARK IV, ADABAS, IDMS, IMS, SYSTEM 2000, or TOTAL.

New facilities for test data generation and file displays are under development.

Reference

DATAMANAGER Fact Book (10.77), MSP Ltd., January 1978.

NAME: DB/DC Data Dictionary

Vendor: IBM Corporation
1133 Westchester Avenue
White Plains, N.Y. 10604

Description: DB/DC data dictionary is a set of data bases containing entries for different subject categories and their interrelationships plus a set of programs for data entry, modification, and reporting.

Entities: The dictionary contains 15 IBM-supplied subject categories: data base, segment, element, system, job, program, module, transaction, PSB, PCB, SYSDEF, user, category, relationship type, and attribute type. In addition, there is a facility for the user to define additional categories, relationships, and attributes.

Input: The dictionary can accept information directly from COBOL or PL/I data descriptions or from IMS DBDS and PSBS. For high-volume input there are preformatted data entry forms for each data entry. Entries may also be made on-line using preformatted display screens.

Data Base: The dictionary data is stored in IMS/VS or DL/I DOS/VS physical data bases.

Reports: The reporting commands allow hard-copy or machine-readable output. The major hard-copy report commands are SCAN and REPORT. SCAN produces a list of entry names, with or without attributes, for all selected entries. REPORT produces a glossary of selected entries. Other commands may be used to produce additional reports, such as a hierarchical list of entries.

Application Program Access: Application programs can retrieve, but not modify, data from the dictionary using a call to a dictionary module.

Other Features: The dictionary can generate and maintain IMS and DL/I structures, e.g., DBDS and PSBS. It can also produce COBOL, PL/I, and BAL data descriptions.

Security routines are included that can be used to control access to the dictionary. The DBA can code authorization information in the User subject category in the dictionary itself for all dictionary users.

There is an interactive display forms facility that can be used for data entry, modification, or display.

Reference

DB/DC Data Dictionary General Information Manual, GH20-9104-2, IBM, October 1978.

NAME: Integrated Data Dictionary (IDD)

Vendor: Cullinane Corporation
20 William Street
Wellesley, Mass, 02181

Description: The IDD consists of a data dictionary definition language, source language preprocessors, a data dictionary reporter, and a central dictionary file. The dictionary contains information on systems, users, programs, and data elements.

Entities: The standard categories supported by IDD include elements, records, files, programs, systems, and users. The user may also define additional classes of information.

Input: The user may describe entities using the data dictionary definition language (DDDL) or may use a source-language preprocessor to capture information on fields, files, and programs directly from the source programs.

Data Base: It does not appear that the IDD data base is dependent on the IDMS data base management system. However, it can be used in conjunction with IDMS.

Reports: The IDD data dictionary reporter provides a set of 41 standard reports of four types: detail reports (e.g., details for a particular class of entity such as elements), cross-reference reports (e.g., records by file), summary reports by entity class, and key reports for each entity class. The user may also generate customized reports to add to this group.

Application Program Access: The dictionary may be accessed by conventional report programs and treated as a standard file.

Other Features: Utilities are provided for backup and recovery of the data dictionary. An option allows the user to access and display dictionary data using an on-line query facility. Security is provided to restrict the user's access to the dictionary.

References

Integrated Data Dictionary, Order No. P406, Cullinane Corp. (undated).
IDMS Concepts and Facilities, Cullinane Corp. 1977.

NAME: The Model 204 Data Dictionary

Vendor: Computer Corporation of America
575 Technology Square
Cambridge, Massachusetts 02139

Description: The Model 204 data dictionary allows the user to store and retrieve information on data items and processes of interest both within and external to the Model 204 data base system.

Entities: Information is maintained on file groups, files, logical record types, fields, load modules, programs, procedures, and logical systems.

Input: Data is entered into the Model 204 dictionary using on-line transactions in the Model 204 User Language for each entity described.

Data Base: The dictionary is a Model 204 file.

Reports: The Model 204 dictionary contains commands to DISPLAY or LIST specified entities. Three types of reports are also provided: cross-reference, directory, and dictionary. The cross-reference displays the relationships in which an entity participates. The directory report shows the logical and physical attributes of an entity. The dictionary lists the descriptions of a set of entities specified by the user. The dictionary and directory reports can be requested for groups, files, record types, or fields.

Application Program Access: Application programs using the Model 204 system may access the dictionary provided they have proper authorization.

Other Features: Prompting is provided for on-line data entry.

Reference

The Model 204 Data Dictionary, CCA, January 1979.

NAME: UCC-10

Vendor: University Computing Company
83103 Elmbrook Drive
P.O. Box 47911
Dallas, Texas 75247

Description: UCC-10 serves as a central documentation source for data base and data communications data definitions, provides cross-reference facilities for analysis of the data definitions stored, and automatically generates all required IMS control blocks.

Entities: The central entity supported by UCC-10 is the field, or data element. However, four classes of additional entities are supported, three of which are interrelated by the definition of common fields. The four classes are data base entities (e.g., data base, data set group, segment), program and application entities (e.g., application, job, program, PSB, logical terminal), message format entities (e.g., message, message segment, format, device), and communication control block entities (e.g., physical terminal, configuration, station, control unit). Meaningful relationships among these entities, some unidirectional and some bidirectional, are also maintained.

Input: UCC-10 can receive input in batch or on-line mode. Preformatted screens are available for on-line input; keyword-type transactions may be used either on-line or batch. High-volume batch input is accommodated by a fixed-format preprocessor. Conversion routines are provided for accepting data directly from existing IMS, COBOL, or PL/I data definitions.

Data Base: UCC-10 is supported by the IMS DBMS package.

Reports: UCC-10 provides over 200 reporting options to generate glossary, dictionary, or cross-reference type reports. A keyword in context (KWIC) capability is provided so that standard names and textual information can be searched and retrieved by keyword. UCC-10 can generate all IMS required control blocks including SYSGEN and message formats as well as the usual data base and program control blocks.

Application Program Access: UCC-10 can be accessed by any batch IMS application or any IMS-supported terminal. An interface is provided to user-defined security routines to protect dictionary contents.

Other Features: UCC-10 edits all incoming data both for dictionary standards and for IMS standards.

Definitions may be designated as test or production. Production definitions are protected from on-line update. Test definitions can be used to generate test IMS environments. A simple MOVE command is provided for changing definitions from test to production status.

Default values are provided for 80% of the attributes of a dictionary entry to simplify data input.

UCC-10 maintains IMS Terminal Security data.

Reference

UCC-10, the Data Dictionary/Manager, University Computing Center, (undated).

References

CHAPTER 1

1. AFIPS, *Information Processing in the U.S. A Quantitative Survey,* American Federation of Information Processing Societies (AFIPS) Press, Montvale, N.J. 07645, 1978.
2. Anthony, R., *Planning and Control Systems: A Framework for Analysis,* Division of Research, Graduate School of Business Administration, Harvard University, Boston, 1965.
3. Churchill, N., J. Kempster, and M. Uretsky, *Computer-Based Information Systems for Management,* National Association of Accountants, New York, 1969.
4. Nolan, Richard L., Managing the computer resource: A stage hypothesis, *Communications of the ACM* **16**(7), pp. 399–405, July 1973.
5. Fry, James P., and Edgar H. Sibley, Evolution of data-base management systems, *Computing Surveys* **8**(1), pp. 7–42, 1976.
6. CODASYL Data Base Task Group, *April 1971 Report.* (Available from Association for Computing Machinery, 1133 Avenue of the Americas, New York 10036.)
7. Bachman, C. W., and S. B. Williams, A general purpose programming system for random access memories, *Proceedings of the American Federation of Information Processing Societies Joint Computer Conference* **26,** pp. 411–422, Spartan Books, New York, 1964.
8. IBM, *System/360 Bill of Material Processor (360-ME-06X) Application Description,* GH20-0197-3, fourth edition, February 1971, IBM Technical Publication Department. 112 East Post Road, White Plains, N.Y. 10601.
9. Sibley, Edgar H., and Alan G. Merten, Implementation of a generalized data base management system within an organization, *Management Informatics* **2**(1), pp. 21–30, 1973.
10. Nolan, Richard L., Computer data bases: The future is now, *Harvard Business Review,* pp. 98–114, September–October 1973.

CHAPTER 2

1. The "data administrator" function, *EDP Analyzer* **10**(11), pp. 1–14, 1972.
2. Lyon, John K., *The Database Administrator,* Wiley-Interscience, New York, 1976.
3. GUIDE-SHARE, *Requirements for a Database Management System,* Joint GUIDE-SHARE Data Base Requirements Group Report, GSD 23-041, November 11, 1970.
4. CODASYL Systems Committee, Data administration function, in *Feature Analysis of Generalized Data Base Management Systems,* May 1971. (Available from Association for Computing Machinery, 1133 Avenue of the Americas, New York 10036.)
5. Steiger, William H., The data administrator function, draft for CODASYL Systems Committee report, July 8, 1970.
6. Lyon, John K., The role of the data base administrator, *Data Base* **3**(4), pp. 11–12, 1971.
7. Nolan, Richard L., Computer data bases: The future is now, *Harvard Business Review,* pp. 98–114, September-October 1973.
8. GUIDE, *Establishing the Data Administration Function,* June 1977. (Available from GUIDE International, 111 E. Wacker Drive, Chicago, Ill. 60601.)
9. GUIDE, *Data Administration Methodology,* January 1978. (Available from GUIDE International, 111 E. Wacker Drive, Chicago, Ill. 60601.)
10. DeBlasis, Jean-Paul, and T. H. Johnson, Data base administration: Classical patterns, some experiences, and trends, *Proceedings of the American Federation of Information Processing Societies National Computer Conference,* pp. 1–7, AFIPS, Montvale, N.J., 1977.
11. Leong-Hong, B., and B. Marron, *Database Administration: Concepts, Tools, Experiences, and Problems,* National Bureau of Standards, Special Publication No. 500-28, March 1978.
12. Weldon, J. L., The practice of data base administration, *Proceedings of the American Federation of Information Processing Societies National Computer Conference,* pp. 167–170, AFIPS, Montvale, N.J. 1979.
13. McCririck, I. B., *A Survey of the Data Administration Function in Large Canadian Organizations,* MSBA thesis, University of British Columbia (2075 Westbrook Place, Vancouver, B.C., Canada V6T1W5), June 1979.

CHAPTER 3

1. GUIDE, *The Data Base Administrator,* April 1973. (Available from GUIDE International, 111 E. Wacker Drive, Chicago, Ill. 60601.)
2. Turner, Jon A., *Organizational Evolution of Data Base Administration,* Auerbach Data Base Management Portfolio No. 22-05-04, Auerbach Publishers, Pennsauken, N.J. 1976.
3. Davis, Gordon B., *Computer Data Processing*, second edition, McGraw-Hill, New York, 1973.
4. Dearden, John, How to organize information systems, *Harvard Business Review,* pp. 65–73, March–April 1965.
5. Weldon, J. L., *Data Base Administration: Organization and Tasks,* New York University Graduate School of Business Administration Working Paper No. 78-143(CA), December 1978.

CHAPTER 4

1. Brebach, G. T., *An Approach to the Organizational Evolution of the DBA Function,* Auerbach Data Base Management Portfolio No. 22-05-04, Auerbach Publishers, Pennsauken, N.J., 1976.

2. Chamberlain, Robert B., *Job Descriptions for DBA Staff,* Auerbach Data Base Management Portfolio No. 22-05-05, Auerbach Publishers, Pennsauken, N.J., 1978.
3. Weldon, J. L., *Data Base Administration: Organization and Tasks,* New York University Graduate School of Business Administration Working Paper No. 78-143(CA), December 1978.
4. IBM, *The Role of IMS at Equitable Life,* Applications Brief GK20-1040-0, September 1977. (Available from IBM Corporation Data Processing Division, 1133 Westchester Avenue, White Plains, N.Y. 10604.)

CHAPTER 5

1. The cautious path to a data base, *EDP Analyzer* **11**(6), pp. 1–13, 1973.
2. Beckhard, R., Strategies for large system change, *Sloan Management Review* **16**(2), pp. 43–55, 1975.
3. DeBlasis, Jean-Paul, and T. H. Johnson, Data base administration: Classical patterns, some experiences, and trends, *Proceedings of the American Federation of Information Processing Societies National Computer Conference,* pp. 1–7, APIPS, Montvale, N.J., 1977.
4. Ross, R. G., Placing the DBA, *Journal of Systems Management,* **27**(5), pp. 25–33, May 1976.
5. Weldon, J. L., *Data Base Administration: Organization and Tasks,* New York University Graduate School of Business Administration Working Paper No. 78-143(CA), December 1978.
6. Walton, R. E., and J. M. Dutton, The management of interdepartmental conflict: A model and review, *Administrative Science Quarterly* **14**, pp. 78–84, March 1969.
7. March, J. G., and H. A. Simon, *Organizations,* John Wiley & Sons, New York, 1958.
8. Browne, P. J., and R. T. Golembiewski, The staff–line concept revisited: An empirical study of organizational images, *Academy of Management Journal* **17**(3), pp. 406–417, September 1974.
9. Kelman, H. C., Compliance, identification, and internalization: Three processes of attitude change, *Journal of Conflict Resolution* **2**, pp. 51–60, 1958.
10. Presthus, R. V., Authority in organizations, in *Concepts and Issues in Administrative Behavior* (S. Maillick and E. H. Van Ness, eds.), pp. 122–136, Prentice-Hall, Englewood Cliffs, N.J., 1962.
11. Bates, F. L., Power behavior and decentralization, in *Power in Organizations* (M. N. Zald, ed.), Vanderbilt University Press, Nashville, Tenn., 1970.
12. French, J. R. P., and B. Raven, The bases of social power, in *Studies in Social Power* (D. Cartwright, ed.), pp. 150–167, University of Michigan Press, Ann Arbor, Mich., 1959.
13. Hickson, D. J., C. R. Hinings, C. A. Lee, R. E. Schneck, and J. M. Pennings, A strategic contingencies' theory of intraorganizational power, *Administrative Science Quarterly,* **16**(2), pp. 216–229, 1971.

CHAPTER 6

1. Radford, K. J., *Information Systems in Management,* Reston Publication Company, Prentice-Hall, Reston, Va., 1973.
2. GUIDE, *The Data Base Administrator,* Report of the GUIDE DBA Project, 1973. (Available from GUIDE International, 111 E. Wacker Drive, Chicago, Ill. 60601.)
3. Weldon, J. L., *Data Base Administration: Theory and Practice,* New York University Graduate School of Business Administration Working Paper No. 75-75, September 1975.
4. GUIDE, *Establishing the Data Administrator Function,* GUIDE EDAF Project Report. (Available from GUIDE International, 111 East Wacker Drive, Chicago, Ill. 60601.)

5. The cautious path to data base, *EDP Analyzer* **11**(6), June 1973.

6. Tillinghast, J., *Establishing a Framework for Data Base Planning,* Auerbach Data Base Management System Portfolio No. 21-02-02, Auerbach Publishers, Pennsauken, N.J., 1976.

7. McFadden, F. R., and J. D. Suver, Costs and benefits of a data base system, *Harvard Business Review,* pp. 131–139, January–February 1978.

8. Cohen, Leo J., *Pre-Data Base Survey,* Performance Development Corp., 1101 State Road, Princeton, N.J. 08540., 1978.

9. Robinson, S. L., *Justifying a Data Base System,* Auerbach Data Base Management System Portfolio No. 21-02-01, Auerbach Publishers, Pennsauken, N.J., 1977.

10. Sibley, E. H., and A. G. Merten, Implementation of a generalized data base management system within an organization, *Management Informatics* **2**(1), pp. 21–31, 1973.

11. Planning for DBMS conversions, *EDP Analyzer* **16**(5), May 1978.

12. Bush, R. L., and K. E. Knutsen, Integration of corporate and MIS planning: The impact of productivity, *Data Base* **9**(3), pp. 4–8, Winter 1978.

CHAPTER 7

1. Date, C. J., *An Introduction to Data Base Systems,* Addison Wesley, Reading, Mass., 1977.

2. Tillinghast, J., *Establishing a Framework for Data Base Planning,* Auerbach Data Base Management Portfolio No. 21-02-02, Auerbach Publishers, Pennsauken, N.J., 1976.

3. CODASYL Systems Committee, *Feature Analysis of Generalized Data Base Management Systems,* Technical Report, May 1971. (Available from Association for Computing Machinery, 1133 Avenue of the Americas, New York, 10036.)

4. CODASYL Systems Committee, *Selection and Acquisition of Data Base Management Systems,* Technical Report, March 1976. (Available from Association for Computing Machinery Order Dept., P.O. Box 65145, Baltimore, Md. 21264.)

5. Dowkont, A. J., W. A. Morris, and T. D. Buettell, *A Methodology for Comparison of Generalized Data Management Systems:* PEGS (Parametric Evaluation of Generalized Systems), AD No. 811682, March 1967, NTIS, Springfield, Va. 22151.

6. Fong, Elizabeth, A benchmark test approach for generalized data base software, *Proceedings of COMPCON Fall Conference,* pp. 246–249, Institute for Electrical and Electronic Engineers–Computer Society, N.Y., September 1975.

7. Rustin, R., Data base management system performance estimation: An elementary approach, *Proceedings of the Fifth Texas Conference on Computing Systems,* pp. 115–126 (University of Texas, Austin, Texas, October 1976.)

8. Yao, S. B., An attribute based model for database access cost analysis, *ACM Transactions on Data Base Systems* **2**(1), pp. 45–67, March 1977.

9. Benevy, D., Data base modeling, a presentation made at INFO 75, New York, September 1975.

10. Scheuermann, P., Concepts of a data base simulation language, *Proceedings of the Association for Computing Machinery SIGMOD Conference,* pp. 114–146, Association for Computing Machinery, New York, August 1977.

CHAPTER 8

1. Lyon, John K., *An Introduction to Data Base Design,* John Wiley and Sons, New York, 1971.

2. Rund, Donna S., *Data Base Design Methodology, Parts I and II,* Auerbach Data Base Management Portfolio No. 23-01-01, 02, Auerbach Publishers, Pennsauken, N.J., 1977.

3. ANSI/X3/SPARC Study Group on Data Base Management Systems, Interim Report 75-02-08, *ACM FDT* **7**(2), 1975.
4. Weldon, J. L., *Trade-offs in Data Base Design,* Auerbach System Development Management Portfolio No. 35-02-03, Auerbach Publishers, Pennsauken, N.J., 1976.
5. Meltzer, H. S., Current Concepts in Data Base Design, unpublished notes from presentation to GUIDE 37, Boston, Mass., November 2, 1973.
6. Date, C. J., *An Introduction to Database Systems,* second edition, Addison-Wesley, Reading, Mass., 1977.
7. The database administrator function, *EDP Analyzer* **12**(10), 1974.
8. GUIDE, *The Data Base Administrator*, report of the DBA Project of GUIDE International, 111 E. Wacker Dr., Chicago, Ill., 1973.

CHAPTER 9

1. ANSI/X3/SPARC, Interim report of the ANSI/X3/SPARC study group on data base management systems, *ACM SIGMOD* **7**(2), 1975.
2. Codd, E. F., A relational model of data for large shared data banks, *Communications of the ACM* **13**(6), pp. 377–387, June 1970.
3. Date, C. J., *An Introduction to Database Systems,* Addison-Wesley, Reading, Mass., 1975.
4. Fagin, R., Multivariate dependencies and a new normal form for relational databases, *ACM Transactions on Database Systems* **2**(3), pp. 262–278, Sept. 1977.
5. Bachman, C. W., Data structure diagrams, *Data Base* **1**(2), pp. 4–10, Summer 1969.
6. Yao, S. B., S. Navathe, and J. L. Weldon, An integrated approach to logical data base design, *Proceedings of the NYU Symposium on Database Design,* pp. 1–14, New York University, New York, May 1978.
7. Kahn, B., A structured logical database design methodology, *Proceedings of the NYU Symposium on Database Design,* pp. 15–24, New York University, New York, May 1978.
8. Sheppard, D. R., *Data Base Design Methodology, Parts I and II,* Auerbach Data Base Management Portfolio No. 23-01-01 and 23-01-02, Auerbach Publishers, Pennsauken, N.J., 1977.
9. Teichroew, D., and E. A. Hershey III, PSL/PSA: A computer-aided technique for structured documentation and analysis of information processing systems, *IEEE Transactions on Software Engineering,* pp. 41–48, January 1977.
10. Hammer, M., W. G. Howe, V. J. Kruskal, and I. Wladawsky, A very high level programming language for data processing applications, *Communications of the ACM* **20**(11), pp. 832–840, November 1977.
11. Chen, P. P. S., The entity-relationship model: Toward a unified view of data, *ACM Transactions on Database Systems* **1**(1), pp. 9–36, March 1976.
12. Smith, J. M., and D. C. P. Smith, Database abstractions: Aggregation and generalization, *ACM Transactions on Database Systems* **2**(2), June 1977.
13. Navathe, S., and M. Schkolnick, View representation in logical database design, *Proceedings of the Association for Computing Machinery SIGMOD Conference,* Association for Computing Machinery, New York, June 1978.
14. Mitoma, M. F., and K. B. Irani, Automatic data base schema design and optimization, *Proceedings of the First Conference on Very Large Data Bases,* Association for Computing Machinery, New York, September 1975.
15. Raver, N., and G. U. Hubbard, Automated logical data base design: Concepts and applications, *IBM Systems Journal* **16**(3), pp. 287–312, 1977.
16. Gerritsen, R., A preliminary system for the design of DBTG data structures, *Communications of the ACM* **18**(10), pp. 551–556 October 1975.

17. Weldon, J. L., *View Restructuring of Abstraction Structures*, NYU Graduate School of Business Administration, Working Paper 78-93(CA), August 1978.

CHAPTER 10

1. Buchholz, Werner, File organization and addressing, *IBM Systems Journal*, pp. 86–111, June 1963.
2. Dodd, George G., Elements of data management systems, *ACM Comp. Surveys* **1**(2), pp. 117–132, June 1969.
3. Martin, James, *Computer Data Base Organization*, Prentice-Hall, Englewood Cliffs, N.J., 1976.
4. Lum, V. Y., P. S. T. Yuen, and M. Dodd, Key to address transform techniques: A fundamental performance study on large existing formatted files, *Communications of the ACM* **14**(4), pp. 228–239, 1971.
5. CINCOM Systems OS/TOTAL Application Programmer's Guide, Publication No. P02-1236-00, CINCOM Systems, Cincinnati, Ohio, 1976.
6. Date, C. J., *An Introduction to Data Base Systems*, Addison-Wesley, Reading, Mass., 1977.
7. IBM, *IMS/360 System/Application Design Guide*, 1972.
8. Cardenas, A. F., Evaluation and selection of file organizations: A model and a system, *Communications of the ACM* **16**(9), pp. 540–548, 1973.
9. Siler, Kenneth F., A stochastic evaluation model for database organizations in data retrieval systems, *Communications of the ACM* **19**(2), pp. 84–95, 1976.
10. Yao, S. B., An attribute-based model for data base access cost analysis, *ACM Transactions on Database Systems* **2**(1), pp. 45–67, 1977.
11. Teorey, T. J., and K. S. Das, Application of an analytical model to evaluate storage structures, *Proceedings of the Association for Computing Machinery SIGMOD Conference*, pp. 9–19, June 1976.
12. Weldon, J. L., *Data Storage Decisions for Large Data Bases*, National Technical Information Service, Publication No. AS/A-023874, U.S. Dept. of Commerce, Springfield, VA, 22161, February 1976.
13. Schkolnick, M., Physical database design techniques, *Proceedings of the NYU Symposium on Database Design*, New York University, pp. 99–209, May 1978.
14. IBM, *DBPrototype* II, *Program Description/Operations Manual*, IBM IUP No. 5796-PJK, April 1977.
15. Hoffer, J. A., and D. G. Severance, The use of cluster analysis in physical design, *Proceedings of the Conference on Very Large Data Bases 1975*, pp. 69–86, Sept. 1975.
16. Schkolnick, M., A clustering algorithm for hierarchical structures, *ACM Transactions on Database Systems* **2**(1), pp. 27–44, March 1977.
17. Salton, G., and A. Wong, Generation and search of clustered files, *ACM Transactions on Database Systems* **3**(4), pp. 321–346, December 1978.
18. Morgan, H. L., Optimal space allocation on disk storage devices, *Communications of the ACM* **17**(3), pp. 139–142, March 1974.
19. Gecsei, J., and J. A. Lukes, A model for the evaluation of storage hierarchies, *IBM Systems Journal* **2**, pp. 163–178, 1974.
20. Shneiderman, B., Optimum database reorganization points, *Communications of the ACM* **16**(6), pp. 362–365, June 1973.
21. Tuel, W. E., Optimum reorganization points for linearly growing files, *ACM Transactions on Database Systems* **3**(1), pp. 32–40, March 1978.

22. Yao, S. B., K. S. Das., and T. J. Teorey, A dynamic database reorganization algorithm, *ACM Transactions on Database Systems* **2**(1), pp. 45–67, March 1977.

23. Lum, V. Y., General performance analysis of key-to-address transformation techniques using an abstract file concept, *Communications of the ACM* **16**(10), pp. 603–612, October 1973.

24. Gottleib, D., S. Hagerth, P. Lehot, and H. Rabinowitz, A classification of compression methods and their usefulness for a very large data processing center, *Proceedings of the National Computer Conference,* American Federation of Information Processing Societies, pp. 453–458, 1975.

25. Huffman, D. A., A method for the construction of minimum redundancy codes, *Proceedings of the Institute of Radio Engineers,* pp. 1098–1101, September 1952.

CHAPTER 11

1. Davis, G., *Auditing and EDP,* AICPA, New York, 1968.

2. Yourdon, E., *Design of On-Line Computer Systems,* Prentice-Hall, Englewood Cliffs, N.J., 1972.

3. Martin, J., *Security, Accuracy, and Privacy in Computer Systems,* Prentice-Hall, Englewood Cliffs, N.J., 1973.

4. Tonik, A. B., Checkpoint, restart, and recovery: Selected annotated bibliography, *ACM SIGMOD—FDT* **7**(3–4), pp. 72–765, 1975.

5. Arthur Andersen and Co., LEXICON: *Automation Concept for Business Information Systems, General Description Manual,* third edition (1345 Avenue of the Americas, New York, N.Y. 10019), 1974.

6. Eswaran, K. P., and Donald D. Chamberlain, Functional specifications of a subsystem for data base integrity, *Proceedings of the Conference on Very Large Data Bases* (Framingham, Mass.,), pp. 48–68, Association for Computing Machinery, New York, September 1975.

7. Thomas, D. A., B. Pagurek, and R. J. Buhr, Validation algorithms for pointer values in DBTG databases, *ACM Transactions on Database Systems* **2**(4), pp. 352–369, December 1977.

8. Severance, D., and G. Lohman, Differential files: their application to the maintenance of large databases, *ACM TODS* **1**(3), pp. 256–267, September 1976.

9. Lorie, Raymond, Physical integrity in a large segmented database, *ACM TODS* **2**(1), pp. 91–104, March 1977.

10. Giordano, N. J., and M. S. Schwartz, Data base recovery at CMIC, *Proceedings of the Association for Computing Machinery SIGMOD Conference,* pp. 33–42, Association for Computing Machinery, New York, 1976.

11. Verhofsted, J., Recovery and crash resistance in a filing system, *Proceedings of the Association for Computing Machinery SIGMOD Conference,* pp. 158–167, Association for Computing Machinery, New York, 1977.

12. Ries, Daniel R., and Michael Stonebraker, Effects of locking granularity in a database management system, *ACM TODS* **2**(3), pp. 233–246, September 1977.

13. Eswaran, K. P., J. N. Gray, R. A. Lorie, and I. L. Traiger, The notions of consistency and predicate locks in a database system, *CACM* **19**(11), pp. 624–633, November 1976.

14. Rosenkrantz, Daniel J., R. E. Stearns, and P. M. Lewis II, System level concurrency control for distributed database systems, *ACM TODS* **3**(2), pp. 178–198, June 1978.

15. Macri, P. P., Deadlock detection and resolution in a CODASYL based data management system, *Proceedings of the Association for Computing Machinery SIGMOD Conference,* pp. 45–50, Association for Computing Machinery, New York, 1976.

16. Date, C. J., *An Introduction to Database Systems,* second edition, Addison-Wesley, Reading, Mass., 1977.

17. British Computer Society, CODASYL DDLC Data Base Administration Working Group, June 1975 report. (Available from the British Computer Society, 29 Portland Place, London W1N 4HU.)
18. Walsh, D. A., Structured testing, *Datamation*, pp. 111–118, July 1977.
19. Lohman, Guy M., and J. A. Muckstadt, Optimal policy for batch operations: Backup, checkpointing, reorganization, and updating, *ACM TODS* **2**(3), pp. 109–222, September 1977.

CHAPTER 12

1. Browne, Peter S., Computer security: A survey, *Data Base* (Association for Computing Machinery SIGBDP Newsletter) **4**(3), p. 112, Fall 1972.
2. Protecting valuable data, part 1, *EDP Analyzer* **11**(12), December 1973.
3. Protecting valuable data, part 2, *EDP Analyzer* **12**(1), January 1974.
4. David, Heather M., Computers, privacy, and security, *Computer Decisions*, pp. 46–48, May 1974.
5. Saltzer, Jerome H., Protection and control of information sharing in Multics, *Communications of the ACM* **17**(7), pp. 388–402, July 1974.
6. Griffiths, P. P., and B. W. Wade, An authorization mechanism for a relational data base system, *ACM Transactions on Database Systems* **1**(3), pp. 242–255, September 1976.
7. Fagin, Ronald, On an authorization mechanism, *ACM Transactions on Database Systems* **3**(3), pp. 310–319, September 1978.
8. Stonebraker, M., and P. Rubenstein, The INGRES protection system, *Proceedings of the Association for Computing Machinery Conference*, pp. 81–84, Association for Computing Machinery, New York, October 1976.
9. Kam, J. B., and J. D. Ullman, A model of statistical databases and their security, *ACM Transactions on Database Systems* **2**(1), pp. 1–10, Association for Computing Machinery, New York, March 1977.
10. Yu, C. T., and F. Y. Chin, A study on the protection of statistical data bases, *Proceedings of the Association for Computing Machinery SIGMOD Conference*, pp. 169–181, 1977.
11. Chin, F. Y., Security in statistical databases for queries with small counts, *ACM Transactions on Database Systems* **3**(1), pp. 92–104, March 1978.
12. Data encryption: Is is for you? *EDP Analyzer* **16**(12), December 1978.
13. Bayer, R., and J. K. Metzger, On the encipherment of search trees and random access files, *ACM Transactions on Database Systems* **1**(1), pp. 37–52, March 1976.
14. National Bureau of Standards, *Data Encryption Standard*, Federal Information Processing Standards Publication 46, Washington, D.C., January 1977.
15. Merkle, Ralph C., Secure communications over insecure channels, *Communications of the ACM* **21**(4), pp. 294–299, April 1978.
16. Needham, R. M., and M. D. Schroeder, Using encryption for authentication in large networks of computers, *Communications of the ACM* **21**(12), pp. 993–999, December 1978.
17. Burns, Kevin J., Keys to DBMS security, *Computer Decisions*, pp. 56–62, January 1976.
18. Date, C. J., *An Introduction to Database Systems*, second edition, Addison Wesley, Reading, Mass., 1977.
19. CINCOM Systems, Inc., OS/TOTAL *Application Programmer's Guide*, Publication no. P02-1236-00, Cincinnati, Ohio, 1976.
20. DPMA, *A Briefing on the Impact of Privacy Legislation*, Data Processing Management Association (505 Busse Highway, Park Ridge, Ill. 60068), 1975.
21. Westin, A. F., and M. A. Baker, *Databanks in a Free Society: Computers, Record-Keeping and Privacy*, Quadrangle Books, New York, 1972.

22. Linowes, David F., et al., Technology and Privacy, Appendix 5 to the Report of the Privacy Protection Study Commission, Stock No. 052-003-00425-9, U.S. Government Printing Office, Washington, D.C., 20402, July 1977.
23. Fong, Elizabeth, *A Data Base Management Approach to Privacy Act Compliance,* NBS Report on Computer Science and Technology, NBS Special Publication No. 500-10, U.S. Dept. of Commerce, June 1977.

CHAPTER 13

1. The "data administrator" function, *EDP Analyzer* **10**(11), November 1972.
2. Get more computer efficiency, *EDP Analyzer* **9**(3), March 1971.
3. Cohen, Leo J., An overview of performance management for data base, Notes from a presentation to New York City Chapter of the ACM Special Interest Group on Management of Data, 1975.
4. Lyon, John K., *The Database Administrator,* John Wiley and Sons, New York, 1976.
5. B.C.S./CODASYL DDLC Data Base Administration Working Group, June 1975 Report. (Available from the British Computer Society, 29 Portland Place, London Q1N4HU.)
6. Ghosh, S. P., and W. G. Tuel, Jr., A design of an experiment to model data base system performance, *IEEE Transactions on Software Engineering* **SE 2**(2), pp. 97-106, June 1976.
7. Yao, S. B., An attribute-based model for database access cost analysis, *ACM Transactions on Database Systems* **2**(1), pp. 45-67, March 1977.
8. Borovits, I., and P. Ein-dor, Cost/utilization: A measure of system performance, *Communications of the ACM* **20**(3), pp. 185-191, March 1977.
9. Sherman, S. W., and R. S. Brice, Performance of a database manager in a virtual memory system, *ACM Transactions on Database Systems* **1**(4), pp. 317-343, December 1976.
10. Brice, R. S., and S. W. Sherman, An extension of the performance of a database manager in a virtual memory system using partially locked virtual buffers, *ACM Transactions on Database Systems* **2**(2), pp. 196-207, June 1977.
11. Lucas, Henry C., Jr., Performance evaluation and monitoring, *ACM Computing Surveys* **3**(3), pp. 79-91, September 1971.
12. IBM, *IMS DC Monitor,* GB21-1336-0, IBM Corp., Productivity Application Development (1501 California Ave., Palo Alto, Ca. 94304), 1974.
13. IBM, *Data Communications Analyzer* (DCANALYZER), G320-1532-0 (IBM Data Processing Division, 1133 Westchester Ave., White Plains, N.Y. 10604), December 1973.
14. Rustin, R., Data base management system performance estimation: An elementary approach, *Proceedings of the Fifth Texas Conference on Computing Systems,* pp. 115-126, University of Texas, Austin, Texas, October 1976.
15. Scheuerman, Peter, Concepts of a data base simulation language, *Proceedings of the Association for Computing Machinery SIGMOD Conference,* pp. 144-146, Association for Computing Machinery, New York, August 1977.

CHAPTER 14

1. The British Computer Society Data Dictionary Systems Working Party Report, *Data Base* **9**(2), Fall 1977.

2. Plagman, B. K., and G. P. Altshuler, A data dictionary/directory system within the context of an integrated corporate data base, *Proceedings of the AFIPS Fall Joint Computer Conference,* pp. 1133–1140, American Federation of Information Processing Societies, Montvale, N.J., 1972.
3. Uhrowiczik, P. P., Data dictionary/directories, *IBM System Journal,* no. 4, pp. 332–350, 1973.
4. GUIDE, *Requirements for the Data Dictionary/Directory within the* GUIDE/SHARE *DBMS Concept,* Report of the Data Dictionary/Directory Project, Nov. 1, 1974. (Available from GUIDE International, 111 E. Wacker St., Chicago, Ill. 60606.)
5. Leong-Hong, B., and B. Marron, *Technical Profile of Seven Data Element Dictionary/Directory Systems,* U.S. Dept. of Commerce, Institute for Computer Sciences and Technology, National Bureau of Standards, Feb. 1977.
6. Installing a data dictionary, *EDP Analyzer* **16**(1), January 1978.

CHAPTER 15

1. Standards, practices, and documentation, in the *Auerbach Data Processing Manual* (Auerbach Publishers, 6560 North Park Drive, Pennsauken, N.J. 08109).
2. The benefits of standard practices, *EDP Analyzer* **13**(8), August 1975.
3. *Acronyms, Initialisms, and Abbreviations Dictionary,* volumes 1–3, fifth edition (Gale Research Co., Book Tower, Detroit, Mich. 48226), 1976.
4. Muehl, J. R., *DB/DC Data Dictionary Implementation Guide,* IBM Technical Bulletin, ref. no. G320-6017, (IBM Palo Alto System Center, Palo Alto, Calif.), July 1978.
5. Couger, J. P., and Robert Knapp, *System Analysis Techniques,* J. Wiley and Sons, New York, 1974.
6. Hartmann, W., H. Matthes, and A. Proeme, *Management Information Systems Handbook,* McGraw-Hill, New York, 1969.
7. Tillinghast, J., *System Development Life Cycle for Data Base Development,* Auerbach Data Base Management Portfolio No. 23-02-01, Auerbach Publishers, Pennsauken, N.J., 1976.
8. Ross, D. T., and K. E. Schoman, Jr., Structured analysis for requirements definition, *IEEE Transactions on Software Engineering* **SE-3**(1), pp. 6–15, January 1977.
9. Ross, D. T., Structured analysis (SA): A language for communicating ideas, *IEEE Transactions on Software Engineering* **SE-3**(1), pp. 16–34, January 1977.
10. Teichroew, D., and E. A. Hershey III, PSL/PSA: A computer-aided technique for structured documentation and analysis of information processing systems, *IEEE Transactions on Software Engineering* **SE-3**(1), pp. 41–48, January 1977.
11. Kahn, B. K., A structured logical data base design methodology, *Proceedings of the NYU Symposium on Database Design,* pp. 15–24, New York University, New York, May 1978.
12. The analysis of user needs, *EDP Analyzer* **17**(1), January 1979.

CHAPTER 16

1. Weldon, J. L., *Data Base Administration: Organization and Tasks,* NYU Graduate School of Business Administration, Working Paper No. 78-143 (CA), November 1978.
2. Lowell, F. M., *The Data Base Administration Function: Three Case Studies,* MBA Thesis, NYU Graduate School of Business Administration, New York, June 1979.

Index